Framing Internet Safety

The John D. and Catherine T. MacArthur Foundation Series on Digital Media and Learning

Framing Internet Safety

The Governance of Youth Online

Nathan W. Fisk

The MIT Press
Cambridge, Massachusetts
London, England

This book was set in Stone Sans and Stone Serif by Toppan Best-set Premedia Limited. Printed and bound in the United States of America.

Library of Congress Cataloging-in-Publication Data

Names: Fisk, Nathan W.
Title: Framing Internet safety : the governance of youth online / Nathan W. Fisk.
Description: Cambridge, MA : MIT Press, [2016] | Series: The John D. and Catherine
    T. MacArthur Foundation series on digital media and learning | Includes
    bibliographical references and index.
Identifiers: LCCN 2016018210 | ISBN 9780262035156 (hardcover : alk. paper)
Subjects: LCSH: Internet and youth. | Internet—Moral and ethical aspects. |
    Internet—Social aspects. | Computer crimes—Prevention.
Classification: LCC HQ799.9.I58 F57 2016 | DDC 302.23/10835—dc23 LC record
    available at https://lccn.loc.gov/2016018210

10 9 8 7 6 5 4 3 2 1

Contents

Series Foreword

In recent years, digital media and networks have become embedded in our everyday lives and are part of broad-based changes to how we engage in knowledge production, communication, and creative expression. Unlike the early years in the development of computers and computer-based media, digital media are now commonplace and pervasive, having been taken up by a wide range of individuals and institutions in all walks of life. Digital media have escaped the boundaries of professional and formal practices and the academic, governmental, and industry homes that initially fostered their development. Now they have been taken up by diverse populations and noninstitutionalized practices, including the peer activities of youth. Although specific forms of technology uptake are highly diverse, a generation is growing up in an era when digital media are part of the taken-for-granted social and cultural fabric of learning, play, and social communication.

This book series is founded on the working hypothesis that those immersed in new digital tools and networks are engaged in an unprecedented exploration of language, games, social interaction, problem solving, and self-directed activity that leads to diverse forms of learning. These diverse forms of learning are reflected in expressions of identity, in how individuals express independence and creativity, and in their ability to learn, exercise judgment, and think systematically.

The defining frame for this series is not a particular theoretical or disciplinary approach, nor is it a fixed set of topics. Rather, the series revolves around a constellation of topics investigated from multiple disciplinary and practical frames. The series as a whole looks at the relation between youth, learning, and digital media, but each contribution to the series might deal with only a subset of this constellation. Erecting strict topical boundaries would exclude some of the most important work in the field. For example, restricting the content of the series only to people of a certain age would mean artificially reifying an age boundary when the phenomenon demands otherwise. This would become particularly problematic with new forms of online participation where one important outcome is the mixing of participants of different ages. The same goes for digital media, which are increasingly inseparable from analog and earlier media forms.

The series responds to certain changes in our media ecology that have important implications for learning. Specifically, these changes involve new forms of media literacy and developments in the modes of media participation. Digital media are part of a convergence between interactive media (most notably gaming), online networks, and existing media forms. Navigating this media ecology involves a palette of literacies that are being defined through practice but require more scholarly scrutiny before they can be fully incorporated pervasively into educational initiatives. Media literacy involves not only ways of understanding, interpreting, and critiquing media but also the means for creative and social expression, online search and navigation, and a host of new technical skills. The potential gap in literacies and participation skills creates new challenges for educators who struggle to bridge media engagement inside and outside the classroom.

The John D. and Catherine T. MacArthur Foundation Series on Digital Media and Learning, published by the MIT Press, aims to close these gaps and provide innovative ways of thinking about and using new forms of knowledge production, communication, and creative expression.

1 Introduction

Online safety? How about real-life safety?
—Student survey participant

For decades, parents, schools, and legislators have attempted to balance the potentials of new personal computer and networking technologies with the risks that they pose to young people. Somewhere amid the pornography, sexual predators, and cyberbullies, a new technological sphere of childhood development has emerged, providing users with unprecedented access to information, tools of creativity, and diverse social networks. Today, discussions of youth and technology invariably mention both the bright potentials and dark horrors of online life, outlining an urgent need for security as connections to information technologies increasingly become markers for both personal and societal development. With such high stakes, interlocking systems of technologies, educational programs, and regulations have been designed to monitor, interpret, and police the social lives of children and teenagers. Tightening the connections between the institutions of childhood (the school and home) these technologies of youth Internet safety operate to produce the competitive cyber citizenry and workforce of the twenty-first-century economy. Unsurprisingly, dissenting voices are rare. Who would be against protecting young people?

Concerns over youth Internet safety serve as a grounding from which to govern information technologies and, by extension, the forms of sociality and society they make possible. The questions become, What forms of existence and social life do the discourses of youth Internet safety produce? How do concepts of youth Internet safety affect youth, adults, and technologies? Although many academic studies have looked at the safety of youth online, there has been relatively little critical examination of the mechanisms of protection themselves—the discourses and technologies of youth Internet safety. This book critically examines youth Internet safety as a productive force rather than a force of restriction. I argue throughout the book that it is through the mobilization of seemingly "online" threats that the governing potentials of information technologies are explored, allowing for the everyday lives of youth to be further monitored and policed. As each youth Internet safety "panic" becomes conceptually possible, so too do mechanisms for leveraging information technologies to surveil and modulate the social lives of youth.

Concerns over youth Internet safety can be linked to a broader crisis of disciplinary governance that is made visible as information technologies problematize the boundaries and power relations that constitute the home and school. In this sense, youth Internet safety "panics" mark a transition of societal governance from Michel Foucault's (1977) mechanisms of *discipline* to Gilles Deleuze's (1992a) mechanisms of *control*. This transition is fundamentally one of technological change, from the ordered spaces of the home and school to the lines of continuous surveillance made possible by mobile parenting applications. Concerns over youth Internet safety are not merely about the lives of youth or the online spaces they populate. Instead, they serve to constitute youth and information technologies in ways that necessitate action, reconfiguring power relations and subjectivities as part of a broader mechanism of governance.

None of this diminishes the lived reality of the risks that young people face online. Supported by information technologies, youth around the globe are unwillingly exposed to obscene content, groomed and manipulated by predators, and harassed by anonymous individuals. In fact, some of the participants in the study that supports this book have reported and reflected on such experiences. However, disconnecting the offline, situated lives of youth from the elements of their lives that are made public through online interactions does a specific form of discursive work. By imagining a form of online life that is distinct from offline social context, the attentions of concerned adults and youth alike are turned away from the social conditions that make young people vulnerable and likely to engage in risky behaviors. By drawing attention to behaviors that become visible through information technologies, the concepts of youth Internet safety mask and protect existing institutions and power relations from criticism while further opening the lives of youth to forms of surveillance and control. Youth require adult supervision and guidance, but focusing on technologies and individual young people often moves the adults responsible for youth safety to invisibly reproduce the conditions that place youth at risk.

The practice of securing children and teenagers in their lives online becomes a means for conceptualizing and producing a particular form of society while obscuring any discussion of what we might want for society in the process. Through the concepts of various online risks, we move to establish the positions and relations that produce the cybercitizens of the future. In *Framing Internet Safety: The Governance of Youth Online*, I examine youth Internet safety as a technology of governance that penetrates and modulates the everyday lives of both young and adult users through the potentials afforded by information technology. Through anticipating a particular form of future that is populated by future generations of adults, we chart the conditions for the present (Adams, Murphy, and Clarke 2009; Haraway 1994). By a project of reverse engineering, the various mechanisms and lines of power that constitute youth Internet safety discourses can be traced from the large-scale policy narratives down to the everyday lives of children, teenagers, and adults.

Technologies of Governance

Today it is nearly impossible to speak of childhood—the experiences of being a kid, tween, teen, or one of many new phases of extended non-adulthood—without mentioning information technology. It no longer seems remarkable that young people live much of their lives on, with, or through information technologies. From the early days of personal computers, mobile devices, and social networks, young people have been commonly understood to be naturally drawn to and a driving force for new technologies. Similarly, visible consumer technologies, as a form of positional good, are themselves portrayed as youthful (Schulte 2008). Information technologies are portrayed as developmental necessities that provide young people with access to new forms of entertainment, communication, and education. It is the very moment at which personal information technologies begin to appear as old or tired that they become obsolete relics of the past. Further, it is through the widespread and rapidly changing use of information technologies that young people mark themselves as a distinct generation, widening the generation gap as information technologies change the very way their brains are "wired" (Small and Vorgan 2008). These discourses of youth and technology, whether they are positive "booster" discourses or negative "debunker" discourses (Holloway and Valentine 2001), operate as elements of the now familiar discourse of the digital native (Prensky 2001a, 2001b).

Despite considerable criticism of the term *digital native* (Bennett, Maton, and Kervin 2008; Gardner and Davis 2013; Thomas 2011), the concept has undoubtedly affected a generation of legislators, school administrators, and parents. By widely using mobile phones, accessing the Internet, and engaging with social networking sites, young people have changed the ways that they socialize and interact with the world (Rainie 2014). Perhaps among the lesser discussed aspects of the relationship of youth to technology are the social forces that bring them to adoption in the first place. Increasingly, scholars of youth and the Internet have drawn connections between the draw of information technologies and the highly constrained independent mobility of youth (boyd 2014; Livingstone 2002). As Mizuko Ito et al. (2009, 38) describe,

Young people who have ready access to mobile phones or the Internet view online communication as a persistent space of peer sociability where they exercise autonomy for conversation that is private or primarily defined by friends and peers. Although in most cases they would prefer to hang out with their friends offline, the limits placed on their mobility and use of space means that this is not always possible.

The spaces where young people can be free of adult supervision and "be themselves" are shrinking rapidly (Alparone and Pacilli 2012; Derbyshire 2007; Hillman 2006; Karsten 2005; Karsten and van Vliet 2006; Santos et al. 2013; Woolley and Griffin 2015). Despite a steady decline in violent crime against youth (White and Laurisen 2012), fears over child predation and crime have led parents and responsible adults to restrict the ranges of youth mobility, reducing the ability to walk to school, and severely limiting their travel beyond the spaces of the school and home (Spilsbury 2005; McDonald et al. 2011). Those spaces that youth are allowed in without direct supervision are increasingly marked by technological surveillance, ranging from surveillance cameras to smartphone enabled GPS tracking. Further, the spaces of youth have increasingly fallen under institutional control as schooling extends into earlier and later periods of life and leisure time becomes increasingly structured and tied to educational and developmental objectives (Prout 2003; Wyness 2000). In this view, kids do not necessarily have a natural inclination toward technology: they are simply looking for spaces where they can socialize with one another. In a recent interview, youth researcher danah boyd described her shock at the extent to which these spaces had become even more limited (Bergstein 2013):

It was shocking how heavily constrained their mobility was. I had known it had gotten worse since I was a teenager, but I didn't get it—the total lack of freedom to just go out and wander. Young people weren't even trying to sneak out [of the house at night]. They were trying to get online, because that's the place where they hung out with their friends.

A lack of mobility further situates youth in ways that make their drive for social connection with one another—hanging out free from supervision—easily commodified. This can be seen in the proliferation of social networks and applications that jockey for young people's attention and acceptance. These services and applications are designed to appeal to youth as adult-free spaces and as new spaces where cool things are happening and everyone is hanging out. By offering "free" ways to maintain a copresence with friends, the administrators of social networks, games, and applications can harvest the various forms of data that youth produce through the process of socializing. When young people are encouraged to "engage" with the services, they post material about themselves, their lives, and their friends, which increases the amount of data available to the service providers and drives more youth to the service by making it appear populated. After these services are established as sites of youth sociality, young people find it difficult to abandon them—even when they know that adults are monitoring the spaces (Madden 2013).

When adults try to protect youth by further restricting their offline independent mobility, they make young people's everyday lives more and more available to adult surveillance and policing. Youth Internet safety discourses problematize youth online social interactions and mark out newly visible forms of social interaction as both distinct from offline "real" life and inherently risky. The risk constituted around online sociality is that of failing to fully realize the potential offered by both information technologies and youth themselves, demanding action by "trusted adults" at all levels of society. Claudia Castañeda (2002, 80) locates this potentiality in the discursive construction of the child:

figurations of the child as a potentiality include a mechanism by which this possibility might be either realized or squandered. The risk of failure is therefore inherent in the child's potentiality. So, too, the child's value as a potentiality lies partly in the opportunities it affords—indeed requires—for external control and direction. The child is figured as a potentiality in need of control for the realization of that very potential—for while development is full of potential, its outcome is also never simply guaranteed.

One could replace *child* with *technology* in the above statement, to a similar end. The strategic need to realize the potential of childhood is not a recent historical development, and the school and home have operated as central mechanisms through which to achieve that potential. Schools and families are technologies that produce particular kinds of citizens who have been imagined to meet the needs of an anticipated future.

Examining the questions of what the work of youth Internet safety discourses is and what kinds of social life they make possible requires examining the mechanisms that allow those safety discourses to operate on populations of youth and the adults charged with protecting them. Foucault (1980, 194) develops the concept of the discursive apparatus (*dispositif*) to describe these complex "systems of relations" that govern societies. For Foucault, apparatuses are the interlinking material-discursive mechanisms of control that constitute and circulate subjectivities and power relations in ways that circumscribe everyday life. Strategy is central to the operation of apparatuses, not in the sense that an overarching power positions and manipulates the elements of the apparatus but rather in the sense that each element operates in ways that respond through various techniques to a dominant urgent need. Further, apparatuses both rely on and produce dominant knowledges, as Foucault (1980, 196) describes:

the apparatus is essentially of a strategic nature, which means assuming that it is a matter of a certain manipulation of relations of forces, either developing them in a particular direction, blocking them, stabilizing them, utilizing them, etc. The apparatus is thus always inscribed in a play of power, but it is also always linked to certain coordinates of knowledge which issue from it but, to an equal degree, condition it. This is what the apparatus consists in: strategies of relations of forces supporting, and supported by, types of knowledge.

The concept of the apparatus, while not explicitly referenced, can be seen to develop from Foucault's work in *Discipline and Punish: The Birth of the Prison* (1977), where he traces the historical shift in the eighteenth and nineteenth centuries from an order of sovereign power to that of a disciplinary apparatus. This shift from sovereign society to disciplinary society was marked by the circulation and accumulation of a carceral logic that was made visible through the emergence of a variety of new institutional forms. To varying degrees, these institutions relied on a specific mode of confinement as they ordered and made visible individuals in space and time. The prison, military, clinic, school, and family are all examples of carceral technologies that, in service of the state, efficiently order and govern populations.

Within these systems of governance, power is seen by Foucault as a flow and as the operating of the mechanism itself, neither located in any one position nor wielded by individuals. Pervasive and ever present, power in this sense is deeply inseparable from the formation of knowledge. Surveillance becomes a focus for operations of power, making individuals visible and allowing them to be known and operated on. Foucault (1980, 39) described this as the capillary action of power:

in thinking of the mechanisms of power, I am thinking rather of its capillary form of existence, the point where power reaches into the very grain of individuals, touches their bodies and inserts itself into their actions and attitudes, their discourses, learning processes and everyday lives. The eighteenth century invented, so to speak, a synaptic regime of power, a regime of its exercise within the social body, rather than from above it. The change in official forms of political power was linked to this process, but only via intervening shifts and displacements. This more-or-less coherent modification in the small-scale modes of exercise of power was made possible only by a fundamental structural change.

As such, power is ever advancing, seeking to penetrate deeper into the everyday existence of individuals and to capitalize on new governing potentials. This capillary action of power can be observed through the construction of youth Internet safety incidents that operate through legislators, administrators, and parents to further open the lives of youth to surveillance and control. Through the capillary dispersion of suspicion and distrust, youth Internet safety discourses make everyday practices visible as risky or otherwise in need of adult intervention. As described by Nancy Campbell (2004, 79), of key importance is the decentralization and deinstitutionalization of distrust, the capillary dispersion of distrust and suspicion throughout the carceral society, and the role of distrust in underwriting the development of certain kinds of knowledge systems and technologies, forms of social and cognitive order, and the functional dispersion of police practices to individuals such as parents, teachers, and peers.

Elements of the disciplinary society outlined by Foucault remain highly dominant in the institutions that control and monitor youth today, most notably in the ways they are regimented and made visible in the spaces of the home and school. As I make clear throughout this book, youth Internet safety discourses are frequently disciplinary in nature, both making visible and circumscribing virtual spaces and youth subjects. In various contexts, the discourse of youth Internet safety (Foucault 1980, 193–194)

can figure at one time as the program of an institution, and [in] another it can function as a means of justifying or masking a practice which itself remains silent, or as a secondary re-interpretation of this practice, opening out for it a new field of rationality.

The urgent, strategic needs of youth Internet safety discourses are always apparent: the potentials of young people and information technologies must be protected because visions of the twenty-first-century economy depend on their ongoing and properly guided development.

Expanding on the work of Foucault, Jacques Donzelot (1979) outlines the emergence of the modern family in the eighteenth century as the control and management of populations became central concerns of the state. Through an analysis of historical documents, Donzelot describes the conditions by which children came to be "preserved" in the mid-eighteenth century as part of a broader technology of governance for producing a maximally useful population. Responding to the growing mortality rate among working-class youth and the perceived unreadiness of upper-class young men for the workforce when they reached adulthood, a new form of the family was constituted through what Donzelot describes as the regulation of images. The family was reconstituted around the preservation of children through a set of practices that Donzelot identifies as the spread of household medicine and philanthropy. A variety of experts and pedagogical techniques helped to reorganize the family around children as a means of producing a more stable and prepared labor and military force. Through the regulation of images that were strongly differentiated by class, new spheres of development were drawn around the child. Working-class families were reformed into a relation of circular vigilance so that youth being raised "on the street" could be shepherded back into the family home and school. Upper-class families were reformed by excluding the "negative influences" of working-class domestic servants. These new formations of the family and new pedagogies of family life established young people as useful subjects for the state and as instruments of continued economic viability produced by particular family configurations and modes of surveillance.

The Dispersal of Control

Throughout this book, I draw heavily on the work of Jacques Donzelot both to reconnect youth Internet safety discourses to historical configurations of the family that persist today and to consider the ways in which Internet safety discourses move to reconfigure families around information technologies. In chapter 4, I develop the term *pedagogies of surveillance* to describe the ways in which the youth Internet safety materials that are provided to parents position them as agents of surveillance within the home and in online spaces. Similarly, in chapter 6, I use Donzelot's concepts of protected liberation and supervised freedom to explain the supervision practices of parents and guardians. Finally, in chapter 5, I use Donzelot's work on the reconfiguration of families to explain the ways in which youth Internet safety curricula (primarily organized around the problem of cyberbullying) further distribute the practice of surveillance to young people themselves by encouraging them to avoid "being a bystander." If, as described by Donzelot, the family and school are technologies of governance, then the problematization of youth sociality through the production of youth Internet safety incidents modifies those technologies in predictable and productive ways. By regulating images of what it now means to be a "good" parent, teacher, or kid online, we reconfigure the positions of adults and youth and reconstitute and expand the spheres of childhood development to encompass the technologies that mediate the lives of both young people and adults.

The reconfiguration of the family and the efforts to protect youth online can be considered as part of a "generalized crisis in relation to all the environments of enclosure—prison, hospital, factory, school, family" (Deleuze 1992a, 3–4). Made possible by the widespread adoption of information technologies, this generalized crisis marks the transition from the disciplinary society to a new configuration of governmentality. Deleuze (1992a) describes this new "monster" as the societies of control that slowly replace the ordered spaces and visibilities of disciplinary technologies with those of smooth, continuous lines of information. Nikolas Rose (2000, 325) expands on Deleuze's brief outline of the societies of control,

Control is not centralized but dispersed; it flows through a network of open circuits that are rhizomatic and not hierarchical. In such a regime of control, we are not dealing with subjects with a unique personality that is the expression of some inner fixed quality, but with elements, capacities, potentialities. ... Conduct is continually monitored and reshaped by logics immanent within all networks of practice. Surveillance is "designed in" to the flows of everyday existence.

A distinguishing feature of control technology, therefore, is the enabling of continuous choice based on an internalized set of rules. It is perhaps no coincidence that Deleuze (2007) describes the highway—long used as a dominant metaphor for the Internet by policymakers—as a key example of a control technology. A vast array of ever-present sensors, analytics, and logics have emerged from the control society, problematizing existing institutions and technologies of governance while providing productive new opportunities. As I was finishing this manuscript, I was invited to attend a webinar on identifying at-risk students by using predictive data, and the marketing copy announced to potential attendees that "you can gain insights so rich that Ferris Bueller would never have taken a day off."

Given the dispersed, open circuitry of societies of control, the strategically aligned concept of the apparatus as provided by Foucault begins to break down. As an alternative means of conceptualizing the organization of material and discursive elements, Deleuze and Félix Guattari (1987) propose the concept of assemblage. Assemblages do not align through a broad, strategic coherence but instead dynamically emerge from the largely independent movements of a dispersed set of elements. Extending Foucault's concept of strategy, Michel de Certeau (1984) distinguishes between strategies and tactics as a means to theorize everyday life. Strategies for de Certeau are the systematic, technical alignments of institutions and government, and tactics are the everyday practices of existence that work within, through, and around institutional strategies. Assemblages can be said to emerge from the loose, working organization of both strategic and tactical operations. The concept further provides for a means by which to understand the process of becoming, in that "'Assemblage' in this case is a verb as much as a noun, a process of becoming as much as a state of being" (Palmås 2010, 340).

When I attended presentations for young people and adults and talked with students, parents, and administrators, I soon understood that the everyday operation of youth Internet safety discourses was not always strategic. Although at the macro level, youth Internet safety discourses moved toward specific strategic goals through policies, media discourses, and curricula, the micro interactions were far more ad hoc and were full of functional coincidences and moments of tactical resistance. In this book, I sometimes use the concept of apparatus to describe the strategic coordination of policy and curricula and use the concept of assemblage to conceptualize micro-level working arrangements between adults, youth, and newly developed information technologies. As I describe in chapter 3, the governing potentialities of control technologies first become visible as they interrupt or complicate the efficient functioning of existing disciplinary institutions. Youth Internet safety issues can be seen as a problematization of those interruptions, allowing for the transitionary exploration of control technologies and establishing positions and power relations that further disperse the operation of power.

Similarly, the works of Deleuze and Rose have been taken up by a number of scholars to consider the implications of information technologies for studies of governmentality (Galloway 2004; Poster 2001). Of particular relevance to this project is the work of Raiford Guins (2009), who locates technologies of control in forms of contemporary media censorship that provide parents with technologies for monitoring and blocking media consumption practices by their children. Parental control technologies allow for a dispersal of control, shifting the work of disciplinary institutions away from those institutions and instead to the individual decisions of parents— what Guins (extending the work of Rose) calls the "parent function." For Guins, however, the implications of the parent function go beyond simply securing families and move to mobilize the family as a larger strategy of control. As Guins (2009, 10) describes:

Performed as a parental function, family is instead a strategy of rule that operates through culture to further an ethos of security that instrumentalizes cultural practices as they flow freely as solutions to the problematic of securitization. In its enhancement, the "family-machine," as Rose might say, or, as I prefer, the parental function, becomes the normative basis for "goodness" and the administration of ways of being "good" through the surveillance, perfection, and maintenance of disciplined freedom.

Although Guins does not cite the work of Donzelot, there is a resonance between Guins's concept of "disciplined freedom" and the pedagogical practices (supervised freedom, protected liberation) targeted at the family as outlined by Donzelot. The parental function operates as a much broader strategy as developers build forms of parental control in various media technologies, including social networks, video game consoles, and mobile devices. Through the affordances of information technologies, security becomes individualized. Where Guins focuses primarily on parental control, I argue in chapter 7 that youth Internet safety curricula further aim to individualize security through the process of distributing control to youth themselves.

To summarize, the adult surveillance of children and teenagers in their everyday practices—made visible as they hang out by using publicly visible online services—further reduces the spaces where they can be free of the adult gaze. Although adults usually do know best and youth typically want them to know best, there is value to having spaces where young people can learn lessons for themselves. This is perhaps particularly true in cases where adults are "better off not knowing" (see chapter 6) about what young people are up to. At one time, young people were able to "get away with" engaging in activities that are appropriate for the young but are inappropriate under adult supervision, but they now must be concerned that such activities will fall under the increasingly persistent gaze of adult surveillance. Similarly, the wider visibility of such events places adults in a web of mutual surveillance as well, bringing the gaze of other adults and authorities to bear on the disciplinary practices of parents. In this way, youth Internet safety discourses are highly productive. The production of youth Internet safety problems necessitates surveillance practices that are made possible by new information technologies—frequently through the further dispersal of power that seeks to control the everyday lives of individuals, both online and off.

Reverse Engineering

Conceptualizing youth Internet safety as a discursive apparatus requires an examination of the heterogeneous, strategically coordinated elements that are intended to protect young people online—including policies, curricula, gray literatures, technologies, institutions, and the linkages that bind them together. As Deleuze (1992b, 159) describes, "Untangling these lines within a social apparatus is in each case like drawing up a map, doing cartography, surveying unknown landscapes, and this is what [Foucault] calls 'working on the ground.'" This book traces the lines of capillary power, starting with the broad, strategically aligned discourses of legislators and Internet safety curricula, moving through the institutions of the school and family, and ending with the everyday microphysics of tactical discourse among youth and adults. In analyzing the discursive assemblage of youth Internet safety, this book reflects the organization of an assemblage where each piece works together and also stands on its own. The chapters are arranged in order of scale from macro (research/policy) to micro (adults/youth) and in loose chronological order (most evident in the chapters on policies and youth curricula).

Support for this book was drawn from a mixed-methods research project that took place in six school districts in New York state. Within each district, focus groups were held with parents and young people (students in grades 6 to 9 and grades 10 to 12 were interviewed separately), interviews were conducted with school administrators, and an online survey with both quantitative and qualitative elements was given to students (n = 3,337). Each chapter loosely groups different actors as they became apparent through an analysis of the data. Chapter 3 focuses on news media and legislative discourses of youth Internet safety, which were found to exist in a dialectical relationship in which they variously supported and opposed each other at different historical moments. School administrators (broadly defined as the various school staff members I interviewed in each district) have no chapter of their own and instead are included in the chapters on pedagogy, adults, and youth.

I begin the next chapter by discussing my own experiences with researching youth Internet safety because they became an important part of the analysis when the project began to be circumscribed by the very processes I was seeking to analyze. I describe the ways in which the project was colonized by the methods of developmental psychology to produce specific forms of knowledge about young people and the Internet and provide an overview of sociological approaches to childhood as a critical response to developmental psychology. In chapter 3, a historical analysis of youth Internet safety policies in the United States situates past panics in patterns of technological adoption by youth. Instead of conceptualizing youth Internet safety in terms of moral panic (see Buckingham and Strandgaard Jensen 2012), I explain the emergence of key youth Internet safety issues as part of the securitization of information technologies, focusing on the productive elements of federal youth Internet safety policies. Chapter 4 outlines what I describe as pedagogies of surveillance and examines a process that uses youth Internet safety curricula to position adults to become agents of surveillance. I argue that instead of being ready participants in surveillance activities, adults must be trained to make sense of both youth and information technologies in ways that produce actionable, institutionally legitimate data. In chapter 6, I turn to the youth Internet safety curricula that are aimed at youth audiences and focus on the shift away from Internet safety from cyberbullying and to newer concepts of online reputation management. Chapters 6 and 7 move to "the ground" of the everyday practices of adults and young people as described by focus group and student survey participants. In chapter 6, parent focus group participants explain their strategies for monitoring their children online, making visible the ways in which these practices subject young people and their parents to online surveillance. Chapter 7 presents the results of the student survey, returns to the issue of cyberbullying (by explaining the ways that young people and adults use youth Internet safety terms to constitute particular power and knowledge relationships), and recommends a "cybersafety of everyday life" that connects youth Internet safety concepts to dominant trends in national infrastructure protection and corporate information assurance.

Children and teenagers face considerable risks in their everyday lives and need adult support as they navigate those risks, and information technologies have presented new possibilities for victimization and crime. But my work here does not suggest that adults are tyrannically cracking down on young people's freedoms or that they are not committed to youth safety and positive use of information technology. As Rose (1990, 125) notes, the extension of social regulation to the lives of children actually had little to do with recognition of their rights. Children came to the attention of social authorities as delinquents threatening property and security, as future workers requiring moralization and skills, as future soldiers requiring a level of physical fitness—in other words, on account of the threat which they posed now or in the future to the welfare of the state. The apparent humanity, benevolence, and enlightenment of the extension of protection to children in their homes disguised the extension of surveillance and control over the family.

As a colleague from an earlier project on youth Internet safety once told me, "No one can say no" to the protection of children. For this reason, programs concerned with the safety of children must be critically examined so that the assumptions and relations of power that they produce can be understood.

2 Predators and Proposals: Doing Research on Youth and Technology

Throughout this book, youth Internet safety appears as a site of contested production (Brown 2005). Legislative and media accounts of young people's online activities variously align and conflict with one another. At Internet safety presentations, law enforcement agents and curricula developers destabilize the situated knowledges of parents by asking them, "What is your child doing online?" Young people and their parents argue over who better interprets youth social interactions online. And because they are embroiled in dramatic performance, young people struggle to maintain interpretive control through the frames of cyberbullying and victimization. "Who knows better" ends up being a question of who produces and controls the spaces of youth Internet safety. In this chapter, my own research project becomes a contested site of production as I examine the works of Michel Foucault and some concepts from the field of childhood studies.

As Valerie Walkerdine (1984, 155) describes, "Particular disciplines, regimes of truth, bodies of knowledge, make possible both *what can be said* and *what can be done.*" The institutions, technologies, and knowledges of developmental psychology and the educational system are mutually constitutive as they shape the forms of legitimate knowledge about children and their lives. The institutions that mediated my research were strategically aligned in ways that reinforced the dominant position of developmental psychology and, by extension, a particular mode of constituting youth subjects. Changes in methods, levels of mediation, and modes of analysis were all implicated in the ways in which childhood and adulthood are constituted. By conducting research with, rather than on, young people, I became positioned outside of my own project—although not outside of institutional discourses—as the social scientific predator. This chapter first describes the historical linkages between the modern institutions

of education and developmental psychology and then reviews the commitments of the new sociology of childhood. Following this, I explain my
experiences as a researcher who undertook a largely qualitative research
project using the work of Foucault and childhood studies as a conceptual
frame.

This chapter is not an attempt to describe a conspiracy against my
research project or to otherwise criticize ethical standards and practices in
research. Despite being hemmed in by dominant disciplines and occasionally messy, the project ultimately succeeded in accomplishing what I set
out to achieve. Researchers never capture all of the data they would like to,
and the project described here was no different. Although the processes and
institutions that were part of this project often served defensive purposes, I
believe that the people who were involved were working for what they saw
as the best interests of children—a point that, in part, led me to shift the
project's framework away from moral panic and toward securitization. Even
beyond the best interests of children, the work that was put into my project
by others met the highest standards of quality and professionalism. Despite
all of this, working in the best interests of children (which always appear
as self-evident within youth Internet safety discourses) is itself a strategic
position that resists analysis and criticism. As mentioned previously in the
introductory chapter, "No one can say no."

Technologies of Development

The field that has come to be known as the sociology of childhood emerged
largely from the work of British social anthropologists in the late 1970s and
1980s and focuses on interrogating the "natural" categories of childhood
and adolescence. This work reflects concerns with the dominant Western
conceptualizations of childhood that are driven primarily by the work of
psychologist Jean Piaget (1971). Developmental psychology conceptualizes
children's growth as a series of transition-bounded stages, where each stage
is marked by the accomplishment of key skills and behaviors. Within such
a frame, children are not-yet-social and are in an ongoing process of becoming fully functional adults. The concepts of developmental psychology rely
on statistical analysis, and data are collected from children within particular age ranges to determine the various skills and behaviors that mark normal development. As is discussed in the following chapters, developmental

concepts of childhood are then used to explain or otherwise dismiss youth perspectives as coming from a position of biological underdevelopment or undersocialization.

This form of developmental psychology remains the primary frame through which judgments about scientific legitimacy concerning research with youth subjects are made, often with an emphasis on the production of actionable data. Undertaking a project involving youth that falls outside the concepts, methods, and analytic techniques of this approach appears, at best, to produce biased, nongeneralizable, invalid, or otherwise irrelevant data. At worst, such projects are rendered inconceivable, made invisible by dominant discourses of childhood.

This is evident in the forms of research that concern youth. In a broad historical analysis of sociological publications, Anne-Marie Ambert (1986) attributed the relative absence of research on childhood (which was more pronounced in the United States) to the low value attributed to work on children and childhood by male-dominated positivist sociology. As Ambert (1986, 16) suggests, "One does not become a household name in sociology by studying children." Not until the 1990s did a critical sociology of childhood emerge and begin to gain traction as a field of study. As originally noted by Allison James and Alan Prout (1997, 9), the sociology of childhood criticizes developmental concepts and embodies a "particularly western conceptualization of childhood for all children which conceals the fact that the institution of childhood is a social construction" through positivist "technologies of knowledge." Key to the paradigm is a view that young people are valuable as research subjects in their own right and play active roles in the production of social arenas. This view seeks to take children and teenagers seriously as human agents. As James and Prout explain, however, the notions of development and socialization have resisted criticism throughout the decades, maintaining entrenched positions within and reproduced by dominant social institutions.

Unsurprisingly, the concepts of developmental psychology have historically both relied on and reinforced the school as a form of disciplinary technology, as described in the work of Philippe Ariès (1962) and Michel Foucault (1977, 1978). Although the historical work of both scholars predates the emergence of a formal developmental psychology through the work of Piaget, concepts of natural development and stages of childhood can be traced back to the writings of Charles Darwin (Castañeda 2002).

Building from the basic concepts of life stages, the architectures and governmental logics of the school allowed developmental psychology to further coalesce into a formal discipline. Although perhaps most widely cited (and criticized) for his assertion that the concept of childhood did not exist during medieval times, Ariès charts "the progress of discipline" by outlining the use and eventual decline of corporal punishment within schools from the fourteenth through the nineteenth centuries. Loosely organized school masters were given the authority to hit students with sticks, which provided the conditions for a hierarchical system in which students are under constant observation and marked a conceptualization of children in which weakness is a central concern. As schools became increasingly militarized in the eighteenth and nineteenth centuries, corporal punishment diminished, marking a shift away from the concept of childhood as weakness (which must be beaten out) and toward a concept of childhood as not-yet-adult. Through this transition, the militarization of schools—requiring demarcation by rank—developed a hierarchical set of categories through which to chart the transition from childhood to adulthood.

In *Discipline and Punish*, which was clearly influenced by Ariès's work, Foucault describes the workings of the school as a technology of discipline and examines the architecture, practices, and pedagogies that govern student bodies. For Foucault (1977, 176), the school is

an institution ... in which three procedures are integrated into a single mechanism—teaching proper, the acquisition of knowledge by the very practice of the pedagogical activity, and a reciprocal, hierarchized observation. A relation of surveillance, defined and regulated, is inscribed at the heart of the practice of teaching, not as an additional or adjacent part, but as a mechanism that is inherent to it and which increases its efficiency.

Through the school, a regime of truth forms around the child, institutionalizing and instilling within subjects a particular form of knowledge, which in turn becomes self-validating (James and Prout 1997). As Harry Hendrick (1997, 44) explains,

But in what ways did the school seek to alter children's "nature," thereby creating a virtually new construction of childhood? ... it required upon pain of punishment, usually physical, a form of behaviour, accompanied by a set of related attitudes, which reinforced the child's dependence and vulnerability and, in terms of deference towards established authorities, its social class. ... it further institutionalized the separation of children from society, confirming upon them a separate identity: their proper place was in the classroom. ... Finally, the school emphasized the value of children as investments in future parenthood, economic competitiveness, and a stable democratic order.

Foucault (1977) connects the institutional development of the school to a broader dispersal of disciplinary governance. Through this form of disciplinary governance, populations are divided into categories, organized in space and time, and subjected to various techniques of surveillance. The work of Foucault connects the institution of the school to the governance of populations, demonstrating how schools operate as part of a network of institutions—home, clinic, prison, military—that efficiently produce subjects that are useful to the state. A key element of these technologies is the production of knowledge around subjects through individualization, ordering, documentation, and normalizing judgment, resulting in a form of knowledge that is inseparable from the power that produces it. An entire discourse—statistics—needed to be developed to support this need to characterize, define, and quantitatively know a population. Populations that were statistically defined could be subjected to policy interventions and controls that stabilized and underwrote policy problems. Through the definition of the statistically normal, populations could be judged and acted on. In this "power of the norm," Foucault (1977, 184) locates the emergence of the social sciences from the various institutional forms of disciplinary power—in the case of the school, the emergent disciplines were those of education and developmental psychology. The discipline of psychology was not the only discipline taken up by Foucault, who explains the emergence of the social sciences from a will to categorize and know subjects.

Building on Foucault, Nikolas Rose (1985, 110) describes the emergence of developmental psychology as made possible by the nursery school:

[The clinic and nursery school] allowed the observation and collection of data covering numbers of children of the same ages, by skilled psychological experts, under controlled, experimental, almost laboratory conditions. They thus simultaneously allowed for standardisation and for normalisation—the collection of comparable information on a large number of subjects and its analysis in such a way as to construct norms. A developmental norm was a standard based upon the average abilities or performance of children of a certain age on a particular task or in a particular activity. It thus not only presented a picture of what was normal for children of such an age, but enabled the normality of any individual child to be assessed by comparison with this norm.

Developmental technology and the school cannot be separated from the practices of observation, documentation, and normative judgment. The very architecture of the school is designed to constitute individuals through the division of space and time, rendering them visible to the analytical gaze of teachers and school administrators. Through the collection and analysis of various forms of data, the school itself is then supported, and its mechanisms are made more efficient through corrective practices. Built into the reciprocal data collection and analysis that are constitutive of the school and pedagogical practice are the logics of developmental psychology. In turn, the architectures and practices of school education constitute the figure of the child. As Walkerdine (1984, 155) explains,

Pedagogic practices then are totally saturated with the notion of a normalized sequence of child development, so that those practices help produce children as the objects of their gaze. The apparatuses and mechanisms of schooling which do this range from the architecture of the school ... to the curriculum materials and techniques of assessment.

From a disciplinary perspective, segments of psychology have ostensibly rounded the social turn, largely as a response to the work of Foucault and other critical scholars who drove psychologists to incorporate more social influences. The psychological literature has moved beyond the basic developmental framework developed by Piaget, and psychology is not monolithic. Despite an acknowledgment of social and critical theory within segments of the academic literature, Piaget's concepts continue to have a strong (if often unacknowledged) hold on parents, school administrators, educators, and legislators. Developmental psychology and the technologies of childhood grounded in developmental concepts "form part of the day-to-day running of classrooms, providing the taken-for-granted forms of a pedagogy which teachers frequently do not associate with the name of Piaget, who appears a dimly remembered figure from college days" (Walkerdine 1984, 190). The basic concepts of developmental psychology are maintained in the everyday practices of parents, teachers, and school administrators and constitute a large part of the discourses and technologies of childhood. Today, it is nearly impossible to discuss childhood without invoking developmental concepts—most commonly through the figure of the developing frontal lobe. In this way, the reinforcing mechanisms of the school and the discipline of psychology propagate beyond the walls of the school itself as students, parents, and teachers internalize taken-for-granted developmental concepts. As Rose (2008, 447) explains:

our very ideas of ourselves, of identity, autonomy, freedom and self-fulfillment were reshaped in psychological terms. Human beings in these regions came to understand themselves as inhabited by a deep interior psychological space, to evaluate themselves and to act upon themselves in terms of this belief. They came to speak of themselves in terms of a psychological language of self-description—the language of intelligence, personality, anxiety, neurosis, depression, trauma, extroversion and introversion and to judge themselves in terms of a psychological ethics.

This was readily apparent throughout this project as I spoke with parents, teachers, and school administrators, observed media coverage, and studied Internet safety curricula. The school and other technologies of childhood not only produce and reinforce particular concepts of the child but also act as mechanisms through which those concepts are propagated out into other disciplinary institutions.

This includes concepts of the child within the academic institutions that regulate research practice—the institutional review boards (IRBs) that are mandated by federal law. For researchers in the United States, IRBs have the authority to review and dismiss research projects that they consider to be unethical or to pose risks to human research participants. Established following the National Research Act of 1974 and within a paternalist, biomedical frame, IRBs construct a concept of children as vulnerable subjects (Loveridge and Cornforth 2014; Schneider 2015; Schrag 2010; Swauger 2009). IRBs categorized children and teenagers as being incapable of consenting to participate in research on their own and place research projects involving youth subjects under heightened scrutiny—particularly where sensitive research topics are being raised. Concerning childhood sexuality, Foucault (1988, 276) reconnects this form of child protectionism in developmental psychology to a specific relation of power and knowledge:

Hence there is a legislation that appeals to this notion of a vulnerable population, a "high-risk population," as they say, and to a whole body of psychiatric and psychological knowledge imbibed from psychoanalysis—it doesn't really matter whether the psychoanalysis is good or bad. … The psychiatrist is the one who will be able to say: I can predict that a trauma of this importance will occur as a result of this or that type of sexual relation. It is therefore within the new legislative framework—basically intended to protect certain vulnerable sections of the population with the establishment of a new medical power—that a conception of sexuality and above all of the relations between child and adult sexuality will be based; and it is one that is extremely questionable.

The moral and legal authority held by IRBs has limited the forms of knowledge that can be produced around certain research subjects—including children, who are rendered largely incapable of speaking on a variety of sensitive and important topics. Virginia Morrow and Martin Richards (1996, 97) further explain the concepts of children in discussions of ethics in research:

[Ethical] discussions [of child research] are dominated by a particular conceptualization of children as vulnerable and consequently in need of protection from exploitative researchers, and as the *objects* rather than subjects of research.

As Morrow and Richards explain, the potential recalling—accidental or deliberate—of upsetting experiences itself is framed as a harm for youth subjects. Further, the disclosure of victimization or engagement in criminal activities often triggers mandatory reporting requirements, requiring researchers to violate the confidentiality and anonymity of their research participants under particular conditions. In this way, protecting subjects who are constituted as "vulnerable children" effectively prevents researchers from speaking with them at all. Although children and teenagers are rendered vulnerable through the social positioning of childhood and are in need of a level of ethical consideration, failing to allow them to have some form of voice in the production of knowledge on their own social lives is disempowering. As Michel Callon (1986) suggests, "To speak for others is to first silence those in whose name we speak," but adopting modes of research that do so to a lesser extent is not without its difficulties.

Becoming the Social Scientific Predator

The research that supported this project focused on youth (see boyd 2014; Livingstone 2009) and performed largely ethnographic work with young people to understand the ways in which they, among other stakeholder groups, conceptualized and described risk online. Such a project involved having discussions with young participants about their experiences—a task made understandably difficult by university IRBs in the United States. Regardless of the ways in which researchers critically examine the social construction of childhood, the structure of youth and adult power relations positions young people in ways that make them vulnerable to various forms of harm and abuse—a point that is explored in later chapters.

Even prior to the submission of a research proposal to the IRB at the Rensselaer Polytechnic Institute, conversations about the research with friends, colleagues, and new acquaintances often led to joking about my perhaps being seen as a predator. The most common hypothetical was that I might one day walk through a door, only to be confronted by Chris Hanson, the host of *Dateline NBC*'s *To Catch a Predator* television series. I felt comfortable enough with my own position to play along with the ribbing—which continues to this day among close friends and colleagues. From a research standpoint, however, the joking did a particular kind of discursive work. Although the jokes operated as a metacommentary on the social context of the research, they also operated as a form of criticism of the underlying discourses of online pedophilia. An element of transgression existed as part of the research, and by adopting a stance that critically examined dominant discourses of childhood, I became available for circumscription as a predator myself. This sense—that as a researcher questioning the constructions of childhood I might be taken for or otherwise positioned into the role of a pedophile, predator, or someone who would otherwise bring harm to children—was present throughout the project.

This was true even in the early stages of the research, particularly as I began to frame the project through critical literatures on childhood. I found online a useful interview with Foucault (1988) on childhood sexuality (a quote is reprinted earlier in the chapter), and hoping to uncover more material hosted at the same site, I browsed through linked pages, only to find that I was visiting an online "forum for people who are engaged in scholarly discussion about the understanding and emancipation of mutual relationships between children or adolescents and adults" (IPCE 2010). Much to my discomfort, I found that discussions of the social construction of childhood, sexuality, and trauma are commonly mobilized by controversial "child love" activist groups. Future searches repeatedly returned me to the literature hosted at that site and also provided some key references for this book. Even returning to the quote now is somewhat disturbing to me because it creates a clear link between the critical discussion of age-of-consent regulations and IRB protection of vulnerable research participants. Thankfully, adopting a critical stance on the construction of childhood does not allow researchers to detach themselves from their social context, and scholarly discussions of emancipation have not shifted my stance on the need for a legal age of consent.

Later in the project, I again unwittingly adopted the role of Internet predator as seen through the worst-case frame of youth Internet safety. I became aware of a site that was a competitor to the popular Disney virtual world, Club Penguin. Woogi World was billed as a "safe, educational virtual world for children K–6" (Woogi World 2011): "Woogi World motivates its young students to learn in ways that will prepare them for a 21st century global workplace—all at a lower cost than traditional education. Its Woogi Cyber Hero program is universally rated the best cyber safety resource in the United States."

To explore this virtual world, users must create an identity for the site through parent approval. Acting as both parent and child users, I set up an account, completed the required youth Internet safety quiz, and began using an avatar to explore the virtual space of Woogi World. I was shown a large map of the United States with forty-eight states colored gray and labeled "Ghost Town" and two states (Florida and Arkansas) colored green and labeled "A Few Woogies." I entered Florida, hoping to see a few children interacting with the space (and assuming that I was maintaining ethical standards because of the checks put into place by the technology itself). There I found a virtual fairground that was occupied by my own Woogi avatar and two others representing other users. After somewhat uneventfully browsing through the various activities that were available to Woogi World users, I decided to ask another Woogi if there normally were more users. When I tried to type "Are there usually more people here?," I found that the word *usually* was not allowed by the chat software (neither was the word *normally*). Woogi World had implemented a whitelisting system, allowing only a predetermined set of words to be used to communicate with other users. When the remaining Woogies left the "room" I was in, I followed, poorly attempting to navigate the space and the restrictive whitelist simultaneously. Eventually, I realized that other users might interpret my behavior as a stranger who was chasing them through Woogi World and spouting nonsensically broken questions. Through the performance of strangeness online, I had unwittingly positioned myself in the role of the Internet creep, predator, or troll.

Later, I rewatched "Dangerous Web" (Hansen 2004a, 2004b)—the first of the *To Catch a Predator* television series—as reporter Chris Hansen held a focus group with eight seemingly middle-school-aged children. He was allowed to record each child's statement and reactions. After he showed them footage of a middle-aged man entering a kitchen in search of a four-teen-year-old girl, Hansen asked questions about how the actions of the predator made them feel. I imagined the questions that I as a researcher (rather than a journalist) could have asked them. Similarly, during the data collection phase of my own project, I often wondered if any of the young people that I met (in focus groups and in my everyday life) were over the age of eighteen, which would allow me to interview them one-on-one with-out breaking the IRB's rules. Desperate for additional material as I sought the "emancipated" voice of youth, I was positioned within my own work as a social scientific predator, and "barely legal" took on an entirely new meaning.

Despite grounding my work in an understanding that specific construc-tions of childhood limit victimization of youth in positive ways, I could see that examining concepts of childhood and youth accounts of online risks also can be the domain of relativistic adult-child love advocates, unethi-cally negligent researchers, and online sexual predators. The very actions and activities of doing research with youth—from the literature to the work itself—appear through the dominant discourses of childhood and even from my own perspective as the researcher as risky and potentially predatory.

Risky Proposals

The resonance between the positions of the predator and the exploitative researcher was not lost on my university's IRB when the board began to review my research proposal. At the time, relatively few researchers had spo-ken with young people about their everyday lives online, and even fewer had discussed with them their concepts of online risk or their experiences with Internet safety policies or curricula. More generally, I noticed that the youth I had met and observed previously tended to adopt the language used by adults when discussing youth Internet safety issues, operating as a form of dual consciousness (Herring 2008). The original proposal submitted to the IRB called for a series of student focus groups, in-depth interviews with school administrators, and cybersafety workshops for faculty and admin-istrators in each participating school district. At the same time, looking to expand the scope of the project and obtain additional research support, I applied for grant funding through the National Science Foundation (NSF).

In previous projects, New York State's Boards of Cooperative Education Services (BOCES) had proven instrumental in coordinating data collection and establishing contacts with school districts. One of BOCES's key roles is to conduct institutional research within member school districts. In New York, BOCES operates as a public organization, facilitating the state-mandated pooling of resources in cases where multiple school districts are seeking similar services. The data analysis group specializes in providing services relating to the collection and analysis of educational data within school districts, allowing for a level of outsider access. The methods used by the BOCES data analysis group operate at the intersection of developmental psychology and large-scale data analytics—particularly in the field of education. Conveniently for the project, BOCES had recently issued a directive to facilitate stronger ties between K–12 and college-level institutions. BOCES agreed to assist me in gaining access to school districts and developing interview and focus group protocols. Anticipating the criticisms of the IRB, BOCES representatives agreed to monitor youth focus group sessions for signs of emotional distress in the young participants—an issue that had raised concerns in previous IRB review sessions.

Because my project involved human participants, it was ineligible for an expedited review process, meaning that it required examination and discussion by the full board, which met only at scheduled bimonthly meetings. As the IRB debated the ethical demerits of my proposal, I was awarded NSF grant funding—pending IRB approval. The IRB, however, had a number of concerns about my project, mostly centered on the possibility that young participants could make statements that would harm them in some way. First, young people could incriminate themselves in front of other participants, saying something that could be used against them and violating their anonymity. It became impossible to ensure that focus group participants would uphold the anonymity of their fellow participants because they later could discuss sensitive and potentially embarrassing statements with people outside the session. Further, eliciting such statements was subject to state and federal reporting laws that require investigators and state employees to provide information about potential abuses or crimes to law enforcement authorities, which would violate the confidentiality of youth participants. Young people were seen as unable or unlikely to understand that making a statement openly in front of peers could not remain confidential, even after being told that this would be the case.

Second, discussing youth Internet safety could lead young people to recall uncomfortable or otherwise harmful experiences—mobilizing the special protections offered to youth as a vulnerable category. In addition to triggering legal reporting requirements, the focus group situation led the IRB to deem that as a sociologist, I was unable to identify a distressed youth participant, raising the topic of the vulnerable child and the negligent (or incompetent) researcher yet again. Youth were seen as potentially too frail to discuss past experiences without incident, and I was seen as lacking the requisite training to identify distressed youth. The IRB positioned BOCES analysts with disciplinary training in educational psychology and experience with institutional research as necessary to the project. Only through the disciplinary expertise of psychology could children be truly protected from the potential harms of open-ended qualitative research.

Given these concerns, the IRB escalated an optional collaboration with BOCES to a project requirement. The IRB would not approve the project without the support of experts in developmental psychology who could monitor and otherwise guide the project. In addition, the IRB further expanded BOCES's role by removing me from the role of facilitator in student focus groups and relegating me to that of observer. Only BOCES analysts would be allowed to engage directly with young people throughout the project. They would guide the focus group sessions as I took notes. Further, no sensitive questions could be asked within a focus group setting, given the risks to participants' anonymity and the need to ensure the psychological well-being of young subjects. At this point, the BOCES analysts suggested that rather than asking the more sensitive questions in a focus group—questions that involved the online practices of youth, the forms of bullying they had experienced, and the risky behaviors they reported engaging in on the Internet—we could ask them in a survey. This was clearly the preferred method because it provided additional protections for youth, allowed for more statistically robust conclusions, and provided the basis for reproducible, generalizable data collection. Such data, while of more limited use for the purposes of a discourse analyst, would be considered more institutionally legitimate, and in turn more likely to drive administrative decision making. Although focus group sessions would be retained in the research design, the discussions would be limited to issues of school policy, curricula, and the ways in which youth understand the relative positioning of adults and youth. By facilitating the discussions, the

BOCES analysts could detect any potentially incriminating or traumatizing statements and immediately halt the conversation.

This configuration satisfied the requirements of the institutional review board, but the project was still denied approval, pending confirmation of BOCES participation. That, in turn, was dependent on NSF funding, which itself was dependent on IRB approval. Eventually, this circular dependency was resolved, which allowed the project to move forward. Overall, the approval process took six months and involved many rounds of memos, IRB meetings, and revisions to the proposal. Throughout this process, IRB members often seemed not to grasp the changes that I made to address their criticisms and would repeat their original criticisms. With each round of revisions, I found it necessary to enumerate all changes because a failure to do so would result in continued rejection. Often, simple changes that addressed the criticisms of the IRB would be rejected, even when they were clearly highlighted in revision memos accompanying the new proposal document. By proposing to speak with young people about their experiences, I evidently had again been placed in the position of the negligent researcher, preparing a project that could place the reputation of my school at risk. I was caught up in a panic surrounding the safety of youth—where worst-case scenarios warped any attempts to modify the project.

Despite proposing a project that centered on issues of youth Internet safety, I was asked repeatedly if it was truly necessary to involve young people in the project—if it was truly necessary to speak with the people whose best interests and safety were at stake. Speaking with youth and taking their perspectives seriously were inherently risky proposals. By seeking to uncover knowledges that had the potential to undermine the privileged position of adults and their capacity to interpret youth social lives, as a researcher I was positioned through the IRB ethical frame as a risky element. Similarly to the ways in which online predators abuse the adult-child relationship to lull youth into a sense of security, as a social scientific predator, I was understood to hold the potential to abuse my power as a researcher to collect data. By taking a patriarchal stance, the IRB acts to manage and limit predatory risks. As described by Susan Boser (2007, 1065), "The IRB exercises power as dominance with the researcher, with the objective of protecting the human participants from the researcher's own power in dominance relation to the participants."

Through the Developmental Frame

Throughout my experiences with survey research—all of which has been collaborative—the operationalization of various concepts through a questionnaire has universally proven to be a site of contestation. Item by item, the disciplinary, methodological, and epistemological commitments of each member of a team of researchers often become painfully clear. My experiences with this particular project involved spending many hours negotiating the minute details of each survey question. In this case, however, there was an additional power imbalance. Because the IRB contracted through BOCES for services and mobilized the formal apparatus of support, BOCES analysts became representatives for the school districts. As such, their role became one of supporting my original project and ensuring the maximum benefit to participating school districts. Although my school's IRB had approved the project through the support of BOCES, the BOCES analysts were able to act as a second and often contradictory interest in the further development of the project.

The original difference in the methodological approaches used by myself and BOCES was the BOCES analysts' focus on generalizability and validity. This move toward generalizability and validity was always couched in terms of providing reports that would benefit the districts within the analysts' counties. The implication was that unless the project was conducted in a manner that met the standards of their disciplinary expertise, there would be no benefit to their constituent school districts. I assume that this was either because the project would not be seen to provide what is commonly understood as "actionable" data or the district administrators would find that the data did not meet their own methodological training grounded in psychology (or both). The methods of data collection and analysis in psychology are so entrenched in the institutional processes of schooling that no other disciplines may produce legitimate or otherwise ethically sound findings. The BOCES researchers had two major concerns—(1) the collection of institutionally relevant data that could be useful to participating school districts and (2) the developmental appropriateness of each survey item that would be presented to the participants (students in grades 6 to 12).

First, the work of collecting data that were valuable to the schools came in the form of additional survey items that addressed some of the concerns of districts themselves. Questions on knowledge of school policies were added, and questions involving the reception of youth Internet safety curricula were rendered through a format commonly used to evaluate school assemblies. A key example of this was the development of a set of questions designed to determine the extent to which young people engaged in multitasking—engaged in multiple simultaneous activities—while using information technologies. The questions asked respondents how many hours they spent engaged in various activities (such as doing school work, gaming, and Web surfing) and then asked them to select which activities they did "at the same time." The survey item was grounded in a concern that the learning process is being interrupted or degraded when students complete homework outside of the school, frequently with unfiltered access to the Internet and mobile devices. This concern was only infrequently mentioned by the administrators and parents I spoke with during interviews and focus group sessions, but it was increasingly reported on by news media that were asking, "But what about homework?" ("Study" 2010) in response to a research report on media multitasking and childhood development (Rideout, Foehr, and Roberts 2010). Multitasking has emerged as a youth Internet safety concern only as the continuous lines of mobile information technologies penetrate the previously disciplined learning spaces of the school and home, problematizing their efficient operation.

Second, negotiations addressed issues of developmentally appropriate terms for the survey. On one level, these negotiations were structural. The length of the survey was reduced based on the limited attention span of young participants. The number of points along Likert scale items was also reduced to make the survey less confusing to participants. The language of the questions was changed and simplified. Many of the questions I originally wrote were simply not askable—even through the mediating, anonymizing mechanism of the survey instrument. Questions regarding experiences with various forms of illegal or risky behaviors were removed from the instrument, leaving only questions regarding victimization. Young respondents could not be asked about their experiences directly in any open-ended way. This became particularly difficult when I received the final data set and found that a number of students had shared detailed experiences—often beyond answering the question posed to them—in response to the open-ended response questions. Many of the participants seemingly had wanted to share their experiences, to explain their problems from their own perspective.

This negotiation was in no way one-sided, and in fairness, it is only in retrospect that I have come to understand the ways in which the disciplinary logic of the school shaped the survey instrument. Both the BOCES researchers and I were relying on naturalized developmental concepts. My previous work on youth Internet safety had involved educators who had similar appropriateness and institutional value concerns, and I had largely come to accept them as the normal course of survey development with youth. In many cases, I grew tired of arguing (and increasingly short on time) and began viewing the survey as largely ancillary to the larger project. Both then and now, I remain committed to forms of research that provide meaningful and relevant information for school districts and parents, even though I am now much more aware of the ways in which doing so can reconstitute and reinforce existing power structures.

Data collection for the project began following approval and confirmation by both my university's IRB and the NSF. Gaining access to school districts can be a slow process, and through the assistance and contacts provided by BOCES, six of the fifteen invited districts agreed to participate in the study. Unfortunately, the six districts that agreed to participate were not as evenly spread across urban, suburban, and rural areas as the original fifteen had been. Further, the largest, most urban of the participating districts was able to provide access to only one of its schools, a small middle school. Although the survey data originally were meant to provide a context for the development of the focus group and interview protocols—including those that would be used for participating parents, administrators, and students—I was prevented from using the data until the end of the data-collection period. The BOCES analysts were in full control of the survey data because it was administered to school districts through an online survey service paid for by BOCES and accessible only by them.

After requesting that the data be provided to me as soon as the first district completed the survey, I was told that the data would not be sent until data collection was complete—even though downloading the data from the service provider and sending it were trivial tasks. The analysts would later change their explanation for withholding the data, but I initially was told that access to the data would bias me for future engagements with parents, administrators, and students. The concern was that, armed with an understanding of response patterns in student surveys, I would ask focus group questions that would support the survey results. Further, there was a concern that I would, accidentally or deliberately, relay some of the existing data to other participants, which the analysts felt threatened the confidentiality of the data and the continued objectivity of the focus group discussions. Additionally, by changing my questions to adapt to the incoming survey data, I would violate the capacity to produce results that would be legitimately comparable across school districts. Later, the stated reason for failing to provide me with the data became the "standard service"—namely, that survey data would not be provided until the analysts had the opportunity to clean and analyze the data, a service they were unwilling to provide until all survey data had been collected. I was told that the analysts would not provide the raw data but instead would perform their own analysis, using that to provide feedback for the draft interview guides that I proposed using during the subsequent focus group sessions and interviews. Reluctantly, I accepted their position on the grounds that the BOCES analysts were providing extensive services at reduced cost and that I arguably had little recourse otherwise. Preventing my receipt of the data until collection and cleaning were complete ensured the highest quality of service.

As the surveys wound down, I visited the six participating districts to conduct focus group sessions and interviews. Per the demands of the IRB, BOCES analysts accompanied me in all student focus groups, facilitating the discussion as I recorded notes silently to avoid engagement with the student subjects. As originally proposed to the IRB, all focus group sessions and interviews were to be recorded, with participants having the option to turn off the recorder, per IRB guidance. While driving to the first research site, I casually mentioned my intent to record the student focus group sessions to the BOCES representative who accompanied me and was told that recording would be impossible. To my surprise, although the university IRB had approved recording, BOCES had not. Again, there was a concern that participants might provide sensitive information that would trigger reporting requirements. In addition to being unable to intervene and ask follow-up questions, I would be left with only the notes taken from focus group discussions. For the facilitators, what mattered was not the words but the concepts as reinterpreted by the researcher on the fly. As a discourse analyst, however, the words were precisely what I was looking to capture—the language, structures, and knowledges that young people mobilized to make sense of their online experiences. Once again, the protection of youth further mediated and suppressed their voices in the project.

The methods used by the analysts to facilitate the sessions were markedly different from those that I otherwise would have used in guiding the conversation. From my perspective as a social scientist, the student focus group sessions were extremely rigid. Interactions frequently took place more as a question-and-response exchange—for the safety of the young participants, of course. In fairness, there were moments during the discussions when the facilitator veered away from the prepared focus group protocol to pursue follow-up questions. However, these moments often were cut short to ensure that the protocol was completed in its entirety, again ensuring the continued validity and generalizability of the student responses. Perhaps most important, young focus group participants were never questioned about their use of various terms—particularly those that seemed self-evident. My attempts to provoke follow-up questions by staring meaningfully at the facilitator during sessions proved to be largely unsuccessful at best and counterproductive at worst. Within the focus group sessions, I had again become the outsider—a social scientific predator, a "creep" in the corner who furiously and silently scribbled notes with a strange electronic pen. This view, it seemed to me, was at least somewhat supported by the student participants, who more than once cast wary glances in my direction. I had once again been placed largely outside of my own research project and was unable to participate or intervene in any meaningful way—which meant that the IRB and the BOCES analysts had successfully managed any and all potential risks of the social scientific predator.

Conclusion

Simply put, some forms of research cannot be undertaken under current ethical regulations—a fact which, stated here, feels uncomfortably like something a social scientific predator might say. A National Research Council (2002, 145) study that examined issues concerning youth and pornography acknowledged that this was the case and provided an example involving the media and violence:

Dorothy Singer, co-director of the Yale University Family Television Research and Consultation Center, was not permitted by her Institutional Review Board to conduct a study that would have measured the impact and short-term behavioral responses of children watching the *Power Rangers*. Ironically, shortly after Singer was prevented from doing this study, a local television station videotaped children's activities on the playground after watching a *Power Rangers* episode.

Private organizations and news media are allowed more latitude to discuss highly sensitive topics and perform otherwise potentially unethical experiments with youth, free from the constraints of institutional review boards. Indeed, much of the youth Internet safety curricula relies on such discussions and even videos of youth being prompted to describe incidents of bullying and sexual abuse, often in great detail. As mentioned previously, researchers are prevented from performing similar work out of fear that young participants will recall past traumas, that information that is elicited through the research will require intervention by law enforcement, or that the discussion will inspire young people to engage in such acts. The protective discourse that surrounds youth research reduces meaningful participation by youth. Allison James, Chris Jenks, and Alan Prout (1998, 188) noted this in their own work on childhood:

Strong though the case for [child protection in research] is, as in debates over children's rights an over-emphasis on protection invites the charge that what resides beneath the rhetoric of welfare is the attempt to exclude children from participation. … In research this would mean, for example, a return to the practice of producing data about children but not with them. Such pressures are sometimes spoken about by government-funded researchers in the U.S. where the notion of children speaking independently of their parents might be seized on as an attack on "family values."

As I have argued here, the organization of the field of research on childhood—through the dominant disciplines and the institutions that have emerged from the work of those disciplines—makes more or less possible various research agendas and outcomes. Working from outside the dominant disciplines and discourses of childhood frames the actions of the researcher as risky and potentially predatory. The boundaries and technologies of childhood are, after all, mechanisms through which child development is secured and optimized (which is the focus of several chapters in this book), and transgressing those boundaries threatens the optimal development of the child.

3   Figuring Youth and the Internet: Media and Legislative Narratives of Youth Internet Safety

Since the early 1980s, generations of youth have had access to information technologies, and prevalent media and legislative discourses have taken as their object the protection of children as they play, communicate, and work online. As Douglas Thomas (1998, 386) asks, "If the goal of law enforcement is to 'protect' us from high tech hoodlums, as is so often claimed, the question remains: what is it that is being 'protected'? And what does it mean to be 'protected'? What are the 'positive effects' of protection?" In the case of Internet safety, legislative and media discourses have considered youth and information technologies as they are relative to the future of the nation—as they produce and reconstitute spaces, technologies, and individuals. Cyberspaces, digital natives, floods of vile content, and shadowy Internet predators are examined through these discourses, which ground them in conceptual resources made possible by varying patterns of technology adoption and use.

Various figures and cyberspaces appear in this chapter. During the teenage hacker scare, media and legislative discourses first identified an online space (a world of sensitive data) and located precocious whiz kids within that world. When cyberporn emerged as a policy problem, legislators placed developing children along an information superhighway, where they were surrounded by the red-light districts of cyberspace. During highly publicized sting operations targeting online sexual abuse, the figures of victimized children and shadowy Internet predators were problematized. Online spaces are constituted through these conceptualizations of childhood and technological development, which bound off youth from predatory forms of behavior, content, and individuals.

Efforts to legislate against youth Internet dangers can be understood as what Helen Nissenbaum (2005) and Julie E. Cohen (2012) have conceptualized as the securitization (Buzan, Wæver, and de Wilde 1998) of information technologies, which mobilizes spectacle to establish threats to social order and set the conditions for further action. Through the lens of securitization, media and legislative discourses construct panics involving youth and the Internet, and this strategic process is bounded by the conceptual resources created by social patterns of technology adoption. Threats to youth safety online are constructed as the widespread adoption of particular forms of technology make possible particular governing productivities, both in terms of conceptual availability and technical affordances. Put more simply, social patterns of technology use make forms of "panic" conceptually possible, and those forms of panic set the conditions for various forms of governance. Conceptualized as such, concerns over youth Internet safety can be contextualized within the broader, disjointed shift from disciplinary societies to societies of control that are undergirded by information technologies. Legislative attempts to protect youth online (and media coverage of those attempts) then become visible as exploratory moves to harness the productivities of newly available and widely adopted control technologies. Mark Nunes (1999) notes that, "metaphors [of cyberspace] do not just organize space; they create a space, or more accurately, they substantiate cyberspace as a virtual topography." Through metaphors of information technology, media reports and legislators produce forms of cyberspace, moving from the smooth virtuality of the teenage hacker scare through to the striated information highways of the cyberporn and predator panics.

WarGamesmanship and Whiz Kids

As is often noted by Internet studies scholars and others who write about information technologies, novelist William Gibson (1982) coined the term *cyberspace* to describe a virtual world of information that was layered on the physical world and that allowed individuals to manipulate representations of information flows and databases. Gibson's term drew on Norbert Wiener's (1948) work on cybernetics and reflected a strong resistance to concepts of intellectual property and a suspicion of controls that might interrupt the creative flow of information. Gibson's term later inspired such terms as *cyberporn*, *cybersex*, *cyberbullying*, and *cybercitizens*, becoming one of central means by which people conceptualize and denote action in a virtual space.

The term *hacker* was rarely used by the mainstream press in the early days of computing, and where the term appeared, it lacked the criminal connotations that it frequently holds today. Instead, media reports used the term primarily in ways that connected it with engineering and technical discourses of practice, arguably in much the same ways those being identified as hackers might have. Hackers were Stewart Brand's (1974) artisan computer bums at Stanford University, Steven Levy's (2001) romanticized poets at the Tech Model Railroad Club (TMRC) at MIT, and young computer and game addicts who were mesmerized by the technology (Wolf 1982). Like Gibson's work, this culture of hacking owed much to the intellectual tradition of cybernetics, and it developed in parallel with early computer and information science programs. Hackers of this era championed the flow of information and the open, playful mastery of technology, exemplified by a central tenant of Levy's (2014) original hacker ethic, "Information should be free." Reconnecting this now infamous phrase back to its cybernetic roots, Adrian Johns (2009, 429) notes that

We still live amid the legacies of these mid-century debates about science and society.

We inherit their terms, and the culture of science that shapes our world is the one left to us by them. If we think "information wants to be free," then we voice a sentiment championed by Wiener, Polanyi, and Plant.

In much the same way, the early concepts of hacking carried with them a particular "culture of science" that shaped understandings of information technologies. Hacking culture was simultaneously a response to authoritarian, traditional paradigms of computer science, and a product of the countercultural movement of the 1960s, emerging from "... a postmodern moment that defines a period in which [knowledge] production is being transformed from a stable, material, physical system to a more fluid, rapid system" (Thomas 2002, xvii). David Gunkel (2001, 13) further explains, "Hacking proposes a mode of investigation that both learns how to infiltrate [sociotechnical] systems that have usually gone unexamined and develops strategies for exploring their functions and reprogramming their operations." It would be permutations of this culture of science, this way of knowing technology and the world, that would later guide the development of early personal computers, and ultimately the young (male, suburban) hobbyists, enthusiasts, and gamers who would come to adopt them in increasing numbers.

In the same year that Gibson coined the term *cyberspace*, an *InfoWorld* columnist warned of an oncoming wave of moral regulation surrounding youth and computers (Stein 1982, 41–42):

> The computer kids are skilled and knowledgeable in a field of intellectual endeavor that adults respect and consider "grown up." ...
>
> I expect that many frustrated and confused parents will be running around, wondering just what the younger generation is coming to. They won't understand the computer culture, and they will quickly discover they have no authority over it. ...
>
> But it will be a problem for the vast number of status-quo-oriented adults who yearn for a return to the secure stability of a romantically remembered yesteryear, when they knew they were atop the pecking order.

In fact, there were signs of adult anxieties over computer technologies and their relationship to youth as reported by the press. In one example, the *Christian Science Monitor* warned of the growing "evasive" lifestyles of younger generations as they retreated into the worlds of computers and video games (Wolf 1982):

> The lure of the computer ... soon may begin to serve as a form of social avoidance in which the traditional Enlightenment guidance systems of reading and writing increasingly are left behind. ... If *Pac-Man* addicts come to believe that the threats to life, like the game, are "just circuitry," or that playing *Space Invaders* can deal with real missiles, then a generation may find itself unable to deal with problems that aren't artificial (and should we now add videoficial?).

Similarly, the *New York Times* provided concerned parents with a primer on computers, encouraged them to "overcome our initial distrust or fear of computers" (Schmidt 1983, A3), and suggested that young people could be disciplined by depriving them of access to computers. Scholastic, Inc. began publishing a series of magazines targeted at families that were attempting to make sense of the new technologies. In an interview, the editor for one of the new publications (*Family Computing*) explained that "Parents feel confused about computers and software, and they feel they have no place to turn" (Collins 1983, A48). Computer technologies were increasingly being made available to youth and were framed as integral for developing skills for the computerized workforce of the future. Personal computers could enhance students' learning experiences and bring new teachers and educational materials directly into the home (Blackburn 2012).

Shortly following the 1983 Scholastic announcement, the homes of six teenagers calling themselves the "414 Gang" (so named for the Milwaukee, Wisconsin, telephone area code) were raided by the Federal Bureau of Investigation for the gang's suspected involvement in digital break-ins (Levy 2001; Sterling 1992). The teens targeted the computer systems at a Los Angeles bank, the Memorial Sloan-Kettering Cancer Center, and an unclassified system at the Los Alamos nuclear weapons research facility, among other organizations with a digital presence (Krance, Murphy, and Elmer-Dewitt 1983). The raid by law enforcement officials and subsequent trials were widely publicized. Reporters were unsure of how to describe what these teenagers had done and initially looked to the recently released movie *WarGames* (1983) to provide context. The film features teenager David Lightman (played by Matthew Broderick) as he types his way into various computer systems in search of computer games, most frequently by making educated guesses at simple passwords. Lightman nearly causes World War III after he attempts to play a "Global Thermonuclear War" simulation with a military missile control device. Although the film never applies a meaningful label to the activity of computer intrusion (the word *hack* does not appear in the script), the similarities between the film and the reported activities of the 414 Gang provided a means by which to report on and make sense of the real-life event.

One report in *Newsweek* called the digital break-ins "WarGamesmanship" and speculated that the 414 Gang's activities may have been a publicity stunt for the movie ("Milwaukee Discovers 'WarGamesmanship'" 1983). As reporters began to interview the 414 Gang and other self-professed hackers, the term *hacking* rapidly became the dominant term used to describe the 414 intrusions. At first, the term was used ambiguously to describe both the playful activities of youth and computer hobbyists as well as the activities of criminals. As the reporting intensified and legislators increasingly were represented in the coverage, the noncriminal connotations of the term receded. The *Boston Globe* (1983, 1) provided a guide to the term and connected the 414 Gang's intrusions to the fictional exploits of *WarGames*'s Lightman:

When one of them could start a war—or thoroughly foul up your company's operations—and the word that describes him isn't even in the dictionaries, it's a case of a word usage catching on before the linguists can catch up with it. ... "Hacker gets access to Congress" was the clever headline on a recent *Globe* story. It reported a "computer-literate" 17-year-old's testimony that ... he was able electronically to break into the computer system at the Los Alamos National Laboratory. In the movie *WarGames*, another young hacker almost triggers World War III when he "accesses" the North American Air Defense Command computer.

Reflecting on the events of 1983, legal scholar Jay BloomBecker (1984, 631) commented:

It is hard to overemphasize the extent to which the "414 gang" was a media event. Neil Patrick was featured on the cover of *Newsweek*, on *Donahue*, America's most respected talk show, on *Good Morning America*, in *People* magazine, and in numerous lesser circulation publications.

Congressional hearings on hacking were convened amid the media coverage framing and driving attention to legislative efforts. One of the 414 hackers, then seventeen-year-old Neil Patrick, testified at one hearing between clips from *WarGames*, which were played to "illustrate, the relative ease with which computers can be accessed by the unauthorized user" (Glickman 1984, 17). When Patrick was asked whether he understood the intrusions as criminal acts, he replied that he had no sense of wrongdoing until the moment that law enforcement agents arrived at his doorstep. In a statement eerily similar to those that later surrounded issues of Internet safety, the resulting report noted that (Glickman 1984, 19),

While the computer hacker might never consider "breaking and entering" into any-one's home, he seems to lose those ethics when gaining unauthorized access to sys-tems. This caused Representative Ron Wyden to speculate that there may be a need to include a section on ethics in basic computer courses.

Several bills were drafted by members of Congress, with nine bills aimed at criminalizing computer trespass or fraud in the year following the 414 Gang raid (U.S. Congress, Office of Technology Assessment 1986). In 1984, the Counterfeit Access Device and Computer Fraud and Abuse Act—later known as the Computer Fraud and Abuse Act (CFAA)—was signed into law, criminalizing "unauthorized access" to "protected" government and finan-cial information systems. The CFAA persists as one of the core pieces of criminal legislation of information systems today. It has since undergone a number of revisions and has been roundly criticized for overbreadth, hav-ing been used by prosecutors in a wide range of court cases from incidents of cyberbullying to trade secret disputes.

The reporting around computer crimes did not appear to directly drive the development of legislation. Often in contrast to the later media coverage of hackers (J. Thomas 2005), the media's early framing of the activities of teens with computers was not always in sync with that provided by legislators. At the time, reporters described the ease with which hacking problems could be handled by corporate security (Pollack 1983), published letters about hero hackers (Wesson 1983), and directed attention to insider crimes perpetrated by adults (Dolnick 1983). The report that resulted from the congressional hearings mentioned that the media tended "misrepresent the nature of the computer hacker's actions ... uncritically, if not admiringly" (Glickman 1984, 19) and that this was problematic as teenage computer hacking spread. Further, the intrusions of the 414 Gang into various government and corporate systems were not the first or even the first publicized computer crimes in history (Farr 1975; Parker 1976). At the time, federal and state legislators were aware of these activities and had created computer crime legislation in the years preceding the event. No legislation, however, produced the widespread media coverage or swift legislative response that surrounded the activities of the 414 Gang and other perceived gangs of teenaged hackers.

The problematization of teenage hacking by legislators and the media was not a response to the broad range of computer crimes perpetrated by both adults and young people. Instead, the response represented an intersection of anxieties surrounding youth and technology in a pattern that has been similarly reproduced throughout the history of Internet safety. Personal computers—and by extension the children and teenagers who used them—were largely underdetermined by the adults who purchased them for family use in the 1980s. The *WarGames* film and the media coverage surrounding the 414 Gang were both a product and reinforcement of these anxieties, providing a widely accessible narrative through which to conceptualize computer technologies and young people for the first time. Although earlier narratives of adult computer crime held little relevance for middle-class and affluent households, the relative lack of understanding of youth computer use made possible worst-case narratives of teenage hackers and demanded adult intervention. Undergirded by anxieties over the computerization of the workforce amid an economic recession that peaked in 1982, these narratives discursively constituted a computerized generation within a lawless computerized space, leaving behind underskilled, jobless adults in the "real world." As such, legislative territorialization was necessary as part of a process to establish the computer world as a safe space for commerce and private communication and to bring adult order to cyberspace.

Although earlier coverage of computer crimes perpetrated by adults could be conceptualized as the use of advanced tools to commit fraud and other conceptually established crimes, the break-ins by the 414 Gang involved computers as the subject of the crime (Hollinger and Lanza-Kaduce 1988; Parker 1976). Unlike previous crimes, these took place entirely within the world of the computer, with no physical component outside of the computers and their operators. The media coverage and legislative activity that resulted after the 414 Gang raid (and the *WarGames* movie release) discursively spatialized new information technologies in ways that reestablished dominant notions of property and privacy. As such, hacking and unauthorized browsing were framed as "breaking into" private spaces and criminal "trespassing" (Pollack 1983) rather than as simply accessing relatively insecure content. One *New York Times* article, entitled "The World of Data Confronts the Joy of Hacking" (1983, E20), makes this construction clear by setting up a "confrontation" between a hacker turned security expert (Geoffrey Goodfellow) and the legendary phone phreak Cap'n Crunch (John Draper). In the interview with the expert and the hacker, the article constructs the "world of data" and asks the interviewees, "Is it criminal to *enter* somebody else's computer?" (emphasis added) Goodfellow responds to the question, analogizing computers to physical homes ("The World of Data" E20):

When we were brought up, we were taught about trespassing. If you go to a friend's house and the front door is wide open, I don't really know of anyone who would walk right in to look around. I would stand at the door, ring the doorbell or knock or call out. That type of responsibility or sense of morals has to be slid down onto the computer.

This narrative was easily transferred to legislative discussions, and the congressional hearings preceding the Computer Fraud and Abuse Act devoted much time to discussing the need for clear legal concepts of computer trespass and digital damage (Glickman 1984).

Operating within this new space of the computer were the media figures of a new generation, not unlike those of the digital native prevalent today (Prensky 2001a, 2001b). Stephanie Ricker Schulte (2008) notes that legislative and media discourses widened and reinforced the generation gap, setting younger generations apart as biologically distinct from adults.

As with the digital natives, the distance between the generations was perceived to generate power. Having "grown up with" technologies, children and teenagers were seen to have abilities that parents and guardians could not match. Schulte explains that remedies to the "problem" of this generational gap, such as computer kits and educational camps, provided adults with the tools they needed to monitor and control their children. Young people's newfound mastery of technology was framed as a confrontation with adult authority, and such resistance was framed as a core element of hacker culture (D. Thomas 2002). Within media discourses, the hacker came to represent a new generation, building on preexisting narratives of the "whiz kid"—the hyperintelligent, digitalized everyteen who not-so-innocently wielded the power of new information technologies. The figure of the computer whiz kid was present in the media for years before the 1983 release of *WarGames*, but it became more prevalent in the years following. In addition to being used to describe both the film's fictional David Lightman (Harmetz 1983) and the actual 414 Gang member Neil Patrick, whiz kids were in the fast lane (McKean 1983), official frontrunners of a digital generation (Miller 1980), and in clear need of moral guidance (Denning 1983). A television show entitled *Whiz Kids* (Allen 1983; Shea 1983) was developed for CBS featuring a team of precocious computer hackers who used computer technologies to help the police solve crimes. Press images from both *WarGames* and *Whiz Kids* later were featured in a *Popular Science* article entitled "Catching Computer Crooks" (Eskow and Green 1984), which despite the imagery focused solely on adult criminals.

These perceived abilities of the teenage whiz kid—like the digital native—were vastly inflated compared to the actual abilities of most children and teenagers. Most hacking attempts by young people were successful due not to a complex understanding of computer programming but rather to a lack of basic computer security. By their own admission, members of the 414 Gang accessed computer systems by using an administrative account with a default password available for testing purposes (Witt 1985). *WarGames* provides a somewhat accurate portrayal of this process in a montage that shows Lightman as he makes educated guesses about the password of the nuclear defense system that nearly causes World War III. However, it portrays these basic efforts as requiring youthful ingenuity and technical skills that the adults in the film lack. At the time, computers, modems, networks, and automated technologies were all understood as exoticized elements of youth culture, accessible only to the quick-thinking, computational minds of the next generation. In a room full of adult authority figures, Lightman is the only person who can outthink the machine and save the world. The whiz kid—the collapsed figure of David Lightman and Neil Patrick—simultaneously occupied the position of the innocent high-potential kid next door and the dangerously anti-establishment troublemaker.

In this environment, the laws that were created to criminalize hacking activities can be read as a symbolic action aimed at sending a message to would-be hackers. Richard C. Hollinger and Lonn Lanza-Kaduce (1988, 118) note that

The principal function of symbolic computer crime laws given current power arrangements is that they send clear cultural messages to youthful dissidents in the privileged classes about the importance of property and privacy interests without penalizing them.

Beyond sending a message, these media and legislative discourses moved to refigure traditional adult-child power relations within a newly constructed space of the computer world. Through media and legislative discourses, it was now both possible and necessary for adults to monitor and govern youth computer activities to protect the newly conceptualized "world of data." In this way, as Schulte (2008, 487) describes, "both internet technology itself and its users [were cast] as rebellious teenagers in need of parental control."

"Info Superhighway Veers into Pornographic Ditch"

At the dawn of the "golden age of hacking" (J. Thomas 2005) in the early to mid-1980s, federal legislators and law enforcement officers began taking action against child pornographers and pedophiles online, initially targeting those who used electronic bulletin boards to trade information about minors who were willing to participate in sexual activities. These early actions were best exemplified by the Computer Pornography and Child Exploitation Act of 1985, sponsored by Senator Paul Trible Jr. (R-VA) (Mace 1985). Initially targeting the transmission of child pornography, the bill eventually developed criminal penalties for storing or transmitting "any obscene, lewd, or lascivious writing, description, or picture" via a computer (Computer Pornography 1985b). The bill expanded from protecting children from victimization by child pornography to regulating the larger, legal pornography industry. As Trible (Computer Pornography 1985a, 3) described at a congressional hearing on the bill:

the content of pornographic material has changed markedly. Where simple nudity was once the order of the day, today's pornography features children, bondage, bestiality, and violence. These changes are deeply troublesome. They presage a new and, I believe, more threatening sex industry.

Under concerns about its unconstitutionality, the bill was never passed, although segments of the law unrelated to obscenity were later adopted by the state of Florida. At the same time, increasing numbers of middle-class households gained access to telecommunications networks and electronic bulletin board systems (BBSs) through personal computers, modems, and dial-up services, providing young people with access to early forms of online communication. As more children and teenagers gained online access to content that traditionally had been hidden "underground," media reports of youth access to pornographic and other sexually explicit content were published along with coverage of child pornography. In one early example, a reporter wrote ("There's an X-Rated Side to Home Computers, Parents Warned" 1987, 47):

Usually operated by computer aficionados out of their homes, the boards can provide off-color jokes, adult pictures, formats for trading sexual messages and dating services. All this, just by dialing up the right numbers. Computers also are used by pedophiles, adults with a sexual interest in children.

In this way, the child pornography problem became linked with the growing accessibility of pornographic content online, particularly as developing personal computer technologies allowed for the display of increasingly multimedia content. Although by 1990 there was still relatively little coverage of youth access to pornography online, a familiar narrative had begun to emerge—that young people accidentally found online obscenity while engaged in other pursuits. As a Texas newspaper describes (Abernathy 1990, 1),

High school student Jeff Noxon's homework was rudely interrupted recently when he stumbled across the world's most sophisticated pornography ring. After musing at the novelty of seeing sexually explicit material, he went on to other studies. Noxon glimpsed only part of an electronic catalog of erotic art and literature that grows daily, offering titles such as "Cindy's Torment" and "The Education of Rachel." It's

supported by taxes and brought into town by the brightest lights of higher education. The purveyor of Jeff's surprise and Cindy's slavery is a grand undertaking called
the Internet. It is the world's most capable research tool, but it is an equally efficient
conduit for pornography and a tempting target for computer hackers.

Such stories drew the attention of lawmakers as it became apparent that
networked computers were not simply educational tools but also the unre-
stricted means of accessing adult content. Among the first legislators to
begin voicing concerns was Senator Jim Exon (D-NE), who spearheaded
what became known as the Communications Decency Act (CDA) of 1996.
Exon had cosponsored previous legislation against child pornography and
began pushing for amendments to the Communications Act of 1996 as it
was being developed in the form of the CDA. Through these amendments,
Exon sought to extend the regulations that restricted harassment and indecency via telephone calls to include any telecommunications services that
made such content available to minors. During nearly every discussion
of these issues on the Senate floor, Exon requested that an accompanying news article be read into the record. In the first such instance, in July
1994, Exon referenced an article from the *Los Angeles Times* that described
the illegal use of servers at a government research facility to host pornographic images—although Exon seemingly changed the article's title from
"Computer at Nuclear Lab Used for Access to Porn" (Bauman 1994) to "Info
Superhighway Veers into Pornographic Ditch" (Communications Decency
Act 1994a). Writing a letter to a constituent who apparently was concerned
about online content and crime, Senator Jim Exon stated that (Communications Decency Act 1994b)

All Americans look forward to the arrival of new telecommunications technology.
Families will gain new options for communication and entertainment and students
will gain easy access to a wealth of knowledge. At the same time, recent stories of
computer and telecommunications technologies being used to transmit pornography, to engage in "electronic stalking" and to engage children in pornographic or
indecent electronic conversations send shivers up the spine of all families. ... As I
said in my statement introducing the Decency Amendments, the information superhighway should not become a "red light district."

Exon outlines a particular vision of "new telecommunications technology," "students," and the nation and presents dangers that unregulated
technological spaces might pose to society. In so doing, he notes a variety
of potential problems (notably, stalking, sexual predation, and pornography) that went on to draw national attention. Only one of those problems

captured the attention of the media and other legislators at the time he was writing—cyberporn.

The amendments posed by Exon did not go without criticism, however, and other senators argued that the proposed legislation violated the constitution and established undue chilling effects (Feingold 1995; Kerrey 1995; Leahy 1995). Given the legally problematic nature of Exon's bill—especially the use of vague terms such as *indecent* and *patently offensive* to regulate online speech—it was poorly received by most legislators. Indeed, the chair of the Senate Commerce Committee, which was responsible for the Communications Act as a whole, originally intended to table the bill (Dewitt, Block, Cole, and Epperson 1995). Sensing the possibility of such an action, Exon prepared a "blue binder" of online pornography, which he presented to the Senate, inviting all to view the shocking material he had gained access to. After viewing the binder, even those who were opposed to the specific changes suggested by Exon began to acknowledge a problem with youth exposure to pornography online. Shortly afterward and prior to any congressional hearings on the matter of online pornography, Exon's amendments were put to a vote and passed the Senate with relatively little opposition (84 to 16). The senators, it seemed, were hesitant to appear as supporters of online pornography in the public record. As Senator Russ Feingold (D-WI) described in a later hearing (Cyberporn and Children 1995a),

Members of the Senate reacted as any parent would when they were confronted with the "blue binder" filled with pornography downloaded from the Internet. ... They voted for an amendment they thought penalized pornographers and sexual predators and which purported to protect children.

Following the passing of the bill by the Senate, *Time* magazine published a cover-story article on the problem of youth access to pornography ("Cyber Porn" 1985). The issue featured a pale, dimly lit child, gasping in horror with his fingers at the keyboard. The headline read "CYBER PORN." The article mentions that Senator Exon first drew *Time* magazine's attention to the issue and cited a Carnegie Mellon study in prepublication at the *Georgetown Law Journal* (Dewitt 1995):

What the Carnegie Mellon researchers discovered was: THERE'S AN AWFUL LOT OF PORN ONLINE. In an 18-month study, the team surveyed 917,410 sexually explicit pictures, descriptions, short stories and film clips. On those Usenet newsgroups where digitized images are stored, 83.5% of the pictures were pornographic.

The statistic captured the public imagination and was misquoted for years, generating the now common myth that "the Internet is 80 percent porn." Despite the sensationalistic cover image and the initial focus on the prevalence and popularity of online pornography, the *Time* article was often critical of legislative efforts to regulate such content. Opinions were solicited from constitutional law experts, freedom of speech advocates, and pro-pornography researchers. The article closed with a quote from Electronic Frontier Foundation (EFF) cofounder John Perry Barlow, who stated that the burden of responsibility was on parents—not legislators—to protect youth from online content. Later that month, the *Time* article was referenced and entered into the *Congressional Record*, with legislators seemingly overlooking the critical tone it adopted and instead focusing on the statistics published from the Carnegie Mellon study. Presenting the article in support of an additional antipornography bill that proposed further amendments to the Communications Act, Senator Chuck Grassley (R-IA) stated, "There is a flood of vile pornography, and we must act to stem this growing tide, because … it incites perverted minds" (Cyberporn and Children 1995b). Once again returning to the idea that both children and adults would inevitably be exposed to this "flood of vile pornography," Grassley read a second article into the record. Entitled "An Electronic Sink of Depravity" (Winchester 1995, 9–12), the author describes his experiences as a "typical enough user" who "had stumbled, not entirely accidentally, into a sinkhole of electronic but very real perversion" comprised of graphic stories and messages from "pasty-faced and dysfunctional men with halitosis who inhabit damp basements." The article featured a sketch of a man with the head of a computer monitor, opening his trench coat to suggestively reveal a pale naked body. Later presiding over a hearing on cyberporn, Senator Grassley described the policy problem in his opening statement (Cyberporn and Children 1995b):

Until very recently, parents could breathe easier in their own homes. After all, the home is supposed to be safe and be a barrier between your children and the dark forces which seek to corrupt and destroy our youth. But enter the Internet and other computer networks. Suddenly, now not even the home is safe. … I want to say that computer communications holds much promise, as we all know. The world of Internet and cyberspace is one that should be used to better humankind, not tear it down. I believe that we in Congress must give America's parents a new comfort level in public and commercial networks if these are to be transformed from the private preserve of a special class of computer hackers into a widely used communications medium. This necessary transition will never happen if parents abandon the Internet and computer communication technology remains threatening.

Although Grassley's own amendments were never passed and the Carnegie Mellon study was publicly discredited (Corcoran 1995), the CDA quickly was passed by the House of Representatives. For anyone involved in the debate, inappropriate content and contact undeniably presented problems.

The efforts to regulate cyberporn occurred during a period of heightened interest in what the Bill Clinton administration termed the national information infrastructure (NII). As described by Tarleton Gillespie (2007), under the leadership of Vice President Al Gore, the national information infrastructure model was intended to render cyberspace hospitable to investment and commerce. The NII's utopian vision of the twenty-first-century economy justified regulatory actions concerning social issues that were perceived to benefit from further development of the Internet and information technologies. An "Agenda for Action" described the goals and potentials of the NII (National Information Infrastructure 1993):

The development of the National Information Infrastructure is not an end in itself; it is a means by which the United States can achieve a broad range of economic and social goals. Although the NII is not a "silver bullet" for all of the problems we face … Americans can harness this technology to:

• Create jobs, spur growth, and foster U.S. technological leadership;

• Reduce health care costs while increasing the quality of service in underserved areas;

• Deliver higher-quality, lower-cost government services;

• Prepare our children for the fast-paced workplace of the 21st century; and

• Build a more open and participatory democracy at all levels of government.

This is not a far-fetched prediction. … Our current information infrastructure is already making a difference in the lives of ordinary Americans, and we have just begun to tap its potential.

The regulation of cyberporn was portrayed as a critical step in the securing of the NII. Because creating an Internet that is free of pornographic and indecent content was seen as a necessary step toward harnessing the potential of networked information technologies, any legislator who failed to support Exon's amendments would not only appear to support pornography, but additionally seem uninterested in securing the technological future of the United States.

Only months after the CDA was passed, it was ruled unconstitutional by the United States Supreme Court on the grounds that critical portions of the law violated First Amendment rights (*Reno v. American Civil Liberties Union* 1997). The ruling seemed to reinforce the perceived need for further legislation. Immediately following the ruling, President Clinton (1997) made a statement on the issue:

The Internet is an incredibly powerful medium for freedom of speech and freedom of expression that should be protected. It is the biggest change in human communications since the printing press, and is being used to educate our children, promote electronic commerce, provide valuable health care information, and allow citizens to keep in touch with their government. But there is material on the Internet that is clearly inappropriate for children. As a parent, I understand the concerns that parents have about their children accessing inappropriate material. … With the right technology … we can help ensure that our children don't end up in the red light districts of cyberspace.

Accordingly, Congress made a second attempt to regulate youth access to pornography in the form of the Child Online Protection Act (COPA) of 1998. COPA moved to restrict minors from access to online "material that is harmful to minors" or that depicted actual or simulated sexually explicit content "in a manner patently offensive with respect to minors" (Child Online Protection Act 1998). The Supreme Court also quickly struck down this second act as unconstitutional. Finally, in 2000 the Children's Internet Protection Act was passed. It required public libraries and schools that receive telecommunications federal funding (through e-rate discounts) to implement online content filtering systems and to enact safety policies for the management of inappropriate content, hacking, and disclosure of personal information (Children's Internet Protection Act 2000a). This legislation was linked to the protected development of youth, and a congressional report provided an explicit stance on pornographic content (Children's Internet Protection Act 2000b):

Natural sexual development occurs gradually, throughout childhood. Exposure of children to pornography distorts this natural development by shaping sexual perspective through premature exposure to sexual information and imagery.

As with the criminalization of hacking, legislative and media discourses around cyberporn figured both youth and technology. Through concerns over cyberporn, primarily using the frame of the information superhighway, these figurations became more clearly defined as they placed youth and technology along a developmental track towards a particular vision of the future. This future held promise for the developmental progress of youth, the economy, and the nation, with heightened levels of economic activity, better access to education and health care, and a more strongly democratic government, per President Clinton's statement referenced earlier in the chapter. The fear seemed to be that without legislative action that redistricted the Internet, parents and children would be "scared away" from or "abandon" the potentials offered by the Internet and information technologies. Further, without the potentials of the Internet, young people would fail to have safe access to the technologies of the future and therefore would fail to develop their own potential as a generation. As Vice President Al Gore noted during opening statements at a national Internet Online Summit (1977),

There is a view, which I consider an absurd view, that defines "children" as "nothing more than miniature adults," not really in need of special protection from material that their parents believe they're not ready to process and handle. Well, children are not "miniature adults." Their minds are developing and growing and evolving. And they are especially vulnerable to some kinds of images and information that, of course, ought to be freely available to adults who have matured and developed and have the full rights of citizenship to choose whatever they want to see and listen to and read and look at. Children are in a different category, and that ought not be a controversial conclusion. ... In short, we must meet this 21st-century challenge in a 21st-century way, not by using the heavy hand of government in ways that would harm and squelch this exciting new resource, and certainly not by ignoring the dangers and allowing our children to roam free and unsupervised on the Internet.

It is perhaps no accident that Gore's statement came amid a growing interest in a new sociology of childhood. For Gore, speaking the discourse of the national information infrastructure, developing youth (symbolizing the social stability of the nation) become intertwined with developing information technologies (symbolizing economic and technological dominance). Developing youth and developing information technologies are bound together in a way that stifles any form of criticism or dissenting opinion.

Implicit in the concerns voiced by legislators is a sense of what children and teenagers are and how they develop, and this sense is so widely held and clearly inviolable that both the Communications Decency Act (CDA) of 1994 and Child Online Protection Act (COPA) of 1998 were signed into law despite an understanding by legislators that they were largely unconstitutional undertakings. Made clear was the concept that all porno-graphic content would permanently damage the fragile developing minds of youth. The "flood of vile pornography ... incites perverted minds" (Protection of Children from Computer Pornography Act 1995, S9017). This was an explicitly developmental concern, as described by Senator Strom Thurmond (R-SC) (Cyberporn and Children 1995c),

Our children are the future of this country. What they see and what they hear and what they do determine the type of citizens they make. We must have the right environment for them, and we must guard in every way to see that they have the right associates. ... The indecency, the outlandishness of pornography being presented where children can reach it should not be allowed under the law.

Any other position within the debate was made untenable. If legislators questioned the harm caused by pornographic content or even pointed out that the question was never raised, they would be placed in the politically difficult situation of seeming to support youth access to pornography and the production of perverted minds. The manner in which viewing porno-graphic content was conceptualized and placed within the new space of the information superhighway further defined the developing figure of the child. In this view, children and teenagers are innocent figures devoid of sexual desire and cannot be described in a way that suggests that they would willingly seek out pornographic content online. As such, the language of "stumbling" repeatedly appears, describing the ways that young people—tasked with the performance of normal development through information technologies by adults—accidentally view "inappropriate," "adult," or "vile" online content. Having stumbled on this content, under-developed minds are incapable of properly framing or processing adult information. Young people do not consume or view adult material—indicating a capacity for interpretive processing—and instead are exposed to adult material. This perspective was made apparent in the language of the CDA and COPA, which criminalized the use of a computer to *send* or *display* content, counted as individual instances of *posting* rather than viewings of material by youth. The language of consumption would otherwise lend too much agency to youth, opening the dangerous possibility that they might actively seek obscene content. As described by David Oswell (1999, 59) in an analysis of Internet safety policies in the United Kingdom,

it seems significant that in regulatory thinking the agency of the child has remained invisible. The child is spoken for, and represented, but rarely, if ever, given a voice.

In policy calculations concerning Internet content regulation, the child is clearly the object, rather than the agent, of representation. If the child is constituted outside of itself, in the field of discourse and government, then agency simply cannot be assumed.

So, too, did "stumbling" off the information superhighway conceptualize a particular form of developing cyberspace. At the time of the proposed CDA amendments, personal computers were rapidly moving away from text-based interfaces in favor of easier to use graphical operating systems, and the World Wide Web was beginning to take hold as the primary representation of the Internet. Microsoft had just begun to ask computer users "Where do you want to go today?" as part of an advertising campaign for Windows (Wieden and Kennedy 1994).

The information superhighway represented a new step in the development of the Internet—later referred to as Web 1.0 or the read-only Web. Accordingly, most computer users interacted with the early Web primarily by accessing content, not creating it. These new forms of adoption patterns made possible a concept of an Internet that was so full of pornographic content that users could not help but be exposed to it during everyday Web surfing. As Schulte (2008) describes, information technologies were figured as teenaged and in need of parenting through the criminalization of hacking, but the cyberporn panic perhaps ushered in a phase of emerging adulthood. The Internet was in need of protected spaces within which its potential could be developed away from the domains of the unregulated adult market. It must be prevented from "Veer[ing] into [a] Pornographic Ditch" (Communications Decency Act 1994a). What was once the space of the "world of data" became that of cyberspace, which increasingly was circumscribed by the information superhighway of the Clinton administration.

The discursive mechanism of this circumscription is apparent in references to the metaphorical online "red-light district," either in terms of specific cyberspaces that offer sexually explicit content or in terms of the entire Internet as a space within which sexually explicit content is unavoidable. These spaces are tolerated by legislators because they are protected by the First Amendment, but they are nonetheless described as being morally "vile" and "indecent," lacking a role in twenty-first-century cyberspace. When cyberspace is conceptualized in this way, the filtering and redistricting of the Internet through legislative efforts become both possible and necessary. It is perhaps no coincidence that as Senators Exon and Grassley were beginning to propose various forms of cyberporn regulation, Mayor Rudolph Giuliani of New York City was controversially enacting zoning resolutions that were designed to shift adult businesses out of Times Square, away from churches and schools, and into selected commercial areas (Simon 1995). But the red-light district and the information superhighway operate as part of a broader set of metaphors that conceptualize the Internet as a Cartesian space, establishing the possibility of virtual architectures and, by extension, disciplinary techniques of governance. As Paul C. Adams (1997, 158–159) explains,

Gore uses the highway metaphor as a basis for radical redesign of the media to support civic society ... advocat[ing] government regulation to ensure that access is not overwhelmed by market forces. ... An architectural metaphor serves less to define a sense of place than to indicate a set of social functions. ... We might worry that the primary function of virtual architecture would be a kind of containment, in which there were no longer an "outside" and populations were everywhere contained and subjugated.

Although the CDA overtly criminalized the sending or display of content to minors through individual acts of posting—again constituting youth as unable to play a role in the active consumption of pornography—in practice, the CDA moved to modify the technical architecture of the Internet (Cannon 1996). To bar access to minors, adult services would have to develop mechanisms that could identify potential users. The redistricting of the Internet via the CDA operated as an initial move to install disciplinary technologies of governance into the developing Internet, moving toward mechanisms for individual identification and regimentation of space within the new virtual world.

Although Vice President Al Gore is attributed with developing and circulating the concept of the information superhighway, the term also was taken up by Gilles Deleuze (1992a) as both support for and evidence of a shift toward a new mode of governance—that of the societies of control. Deleuze (2007, 322) describes the highway as exemplary of a control technology:

Control is not discipline. You do not confine people with a highway. But by making highways, you multiply the means of control. I am not saying this is the only aim of highways, but people can travel infinitely and "freely" without being confined while being perfectly controlled. That is our future.

Given the coincidental timing of the two concepts, it is clear that that the metaphor of the information superhighway influenced Deleuze's thinking on the societies of control (Guins 2009). Nunes (1999) offers a means for theorizing metaphors of virtual space through the work of Deleuze, suggesting that the concept of the information superhighway as developed by Gore and the national information infrastructure substantiates a form of "striated" space—the "linear, point-oriented, and Cartesian ... system of regulated connections between determined points on dedicated lines." Similarly, the metaphor of the online red-light district is that of a striated space where pornographic content is confined away from the informational districts of education and commerce. In contrast, the space substantiated by the metaphor of the pornography-filled Internet can be best conceptualized what Gilles Deleuze and Félix Guattari (1987) describe as "smooth" space that is fluid and free from the demarcations of state control and where users are constantly in danger of exposure to obscene content. The metaphor of the information superhighway makes possible and sets the conditions for the installation of disciplinary control into the newly figured space of the Internet.

Conceptualized as such, the ultimately ineffectual move by legislators to bound off pornographic content through the CDA was not one of moral panic. Instead, it becomes an initial, stumbling foray into harnessing the new potentials and productivities made possible by the Internet as a control technology, using the more familiar operative codes of disciplinary power. Further, the development of highly controversial legislation to address a widely publicized media issue drew public attention to the issue of pornographic and obscene content online. Between the stable regulatory effort of CIPA (demonstrating the willingness of the state to filter public information systems) and the public statements of Gore and Clinton, an image of appropriate parenting practice was placed into circulation. It became clear that even with successful legislation, parents would play an important role in the supervision of online spaces, and developers of filtering technology would provide the tools through which to facilitate such supervision. As Guins (2008, 44) describes:

In line with the instrumentalist view of technology, the state and the market take a "hands-off" approach that refines their role as supplier of tools legislating to enable through self-regulation. In our hands is placed a beneficent technology that will enable parents to exert more control over culture with ease and automatic results. ... Security resides in the home and in the hand of parental control.

Although the legislative efforts of Senators Exon and Grassley undoubt-edly were sincere, the failure of the CDA simply "works" with the distribu-tion of filtering technologies into the home as part of the broader assemblage of Internet safety. Further, these initial experiments with filtering technolo-gies—many of which occurred during the Supreme Court's hearings in *Reno v. ACLU* that ultimately declared the CDA unconstitutional—demonstrated the inefficiencies of attempting to centralize filtering and other similar dis-tricting efforts (Heins 2008).

In the late 1990s and early 2000s, youth Internet safety legislation appeared somewhat infrequently in Congress, and it included the Internet Freedom and Family Empowerment Act of 1995, the Protection of Chil-dren from Computer Pornography Act of 1995, the Protection of Children from Sexual Predators Act of 1998 (passed into law), the Children's Online Privacy Protection Act of 1998 (passed into law), the Dot Kids Name Act of 2001, and the Who Is E-mailing Our Kids Act of 2001. Beginning in 2000, numerous resolutions were made to recognize particular "Children's Inter-net Safety" months. In 2005, however, the news media began to focus on another aspect of Internet safety—online sexual predators. By this time, new generations of youth were taking part in social networking sites such as MySpace and Facebook. Although the existence of sexual predators online had been known to legislators as early as 1994, the rise of social network-ing platforms and advanced search engines made the possibility of online predation increasingly imaginable by the media, legislators, and parents.

Keeping the Internet Devoid of Sexual Predators

On November 11, 2004—the same month that MySpace users reached five million (Scalet 2007)—an announcer for the television show *Dateline NBC* began a now infamous special episode called "Dangerous Web" (Hansen 2004a):

It's a *Dateline* hidden camera investigation no parent will want to miss. This man could be your neighbor. He thinks he's at this house to have sex with a 14-year-old girl. He met her just hours ago in an Internet chat room. The kind your kids may visit every day.

The problem of online predation was framed "as you'll see in our inves-tigation, [an] epidemic." Hosted by reporter Chris Hansen, the *Dateline* program showed how members of its team lured "online predators" by presenting themselves in AOL and Yahoo! chat rooms as teenagers who were "home alone and looking for sex" (Hansen 2004b). *Dateline* employees were unable to do the work of luring themselves, so Hansen partnered with an online vigilante group known as Perverted Justice, who provided expertise in "the teen-speak of the Internet." After chat users were persuaded to meet in person, Hansen and a hidden camera crew waited at a rented home in Bethpage, New York, where they confronted and interviewed the eighteen men who arrived. The men ranged in age and profession, including a television producer and a New York firefighter. One entered the home, asking the female decoy to openly state that she was nineteen. Hansen noted that "They're all over, and yet there's nothing to make them stand out in the crowd. Everyday members of the community. ... They're very inventive. So inventive, that kids might not sense the danger." The footage frequently cut between images of the male "travelers" who were fooled by the sting, edited chat transcripts, and shadowy images of masculine hands on dark keyboards.

As part of the special program, Hansen interviewed a group of students, asking them if they had ever been approached by a stranger online. All of them raised their hands. None of them had told their parents. One girl explained: "Because we're scared of what they'll say ... like, if we'll get in trouble or yell at me, or ground me from never going online ever again." Some of them had actively participated in conversations with online strangers. A student named Laiomi was portrayed as being particularly good at circumventing parental restrictions:

Hansen (narrating): But if parents think they can completely protect their kids by installing standard software or setting ground rules, think again.
Laiomi: There's always ways to bend those rules and stuff like that.
Hansen: So you know how to get around that stuff.
Laiomi: Yeah. ... Rules are made to be broken. (laughing) Sorry!

Later it was revealed that Laiomi was the daughter of an NBC producer who already had set up parental control settings and established rules for Internet use with her daughter. Because these precautions were shown to be insufficient to prevent Laiomi from contacting online strangers, the producer agreed to meet with someone from law enforcement. *Dateline* showed a meeting between the producer and Detective Mike Sullivan, who demonstrated how to install and configure the extensive range of parental control software on the family's computer, including keylogging, full video capture, and automated Internet safety alert systems. After Laiomi is allowed back onto the now fully monitored family computer, Hansen and Sullivan end the show paradoxically by noting that a strong relationship between parents and children protects kids better than any technical fix (Hansen 2004a).

In "Dangerous Web," *Dateline*'s first special segment on this topic, the men who were caught by the unofficial sting operation were free to leave at any time. "Dangerous Web" proved to be immensely popular, and additional specials on Internet predators were planned. The next two episodes were released in November 2005 and February 2006 as a new series (*To Catch a Predator*) focused on sting operations, removing any additional content involving actual youth or safety practices. With each special, the show became increasingly popular, driving additional civilian sting operations across the nation and the eventual cooperation of law enforcement officials. Spin-off shows were developed, highlighting the tapes produced by Hansen's investigations. In 2006, *Dateline* aired nine additional *To Catch a Predator* programs. Although the viewing ratings remained high for the show, with *Dateline* viewership increasing by approximately one million households during the programs, NBC faced pressure from advertisers and critics who questioned the methods used to lure suspects (Stelter 2007). A further incident involving the identification and eventual suicide of a Texas district attorney drew further negative attention to the show. Eventually, pressure mounted as advertisers asked to be removed from the *To Catch a Predator* time slots, and the final episode was aired in December 2007. Use of the term *online predators* by the news media grew exponentially during the years in which the show aired (Marwick 2008).

Between 2006 and 2007, ten bills targeting online predation of youth were introduced in Congress, with names such as the Protecting Children in the Twenty-first Century Act, the Deleting Online Predators Act (DOPA), and the Providing Resources, Officers, and Technology to Eradicate Cyber Threats to Our Children Act (PROTECT Our Children Act). Congressional hearings on online predation focused primarily on social networking sites.

The first congressional hearing, entitled Making the Internet Safe for Kids: The Role of ISPs and Social Networking Sites, was held in June 2006 and included testimony from Chris Hansen and representatives from AOL, MySpace, and Facebook. Kentucky representative Ed Whitfield (Republican) opened the hearing by explaining that the Internet had produced "a 'virtual Sears catalog' for pedophiles" and oriented the hearing around developing methods for assisting law enforcement in investigations and prosecutions of online predators (Making the Internet Safe 2006c). Continuing, Whitfield remarked on the role of Internet service providers (Making the Internet Safe 2006c):

I want to thank also the representatives of the Internet service providers who are here today. We look forward to their testimony explaining what they are doing to assist law enforcement in cases involving this sexual exploitation of children over the Internet and what measures the companies are taking to minimize opportunities to sexually exploit children from their networks.

As with the issue of online pornographic content, this hearing again linked the issue of online predation to that of child pornography, although Hansen provided testimony on predation through chat networks. More hearings were held, including one on the Deleting Online Predators Act and another entitled Sex Crimes and the Internet, and testimony in each linked child pornography and online predation, which in turn was linked to social networking sites. Among the introduced bills, one was signed into law—the Keeping the Internet Devoid of Sexual Predators (KIDS) Act of 2008. Sponsored by Senator Charles Schumer (D-NY) in 2007, the act required registered sex offenders to register online identifiers, allowing social networks to ban them.

Much like the discursive construction of the "world of data" during the 1980s' hacker scare, social networking platforms were positioned by legislators and the media as exotic, technologically complex, and potentially risky. Given the skill needed to develop and maintain a presence on such platforms, it became necessary to attribute children and teenagers with a dangerous level of expertise, but also to see them as being incapable of protecting themselves or understanding the complexities of the cyberspaces that they themselves work to produce (such as online profiles). Within such media and legislative discourses, it is impossible for young people to occupy the positions of the predators or solicitors. Young people—like Laiomi—who choose to communicate with online strangers are understood to lack the developmental capacity to comprehend the potential consequences of doing so. All online strangers, regardless of actual age or intent, are portrayed as being able to convince such youth that they are friends, entrapping them through the grooming process. Ken Lanning, a former Federal

Bureau of Investigation profiler, explains the potential driving factors for youth in the "Dangerous Web" television program (Hansen 2004a):

It may be attention and affection. For another child it may be gifts. For a lot of teenagers it's romance. Just somebody who will ... pay attention to you. Tell you how pretty you are or how nice you are.

Similarly, former predator victim Alicia Kozakiewicz explained the mindset of victims in her testimony to Congress (2007, 9):

Imagine your 13th birthday was last month and for some ridiculous reason your parents still think you are a child. You are sitting home bored and lonely because your best friend decided that you are not so cool anymore and your other best friend has moved far away. That person you have an unbelievable crush on, they think you are the biggest geek. You have a D in algebra despite your best efforts and you won't be making the honor roll this semester. And nobody understands anything at all, nobody ever will. You are alone in this world and you are so bored, so lonely that you are online just chatting.

Both statements are taken as evidence that something must be done to protect youth, who are willing to risk meeting a stranger for intimacy. The fact that troubled young people feel that they have no choice but turn to connections with strangers online is ignored as a natural stage of adolescent development. Instead of addressing the structural conditions that limit the independent mobility of youth, the isolation that comes with a restricted social sphere, and the lack of meaningful work, legislators turned to manage the adults who take advantage of existing power relations. Parents are encouraged to further limit or intensively monitor their children's activities online, and as Sonia Livingstone and Magdalena Bober (2006, 106) explain, "The result is that parents and children are positioned as opponents in a struggle rather than in cooperation to resolve an externally generated problem."

The KIDS Act and media representations of online predators are products of the crisis of the home as a disciplinary space, problematized through the technologies of chat and social networking. The previously private space of the home has been penetrated by the not-yet-continuous gaze of the predator through the construction of youth identities online. Just as the metaphor of the "red-light district" became a central metaphor for the operation of the cyberporn panic, the metaphor of the gateway took a central position in the online predator panic. As Chris Hansen (2007) stated, the "Online enemies [are] already in your home." Strangely echoing

Deleuze (1992, 3) ("We are in a generalized crisis in relation to all environments of enclosure—prison, hospital, school, family"), Texas attorney general Greg Abbott, testifying to the House of Representatives, stated the following (Deleting Online Predators Act 2006, 24):

No one would allow their children to invite a predator over to the house for the evening. The fact is, that is exactly what happens when children log on to these social networking sites and chat rooms. Clearly, safeguards are needed at schools, at libraries, as well as in our homes if we are to protect our children against these predators. Such safeguards are the kinds of protections that Americans have come to expect. Streets, neighborhoods, and playgrounds are essential to our daily lives and are a part of the American social and economic fabric. Nevertheless, we must police our streets, neighborhoods, and playgrounds to ensure their safety.

For Abbott, the information superhighway is used by predators to penetrate the walls of the home, which until now have kept out the corrupting forces of the public. Once again, legislative and media discourses moved to reconstitute these boundaries within cyberspace and to police them through new technologies and law enforcement methods—a task that only the state, partnering with private industry, is capable of undertaking.

The anxieties surrounding online predation were triggered by the construction of a publicly visible online presence of young people—a "virtual catalog" of children who were newly available to pedophiles. No longer were children and teenagers simply stumbling into adult content; they now were constructing online identities that made them targets for sexual deviants. It had not gone unnoticed that these virtual catalogs of young people were also just as available to law enforcement agents. Online profiles were made invisible and carefully protected by the legislative efforts around the online predator. It was not inherently dangerous for youth to provide appropriate levels of information online, as much as it was that predators had access to that information. The figure of the predator established a route for legislators to connect law enforcement to the new resources made available through the widespread adoption of social networking—namely, semistable online identities and the surveillance of everyday life. Law enforcement required tools and access to social networking platforms—not to surveil youth but rather to protect youth from the ever-present threat of online predators. Such an effort necessitated extralegal partnerships between law enforcement and private service providers, which were established often through extralegal and informal agreements, and remain in place to the present day.

Accordingly, legislative attention and action focused primarily on private social networks. Of the three major congressional hearings on sexual predation between 2006 and 2007, members of Congress repeatedly referenced social networking sites as a new space for online predation, and two of the three hearings invited testimony from social networking site representatives. In contrast, the methods of NBC's *To Catch a Predator* television series used chat technologies and only rarely social networks for sting operations. Even the Perverted Justice (2014) Web site notes that it was not until 2007 that the group began "working on identifying sex offenders on MySpace and in 2008, expanded that effort to Facebook." Alice E. Marwick (2008) also notes this disconnect, attributing some of the attention given to MySpace to a series of high-profile cases involving predator activity on the site—although the cases were often misrepresented in the media. Despite the clear connection between the timing of the hearings and the rising popularity of *To Catch a Predator*, more emphasis was placed on social networking sites and their capacity to provide predators with the "virtual catalog" of vulnerable children and less on the anonymous chat rooms more commonly used in successful sting operations. The concern over online predation clearly was mobilized as a means for legislators to regulate social networking platforms indirectly, in comparison to the efforts surrounding cyberporn. At the Making the Internet Safe (2006b) hearing, Representative Bart Stupak (D-WI) explained the following:

But make no mistake about it, regardless of the level of effort expended so far, it is not enough. The problem is growing, Mr. Chairman. ... However, absent are the CEOs who can make the voluntary commitments of the resources and cooperation necessary to clean up the Web.

Similarly, Representative Diana De Gette (D-CO) stated the following (Making the Internet Safe 2006a):

we really do need to get a grip on it, and we all need to do it together: the media, Members of Congress, and the providers. ... ever since our first hearing, I started working on legislation that would require companies that provide broadband service to keep certain records that identify their customers for 1 year. ... I don't think that people who are raping 2-year-old children on the Internet have any right to privacy, and nobody thinks that.

The hearings operated as a signal to social networking providers that legislators were willing to regulate, which placed pressure on the providers to open themselves to extralegal and opaque public-private partnerships. These partnerships are made possible by the successful portrayal of the social networking predator, and they foreshadowed later moves to secure cyberspace primarily through voluntary compliance methods (Department of Homeland Security 2015).

Amid the legislative efforts, nonregulatory partnerships in service of protecting youth from online predators also played out in a variety of arenas. MySpace chose a new chief security officer who was uniquely suited for working with law enforcement on child safety issues (Scalet 2007). At the state level, the New York and New Jersey attorneys general subpoenaed Facebook, seeking information about security and the incidence of sexual predator profiles on the site (McCarthy 2007), signaling their intent to the company. Then Connecticut's attorney general, Richard Blumenthal, along with forty-eight other state attorneys general and the chief privacy officer of Facebook, issued the Joint Statement on Key Principles of Social Networking Sites Safety (2008). The statement operated as a nonregulatory agreement between Facebook and the attorneys general and proposed changes to the technological infrastructure of the site, the development of educational resources for parents, and the establishment of an Internet Safety Technical Task Force (ISTTF). The ISTTF was comprised of industry members and scholars who were "devoted to finding and developing ... online safety tools with a *focus on finding and developing online identity authentication tools*" (Joint Statement on Key Principles 2008, 1, emphasis added). Chaired by researcher John Palfrey, the task force compiled an extensive literature review on youth Internet use and interviewed researchers, industry officials, and law enforcement agents.

Several major research projects were highlighted in the ISTTF literature review and made available to legislators, but each was vulnerable to cooptation and dismissal in various ways. The most widely read was the Youth Internet Safety Survey that was conducted by the University of New Hampshire Crimes against Children Research Center. Funded by the National Center for Missing and Exploited Children (NCMEC), this project gathered data from over three thousand youth Internet users through two national telephone surveys in 1999 and 2005 (Wolak, Mitchell, and Finkelhor 2006). Out of all the findings generated by this project, the one that became widely publicized was that one in five (or one in seven, depending on the survey) young Internet users have been sexually solicited online (Richtel 2006; K. Thomas 2000; Wetzstein 2001). Sexual solicitation was defined by the researchers as an incident "where someone on the Internet attempted to get them to talk about sex when they did not want to or asked them unwanted sexual questions about themselves" (Wolak et al. 2006, 15). This statistic and other alarming findings were broadcast widely by the *Dateline NBC* programs (the "Dangerous Web" segment and the *To Catch a Predator* series) and led legislators to claim that there was an "epidemic" of online sexual predation. However, the research team has repeatedly criticized the use of the one-in-five statistic for such purposes, noting that the simple solicitation of a minor online does not make the minor a victim and that only 4 percent experienced an event that they found disturbing. Further, most solicitation attempts reported by youth were described as having originated from people who were under the age of twenty-five; the adult predator appeared to be a relatively rare phenomenon (Mitchell et al. 2014). In a congressional Internet Advisory Committee Forum, researcher David Finkelhor stated the following (Just the Facts about Online Youth Victimization 2007, 3):

Now, on the case of Internet sex crimes against kids, I'm concerned that we're already off to a bad start here. The public and the professional impression about what's going on in these kinds of crimes is not in sync with the reality, at least so far as we can ascertain it on the basis of research that we've done.

Similar statements by Finkelhor were picked up by news outlets and publicized—although not as prominently (Kornblum 2007) as the original one-in-five statistic. Unfortunately, just as with the "80 percent of the Internet is pornography" statement, the one-in-five statistic can be found in many of the materials outlining the dangers of youth Internet use today.

In December 2008, the final ISTTF report was released to the public. It stated that concerns over online predators were largely unfounded and that additional legislative attention should be directed to cyberbullying. Additionally, a pattern that emerged from the data was that most of the young people who were being victimized also displayed other risk factors offline (Internet Safety Technical Task Force 2008). Danah boyd (2009) reflected on the report, stating that

The patterns are brutally clear. The same issues continue to emerge with each new technology. The kids who are in trouble offline are more likely to be in trouble online and offline psychosocial factors contribute to online risks. Many more youth experience bullying than sexual contact and the realities of "predation" look very different than most people imagine and, thus, require vastly different solutions than most people propose.

Responses to the report by the attorneys general were mixed, and many of the more negative sentiments received wider press coverage. During an interview, North Carolina's attorney general, Roy Cooper—one of the coalition leaders—responded negatively to the report, stating that the task force was meant to study predators, not bullies (Steel 2009):

We did not ask the task force to look at the bullying issues. We asked them to look at ways for us to fight child predators. I am concerned with some of the findings. I think it relied on outdated and inadequate research. ... The report says that not much of the research occurs after 2006, the time that social networking sites exploded. Our main effort here is protecting children from inappropriate adult contact.

Despite having been recognized by many as a troubling issue, cyberbullying did not appear in the dominant discourse. It was not as politically palatable (because it implicated youth in criminal activity), and it did not have the same immediately apparent strategic value as the narrative of the adult Internet predator. As the father of deceased cyberbullying victim Ryan Halligan described to PBS, "At the time I was concerned about what everybody was concerned about: predators and pedophiles, right? I mean, that was what the media was talking about—you heard the horror stories" (*Frontline: Growing Up Online* 2008).

Conclusion

The legislative concerns about online sexual predators ultimately decreased in the wake of federal legislation and the emergence of cyberbullying as a new Internet safety issue—although statistics and concerns about predation continue to circulate via gray literatures and safety curricula. Despite the sentiments of the attorneys general responding to the report of the Internet Safety Technical Task Force, cyberbullying eventually gained the attention of policymakers. Although at the federal level there has been little movement beyond a provision in the Broadband Data Improvement Act of 2008 that linked cyberbullying education to continued e-rate funding, forty-eight states have passed antibullying statutes that cover forms of "electronic harassment" (Hinduja and Patchin 2015). But state laws were widely criticized because they frequently included unfunded mandates and were seen as ineffective in preventing cyberbullying behavior among students in everyday practice (Clark 2013). At the same time, the rise of cyberbullying led adults to feel that bullying had become an epidemic, and it increasingly was framed as a public health issue rather than a crime. As the Web site Stopbullying (U.S. Department of Health and Human Services 2013) suggests to reporters, "In particular, when a youth dies by suicide, it is misleading to cover the story as a crime. Rather, consider covering it as a public health issue." Unlike earlier Internet safety issues, combatting the threat of cyberbullying required "getting the kids involved" (Clark 2013).

As the frame shifted away from seeing Internet safety as a policy problem and toward providing children and teenagers with cyberbullying education via the Broadband Act, various pedagogical techniques were mobilized to combat cyberbullying by changing school cultures, fostering mutual respect, and intervening in bullying incidents. In such a configuration, young people themselves are encouraged to adopt the surveillant gaze and to "take responsibility" for the acts of violence that they witness and experience. This turn to educational efforts—which is revisited in chapter 5—perhaps best marks the transition to control in the governance of youth online.

4 Pedagogies of Surveillance

In a statement that could be referencing inappropriate Internet use by young people (rather than masturbation), Michel Foucault (1978, 42) states:

Wherever there was the chance [that pleasures] might appear, devices of surveillance were installed; traps were laid for compelling admissions; inexhaustible and corrective discourses were imposed; parents and teachers were alerted, and left with the suspicion that all children were guilty, and with the fear of being themselves at fault if their suspicions were not sufficiently strong; they were kept in readiness in the face of this recurrent danger; their conduct was prescribed and their pedagogy recodified. ... The child's "vice" was not so much an enemy as a support. ... Always relying on this support, power advanced, multiplied its relays and its effects, while its target expanded, subdivided, and branched out, penetrating further into reality at the same pace. In appearance, we are dealing with a barrier system; but in fact, all around the child, indefinite lines of penetration were disposed.

Similar campaigns have been waged against many types of online content that are inappropriate for children—such as pornography, sexually explicit conversations, and messages from online predators. Programs that educate parents on the risks faced by children online been developed at the national, state, and local levels by government agencies, private corporations and nonprofit groups. The stated goals of these programs are to help prepare young Internet users to become good cybercitizens and to foster an effective and safe online environment for both educational and business activities. Additionally, they seek to assist parents to understand what their kids are doing online and the potential risks they face when the Internet is used inappropriately. These curricula—course materials, online resources, handouts, assemblies, and presentations—have been provided to children and adults across the states and provide insights into the ways in which youth Internet safety has been problematized by policymakers, school administrators, and parents.

In this chapter, I examine the production and proliferation of adult surveillance practices online through Internet safety discourses. In an analysis of youth Internet safety curricula provided to adults and interviews with parents, law enforcement officers, and school officials, I describe the mechanisms by which adults are positioned as agents of surveillance relative to social networks and youth Internet practices. As I argue, youth Internet safety discourses represent what can be conceptualized as a pedagogy of surveillance—reconfiguring both adult and youth conceptions of online practices in ways that establish "trusted adults" as final arbiters of risk and appropriateness and that cast suspicion on the everyday social practices of youth. Through the pedagogy of surveillance provided by youth Internet safety materials, parents and guardians are encouraged to conceptualize social networking sites and other information technologies used by young people as surveillance tools rather than as social spaces. Additionally, these materials provide adults with a conceptual frame for making sense of youth sociality online by interpreting everyday communications and actions from the standpoint of an imagined twenty-first-century employer.

Pedagogies of Surveillance

Internet safety discourses can perhaps be best understood as mechanisms for what Foucault (1980) describes as the capillary penetration of power, which is a concept commonly used in the field of surveillance studies (Campbell 2004; DiNicola 2006; Lyon 1993; Marwick 2012). Adult surveillance has slowly penetrated formerly unsupervised times and spaces of youth sociality both online and off, as children and teenagers have adopted social networking platforms as part of everyday social practice and have increasingly documented their lives on online video- and photo-sharing sites. As with Foucault's (1978) discussion of onanism discourses above, the central logic of such surveillance is child protection. Similarly, decades of moral panic scholarship have demonstrated the ways in which concerns over children and teenagers are mobilized in productive ways (Clapton, Cree, and Smith 2013; Critcher 2008; Garland 2008; Jenkins 1992; Payne 2008), allowing for "a 'more than usual' exercise of control" (Hall et al. 1978, 221). Further, and more explicitly referencing child surveillance and dataveillance, Lynne

Wrennall (2010, 306) offers the Trojan horse theory of child protection, in which "the discourse of Child Protection is being misused for purposes that have little or nothing to do with enhancing the lives of children."

Jacques Donzelot's (1979) work provides a historical context for modern child protectionism by describing the conditions under which children came to be "preserved" in the mid-eighteenth century through various forms of supervision and containment. This emphasis on preservation came from a realization by the state that the current practices of child rearing were intensely wasteful. Children who were abandoned at foundling hospitals were a financial expense, the child mortality rate was high, and many of those who survived were "corrupted" and unfit for work. The result was a set of pedagogical practices that reconstituted the family around the preservation of children as state resources. Donzelot states that this occurred through the regulation of images as institutional alliances and struggles produced various forms of normative imagery and family education, ranging from the church to modern family planning. Donzelot's discussion of pedagogies of the family throughout history continue to be relevant and are similar to scholarship on youth and the Internet today. Mark Connolly and Judith Ennew (1996, 133) remark that "To be a child outside of adult supervision, visible on city centre streets, is to be out of place." Similarly, referring to issues of youth Internet safety, Sheila Brown (2005, 148) notes that

Children are seen as "in danger" from the Internet because it seems that just as adults do not like young people hanging around on street corners, so they do not like them to have unfettered access to the virtual street corners of cyberworlds. Hence we see "moral panics" surrounding the supposedly deleterious effects of computers on children's development and morals, and the alleged need to control the amount of time children spend on the net, and what they do on it "for their own good."

With Donzelot's work in mind, I begin to consider what I describe as *pedagogies of surveillance* through which individuals become agents of surveillance as they learn to observe, interpret, and police social behavior. In part, this consideration of pedagogies of surveillance is a response to Gavin J. D. Smith's (2012, 108) call for further research on

surveillance-in-action: as a participatory mode of being-in-the-world (in terms of socialization, pedagogy and the interaction order) and as an organizationally based mode of work (in terms of the prioritization and expansion of information collection techniques and corollary emergence of a specialized human/non-human labor force tasked with "reading," categorizing and deciphering this data such that it becomes expert and institutionally-relevant knowledge).

Focusing on pedagogies of surveillance draws attention to the production and proliferation of institutionally legitimate forms of surveillant subjectivities and recognizes that surveillants must be produced through training and education. Similar to what Nancy Campbell (2004, 79) describes as technologies of suspicion, pedagogies of surveillance "constitute a set of empirical modes for producing and interpreting 'data'—results—in ways that conflate prediction with prescription, acting as technological forms of supervision, monitoring, supposed deterrence, and ultimately control." Through these pedagogies, "Surveillance is 'designed in' to the flows of everyday existence" (Rose 2000, 325) as part of a broader society of control.

Pedagogies of surveillance provide conceptual approaches to technologies and experiences that produce institutionally relevant knowledge, often at the cost of "coextensiveness with [a] social field" (Donzelot 1979, 45). Further, focusing on the production of surveillants provides a means for understanding how institutional surveillance techniques are incorporated into everyday life. Smith (2012) characterizes surveillance work as both a mundane activity (in cultural and identity construction) and an organizational activity (in bureaucratic goals). As David Lyon (2007, 13) has noted: "Parents have always been concerned about what their children might be up to, of course, but our [generation] is the first that has deliberately sought techniques used by the military or police in order to monitor their activities." Analyzing pedagogies of surveillance helps to reveal the strategic intertwining between these two activities as particular modes of identity construction become institutionally useful.

Finally, conceptualizing the production of surveillance systems through pedagogies of surveillance allows for a further examination of the forces that allow various technologies to be interpreted and mobilized as surveillance tools by different groups. Just as surveillant subjectivities must be socially produced, so too must surveillance technologies. Drawing from work on technological flexibility (Hess 1995) and adaptation (Eglash et al. 2004) from the field of science and technology studies, the concept of pedagogies of surveillance is predicated on the understanding that "users" approach technology from a particular sociocultural context. An analysis of pedagogies of surveillance points to the discursive reframing of flexible technologies—such as social networking platforms—as institutionally valid tools for knowledge production.

The Construction of Trusted Adults

The NetSmartz curriculum is a popular Internet safety resource that was developed in 2001 by the National Center for Missing and Exploited Children (NCMEC) and funded in part by major corporations such as Walmart and Viacom. With separate sections for parents, teachers, law enforcement, and children in three age groups (kids, tweens, and teens), NetSmartz provides online videos, presentations, games, and classroom materials free of charge and comparable to other forms of Internet safety curricula. Given the standing of the NCMEC and the breadth of materials available, especially the materials for adults who provide Internet safety education to parents and children, the popularity of the program is unsurprising. A woman who participated in a focus group and who has presented NetSmartz material to youth and adult audiences made the following comments:

Where we've come from with drugs: we're trying to get there with Internet safety. We're trying to get there with sexting. ... I go over the laws with them. I get my tools from NetSmartz. They're a great resource. ... It's free! The county always likes things that are free!

Most school administrators I spoke with saw a need to educate parents about youth Internet safety risks. One school principal said the following:

I think that the educating-the-parent piece is incredibly important. The hard thing is enforcing the parents to participate in that. You know, with students here we can do that, but if someone's not supervising them with this media, it's as good as—kids will swear when no one is hearing them swear. ... I fear for that.

Another administrator described the need for parental education, broadly explaining that if youth Internet access was contained to schools, there would be no safety problems:

I do think that if they were just using these things in school, we would be okay. ... I think it's, in my opinion, one of those social responsibilities [that schools] need to take on because it's more interesting to the students than it is to their parents. And the students are the IT people in their homes, and they can pull the wool over their parents' eyes. ... I do think we need to take on more responsibility of educating them about it. ... Anytime we can keep children safe, we need to.

The 2010 version of the NetSmartz presentation for adults briefly discusses the kinds of technologies that kids use to communicate with each other and outlines the positive elements of online communication. The presentation then moves to Internet safety materials and provides ways to identify categories of risky behaviors online. In a tutorial on the functions and features of social networking sites, parents are alerted to the dangers of posting too much information on those sites. Risky behaviors include "'Friending' unknown people," "Posting personal information," "Embarrassing and harassing people," and "Talking about sex." The online narrator in the presentation explains, over a bulleted list of the risky behaviors, that "Kids get away with these behaviors all the time, and doing just one of them might not get your child in trouble, but a combination of these behaviors … is likely to put them at greater risk" (NetSmartz 2010a).

The presentation covers other topics, including cyberbullying, "Crossing the Line" by posting personal or inappropriate information, and engaging with online predators, with each section containing tips on identifying problems and navigating social networks. For example, the section on "Signs of Grooming" provides parents with a diagnostic for identifying possible online sexual predation. Indicators of possible victimization include the relatively average teen behaviors of "Turning away from friends and family" to spend more time online and "Spending a lot of time online" more generally. Reframing any possible resistance by teens to parental concerns over spending private time, both "Getting upset when he or she can't get online," and "Minimizing the screen or turning off the monitor when you come into the room" (NetSmartz 2010a) are additionally marked as potential risk indicators. A 2013 version of the presentation similarly provides a set of behaviors for identifying cyberbullies: "Quickly switches screens or closes programs," "Uses the computer at all hours," "Gets unusually upset if they cannot use the computer," "Laughs excessively while online," and "Avoids discussion about what they are doing" (NetSmartz 2013b). Through such diagnostics, all teens seeking privacy or otherwise enjoying themselves on the computer are made to appear as risky or suspicious.

The presentation ends with a series of monitoring and policing strategies for parents, including increasing control over mobile devices, housing family computers in shared spaces, and installing monitoring and filtering software. A need for active supervision is emphasized, and parents are told to maintain a supervisory presence whenever their children are or could be online. In the video, the narrator attempts to assuage the fears of parents who feel that constant surveillance of their children to prevent them from "sharing too much" may be unwanted (NetSmartz 2010a):

Helping your children filter their comments online may seem like a challenge, especially if you think they don't want you anywhere near their online life. But NetSmartz has interviewed these students who think parental involvement is not that bad.

Following this statement, several students are shown describing the ways in which they are watched by their parents. None of the students explicitly state that they feel comfortable with parental monitoring. Closing the presentation, the narrator tempers the emphasis on supervision, describes the need to maintain open lines of communication with children, and mentions the ways in which overreaction and too much control can be counterproductive (NetSmartz 2010a):

But don't go overboard. Many kids are afraid that if they tell their parents about something that's happened, they'll overreact and pull the plug. If you take away the Internet, your children may be less likely to come to you if they have a problem.

The 2013 version of the presentation no longer includes this narrated statement—although the revised presenter's guide continues to emphasize that these behaviors are indicators that a conversation may be necessary rather than indicators that their children are at risk (NetSmartz 2013a).

Throughout the materials are references to the "trusted adult"—the figure that children and teenagers are expected to report to when they encounter risky situations online. The term remains largely unexplained in the materials provided to parents but is more clearly defined in the materials provided to young people. Trusted adults are "Someone you can talk to about anything; someone you feel happy being around; someone who is a good listener; or someone who has helped you before" (NetSmartz 2010b). The emphasis is placed on the adults in youth lives, and other children are explicitly excluded from the "trusted" category (NetSmartz 2010d). This distrust of youth is likely due to the concern within the NetSmartz materials that other non-adults may potentially use personal or sensitive information to further harm someone in distress. As such, children themselves are positioned as fundamentally untrustworthy. The resource manual that is provided to Internet safety presenters explains that "Trusted adults are educated about the online safety risks and encouraged to: Consider filtering and monitoring options, Establish rules and guidelines at home, Communicate with their children, [and] Share resources with others in the community" (NetSmartz 2010c).

Although the NetSmartz creators and presenters probably consider most well-known adult figures to be trusted adults, adults who have received NetSmartz or other forms of Internet safety training are closer to the ideal. This ideal draws on existing legislative and mainstream media discourses that position parents as being unaware of the risks that young people face online and facing overwhelming forces that threaten the safety of their children. Implicit in the concept of the trusted adult is that in the anonymous world of online communication, no one can be trusted. Young people are encouraged to discuss problems with adults that they can verify to be trustworthy and safe—and only adults known offline are trustworthy. Such problems may include unpleasant incidents that they experience online or issues that they need to discuss. Youth are told that if they talk to people online about personal problems, predators and bullies may use sensitive information to groom or attack them.

Although NetSmartz and many other online resources available to parents encourage dialogue between parents and children as a necessary aspect of managing the risks that youth face online, these elements of the curricula are typically minimized in the presentations offered by school districts and communities. Law enforcement officers, information security groups, district attorneys, and computer crime units frequently offer free presentations for both parents and students. In many school districts I visited, these presentations were the only form of Internet safety education offered by the schools, whether for parents, students, or faculty and staff. The NetSmartz curriculum provided free of charge by law enforcement officers is positioned as the least expensive and therefore the most popular means by which districts are able to provide Internet safety education, often in highly publicized ways. By requesting or accepting presentations by members of law enforcement, school districts often receive local media coverage, further demonstrating a commitment to the community without risking investment in any meaningful structural or cultural change. The risks that children and teenagers face online are made viscerally real through experiences that the presenters have had with harassment, Internet predation, and child pornography investigations. Because of this, presentations provided by law enforcement officers and those close to the judicial process deliver a sense of a real and looming threat that is made credible through the experiences of the presenter, additionally emphasizing the potentially disastrous consequences of inappropriate online behavior. Further, much of the discussion of communication and engagement with youth lives tends to be supplanted by stronger techniques for surveillance and control.

During a parent focus group session in one school district, I had an opportunity to discuss Internet safety issues with two participants who were both parents and law enforcement officers. One had been the chief information officer of a large police department and founded the local chapter of InfraGard, the public/private partnership established by the Federal Bureau of Investigation to protect national information infrastructure. The other focus group participant chose to remain anonymous. Both parents routinely provided Internet safety presentations to both parental and youth audiences. The participants in this focus group produced the most extreme example of the law enforcement view of youth Internet safety. One parent linked social networking sites to organized crime, terrorism, and human trafficking:

When you open the door to the Internet, you open the door to the entire world. And there are cultures out there that think nothing [of], and even worse, despise our way of life. … Social media is a great venue for organized crime—especially international organized crime, especially the human slave trade. … It is becoming almost an underground phenomenon that this is how they find their prey. And kids—that doesn't even enter their heads.

Accordingly, the techniques offered by law enforcement and security experts tend to be significantly restrictive of and intrusive into the social lives of youth online. These techniques can range in intrusiveness from "friending" youth on social network sites solely for surveillance purposes to suggesting that parents construct false identities online in order to run virtual sting operations on unsuspecting youth, ensuring that they think twice before engaging online strangers. Online, anyone could secretly be your parents. As a school resource officer suggested to parents at a public cyberbullying discussion panel hosted by a New York school district (Whiteley 2010):

I think with some of this technology, make a fake account and try to friend them on Facebook. Have a [adult] friend phone and text them, and say "Hey, what are you doing?," and does he respond? If he does, that's a great teaching point. … I'm accused of spying all the time, you know. I'm a cop; it's what I do,

Another participant in the discussion panel, the technology coordinator for the district, provided additional, more technical suggestions on methods for monitoring children online (DiAngelo 2010):

What can I do as a parent from a technological perspective to monitor my child's behavior? There's all sorts of products out there that you can install on your personal computer that will monitor and record every bit of activity that your student's doing. It may be seen by some as an encroachment of their rights, but we have a right as a parent to protect them as well. So you need to balance the two sides of that equation. … Your digital footprint is forever, and I don't believe students can certainly understand or comprehend the ramifications.

Another example of the law enforcement perspective appeared at a parent information session, presented by the New York State Internet Crimes against Children (NYS ICAC) task force, where yet another modified version of the online NetSmartz presentation template was used. The title was changed from "The Internet and Its Risks" to "Your Child's D.I.G.I.T.A.L Life," but the core materials and messages remained largely the same. The presentation itself was revised as part of a larger effort by the New York State attorney general's office to educate New York State residents on youth Internet safety issues (NYS OAG n.d.). Sessions using the same materials continue to be offered at school districts across the state and throughout New York City ("Facebook to Texting" 2013). Despite a title change suggesting a broader discussion about the ways that kids use the Internet in their everyday lives, the information on positive elements of online communication provided by the original NetSmartz materials was removed from the "D.I.G.I.T.A.L. Life" brochure and presentation. At the start of the NYS ICAC session, the presenter asked the audience, "What is your child doing online?," implying that the parents in the room did not know ("Your Child's D.I.G.I.T.A.L. Life" 2010). The same question remains in the opening to NetSmartz presentations to parents even after more recent revisions to the content (NetSmartz 2013b). In this way, adults—even those who are relatively close to the everyday lives of children and teens—are positioned as needing a native guide to the "complex" technological world of youth spaces online, destabilizing their existing understandings of everyday youth sociality. The law enforcement official, the Internet security specialist, the state attorney general, and the school superintendent are positioned as having the expertise that can transform the confused adult into a trusted adult who can effectively surveil youth Internet practices, see through the potentially deceptive practices of youth, and use those experiences to dispense meaningful advice through the frame of adult appropriateness. Similarly, the top-level NetSmartz Web pages for the "Parents and Guardians" and "Law Enforcement" sections exemplify a logic of empowerment, "reconstitut[ing] the public responsibilities of the parent while seemingly preserving his or her private authority" (Baez and Talburt 2008, 1). Parents receive a message that says, "Parenting wired kids can be difficult, especially if you didn't grow up with the same technologies. These resources can help" (NetSmartz n.d.-b), and law enforcement officials receive a message that says, "With today's changing technologies, educating your communities about Internet safety is becoming more and more important. These resources can help" (NetSmartz n.d.-a).

At the NYS ICAC session, the presenter mentioned that "Kids only think they know what they're doing," with the implication that youth required the expertise of trusted adults to show them the realities of what they were doing online and how dangerous their activities online were. As mentioned previously, there is no possibility of a "trusted child" within such curricula, which position youth as inherently untrustworthy and suspicious. In the absence of discussion of lines of communication and the positives of everyday youth sociality online, risky behaviors such as "Friending unknown people, talking about sex, [and] clicking on pop-ups" are positioned as the "truth" about kids' lives online that parents "need to know," with the "D.I.G.I.T.A.L." acronym remaining undefined. This presentation of the material frames everyday youth sociality as suspicious and in need of constant policing. Further, otherwise normal online activities become reinterpreted through the worst-case frames of child predation, cyberbullying, and the imagined gaze of the future employer or college recruiter. Because "Kids only think they know what they're doing," trusted adults must make sense of what they are doing for them. However, trusted adults must be provided with the appropriate frame through which to perform that interpretive work. The move to produce trusted adults represents the dispersion and interlinking of adult supervisory roles. Responsibility for supervising young people and for mobilizing the expertise necessary to reinterpret youth behavior is shifted away from the specific categories of parents and teachers and to a broader category of properly trained trusted adults. As Aaron Kupchik and Torin Monahan (2006, 622) describe, "Students' experiences are thus framed within a climate of distrust under the watchful eye of the state"—or, in this case, the state as extended through a network of other trusted adults positioned as individual agents.

In addition to delegitimating existing adult and youth knowledge of online social interactions, these presentations reinforce concepts of the networked publics constituted by youth safety incidents. Later, the investigator facilitating the NYS ICAC information session noted that she frequently told teens that "If you wouldn't tell someone something to somebody's face, don't say it online." In cases where inappropriate content was involved, she instead asked them, "Do you want your grandma to see that?" She lamented that at one point, the policy was to tell youth Internet users, "Don't post pictures. Well," she said while shaking her head, "we lost that battle." Similarly, a school lawyer provided advice to adults at the previously mentioned cyberbullying panel ("Cyberbullying" 2010):

With respect to privacy, I think my best advice is that once something is in an electric format, it isn't private. ... When we do any kind of legal issues training related to electronic use, ... the one thing you need to remember is the *New York Times* rule. When it comes to electronic communications of any kind, don't say anything that you would be embarrassed to see on the front page of the *New York Times*. Because once you put it in an electronic medium, it is on the front page of the *New York Times* or at least could be. ... If it's electronic, you should assume it is not private. ... That electronic footprint that children leave is forever.

This anticipatory construction of networked publics, envisioning the future employer or college recruiter as a basis for constituting appropriateness, is further used as the rationale by which adults must reframe and police what might appear as "harmless" youthful communications. This particular strand of youth Internet safety discourse, which is referred to as reputation management, is becoming the dominant framework through which earlier Internet safety risks are interpreted and is returned to in later chapters.

Possible Solicitation: Contains GLBT

Throughout the presentations provided to adults, there is a pervasive sense that "fast-moving" technologies are overwhelming parents, outstripping their ability to monitor their children online. This narrative of overwhelmed parents again relies on concepts of the digital native (Prensky 2001a), dividing inept parents from technologically adept young people. Adults are situated as being poorly suited for quickly learning how to navigate new communication technologies having long since lost the brain plasticity that their children retain (Prensky 2001b). These programs are intended to provide the concepts and tools that adults "need" to govern their families, making developmental discourses a strategically viable means for explaining the lack of adult engagement with information technologies. Parents arguably are overwhelmed but not by the technologies themselves—as demonstrated by the increasing number of adults who have adopted Facebook and other social media platforms that once were considered the territories of youth (Duggan et al. 2015). Instead, it is explained, parents are overwhelmed with the amount of data that is now made available to them via information technologies. Many new automated surveillance technologies that assist parents in their supervision efforts have been developed over the past decade, providing simplified ways to gather and interpret the volumes of data that youth produce. It is perhaps no coincidence that the term most commonly used to describe these forms of software is *parental control*.

Parental control technologies today can be traced back to the filtering and control technologies that were developed in the mid-1990s amid concerns over youth access to inappropriate content on television and online. As is discussed in the previous chapter, this was the time of cyberporn reports, the Communications Decency Act of 1996 (CDA), and the Child Internet Protection Act (CIPA) of 2000, which mandated large-scale filtering technologies for public institutions receiving federal funds. Filtering was originally the primary goal of these forms of software, with the primary concerns being those of content rather than of people or publics. In the legislative struggles over the CDA, these technologies were positioned as a means for the state to avoid sweeping and potentially unconstitutional regulation of online content. One *USA Today* article reported on these early technologies and their relationship to the state (Miller 1995, D1):

Kids too young to cross the information highway unsupervised will soon have electronic helpers with names like Crossing Guard, CYBERsitter and Net Nanny to protect them from explicit material, obscenity and other adult traffic. Enough such products are being developed that "the government can by and large leave the Net alone and focus on making sure families know where to get" such products, says Rep. Ron Wyden, D-Ore.

These discourses distributed the work of filtering to parents and families. As concerns over youth Internet safety shifted away from content and toward issues of predation and cyberbullying, parental control technologies were reconstituted and upgraded to respond to those new concerns. For example, just prior to a new release, Net Nanny (2002b) (an early parental control software) prominently displayed the phrase "Filters harmful web sites" at the top of its Web site. With the announcement of version 5.0, Net Nanny (2002a) instead said the following:

Take Control of the Internet with the NEW AND IMPROVED Net Nanny 5. ... the world's leading parental control software, provides responsible adults with the broadest set of Internet safety tools available today. Our award-winning software gives you control over what comes into and goes out of your home, school, library, or business, while respecting your personal values and beliefs.

Shortly thereafter, the site was updated to feature a video segment from the *Today* show on online sexual solicitation of youth in which Net Nanny was mentioned, adding an advertisement for eBlaster: "Automatically Get Sent Copies of ALL Your Child's Emails and Chats" (Net Nanny 2003). Today the site hosts updated software that address the current wave of new threats, including cyberbullying and irreparable reputation damage (Net Nanny 2014b) in addition to an infographic that asks parents: "CYBERBUL-LIES: ARE YOU CREATING THEM?" (Net Nanny 2014a).

Like other providers of parental control technologies, Net Nanny has since shifted to a paid service model, charging parents on a monthly or yearly basis to provide constant monitoring of social networking profiles, personal computers, and mobile devices. Interest in Net Nanny has subsided somewhat, having retained its image as an older filter-based technology, although a range of new services are now offered to assist parents in their supervisory efforts. These services do the work of categorizing and analyzing the lives of youth in invisible ways, by automatically providing alerts to parents who are "overwhelmed" by the amount of data generated by their children online. As with filters such as Net Nanny, the algorithms that support the work of automated supervision are closely guarded secrets—although they can be tested by users of the system. To do so, I registered with the free services Avira Social Network Protection and Minor-Monitor, connected them to a virtual "child" Facebook account to monitor, and populated the account with various posts and images. Avira Social Network Protection is part of a suite of "freemium" antivirus and security applications offered by Avira Operations, and MinorMonitor is a service offered by Infoglide, a "deep security and fraud analytics" (MinorMonitor

2012) technology firm. Infoglide appears to provide access to the Minor-Monitor service to demonstrate the possibilities of its larger data analytic capacities, which the Web site claims are currently used by the Department of Homeland Security and other clients in law enforcement and financial services. Various forms of content were posted to the account page, including literary quotes, attempts to generate false positives and false negatives through conversation, and a list of 770 potentially offensive, violent, and obscene terms from an online slang dictionary (Rader 2015).

Both services provide parents with an analytic dashboard through which to interpret the data generated by their child. The analytic dashboard has become an increasingly common feature of software intended to allow users to process large amounts of data, and can also be seen in financial, military, and law enforcement settings. Both Avira Operations and Infoglide offer dashboards that condense the data generated by a social networking profile into an easily readable format that is presented in a series of smaller windows. An on-the-fly analysis of materials posted to the child's social networking account consists of colored dials and graphs that indicate the current threat level, recent images posted to the account, recent friend requests, and chat transcripts. Avira Operation's Avira Social Network Protection provided a volume-unit-style gauge on the home page and in reports to parents, listing an alert level from green to red and listing the total number of alerts generated. Infoglide's MinorMonitor provided a "sentiment analysis" histogram, with columns representing the number of positive and negative posts made by the monitored account. The dashboard elements provide links that allow parents to explore the data by examining the alerts and warnings that produce the dials and graphs. The Avira Social Network Protection graphic design team produced a more professional-looking product. Opening the reports provides a listing of the potentially risky texts or images posted to the profile, categorized by type of threats. Threat categories varied, but both systems detected profanity, drug references, potential solicitation, bullying, and personal information. Testing revealed a large number of terms and actions that triggered warnings. Here I focus on the most interesting or problematic triggers.

Avira Social Network Protection categorized triggers into a series of top-level categories, including Sex Language Alerts, Cyberbullying/Profanity Alerts, Drinking/Smoking Alerts, Violence/Gangs Alerts, Personal Information Alerts, and MeetUp Alerts. These alerts were categorized as minor (marked by a yellow hazard symbol) or major (marked by a red stop sign), although it was not immediately clear what triggered minor versus major alerts. Each alert displayed the category in bold, the name of the user who posted the offending material, the offending term or action that triggered the alert, and an Explain link. When the cursor hovered over the Explain link, additional information about why a term was flagged was revealed. For example, the Sex Language Alert for using the term *preggers* had this definition: "PREGGERS is a texting code for 'pregnant' and could have negative reputation consequences." Not all alerts were explained with additional details or definitions, but all alerts were stated to alert adults to the potential of "negative reputation consequences." Avira Social Network Protection was less sensitive than Infoglide's MinorMonitor, which may have been due to additional contextual analysis run by the platform. In total, the list of terms triggered seventy-nine alerts. In one particularly confusing example, the word *fuck* was ignored by the system, with two exceptions: the phrases *butt fuck* and *titty fuck*. Within the post containing the 770 offensive terms used to test the systems, *titty fuck* was the only term that generated a severe/red alert; all other triggers were labeled as minor/yellow alerts. It also was one of only three terms (including *pistols* and *rape*) across those tested that triggered severe/red alerts. Avira Social Network Protection additionally monitored personal information and flagged telephone numbers and addresses as Personal Information Alerts. A statement concerning "420 Blaze Ave." was categorized as both the posting of personal information and a possible drug reference.

Infoglide's MinorMonitor was far more sensitive than Avira Social Network Protection and used a tagging system rather than a category system to sort alerts. MinorMonitor's tags were more granular, including Possible Solicitation, Possible Drugs Reference, Possible Bullying or Confrontational Language, Possible Violence or Illegal Activity Reference, Possible Sexual Reference, and Possible Profanity. Terms could be labeled with more than one tag, so a single term could generate multiple alerts. The term *nude*, for example, was simultaneously flagged as both Possible Solicitation and Possible Sexual Reference. Given the sensitivity of the MinorMonitor service, it was often difficult to avoid triggering alerts, to the extent that it is difficult to imagine that parents could use the service to identify potentially risky interactions. The most broadly encompassing of all the tags was that of Possible Drugs Reference, which was applied to the terms *slang*,

Table 4.1

Sample terms flagged by two social media monitoring services—Infoglide's Minor-Monitor and Avira Operations' Avira Social Network Protection, 2014

Term	Alert Level	Alert Type	Service
cris	Minor	Possible drugs reference	MinorMonitor
hating, hate	Minor	Possible bullying or confrontational language	MinorMonitor
decade	Minor	Possible drugs reference	MinorMonitor
blowing up	Minor	Possible violence or illegal activity reference	MinorMonitor
fo	Minor	Possible bullying or confrontational language	MinorMonitor
pistols	Minor	Possible violence or illegal activity reference	MinorMonitor
eyes open	Minor	Possible drugs reference	MinorMonitor
gay	Minor	Possible sexual reference, possible solicitation	MinorMonitor
hurt	Minor	Possible bullying or confrontational language	MinorMonitor
superman	Minor	Possible drugs reference	MinorMonitor
gang up	Yellow	Violence/gangs alert	Avira SNP
(phone number)	Yellow	Personal information alert	Avira SNP
shoot me (an email)	Yellow	Violence/gangs alert	Avira SNP
meet up with you	Yellow	Meetup alert	Avira SNP
(messages from any deleted users)	Yellow	Stranger alert	Avira SNP
blade	Yellow	Violence/gangs alert	Avira SNP
titty fuck	Red	Sex language alert	Avira SNP

shoot, prescription, ski, sleigh ride, white lady, and *green stuff,* among others (although perhaps that demonstrates the broad lexicon of drug slang more than an overbroad tagging scheme).

Perhaps most concerning were the ways that the two services handled references to sexuality and gender. Across both services, nearly all references to sexual orientations or activities that fell beyond the scope of heteronormativity were flagged as potentially risky. Avira Social Network Protection flagged the term *gay,* explaining that "GAY is a condescending/profane term and could have negative reputation consequences." Similarly, *homo, fag, dyke, lesbian,* and *tranny* and some variants of those terms triggered Sex Language Alerts. MinorMonitor produced alerts on these terms but tagged them differently than Avira SNP. The word *gay* was simultaneously tagged as Possible Solicitation, Possible Bullying, and Possible Sexual Reference. By contrast, *lesbian* was tagged as Possible Bullying and Possible Profanity. The term *GLBT* was tagged simply as Possible Solicitation. With these monitoring services, it became nearly impossible to have a conversation that questioned the gender binary or mentioned homosexuality without being flagged. Beyond the fact that such terms were categorized as potentially risky for children and teenagers, the categorization schemes speak to the positioning of homosexuality as profane and as linked to pedophilia within dominant, heteronormative discourses.

Over time, the services and applications available to parents have grown more robust. MamaBear, a paid family safety mobile phone app that recently secured $1.4 million in investment funding, provides location-based tracking in addition to social network monitoring (Perez 2014). Marketed as a service rather than a product, MamaBear updates its product over time to include monitoring capabilities for the newest social networking and chat applications used by young people, providing parents with a means to keep up technologically with their children. As with the global positioning system (GPS) ankle bracelet technologies used by law enforcement, mothers can use maps that establish "safe zones" within which youth are allowed to travel and generate alerts whenever they leave established boundaries or fail to "check in" at set times. One user reviewed the Android version of the application (MamaBear 2015), stating that

I am a child whose mother made her get this, but my sister and I cannot be in the same place. If we are both home, it says one of us is in another town. It tells my mom I will leave home and come back in about 3 minutes when I never even left my room.

Parents magazine (Singer n.d.) provides a list of the "10 best apps for paranoid parents," asking "Are you a hover mom who needs to know where your child is at all times? We've found the apps (including ones with GPS tracking) that will give any parent more peace of mind." There is an increasingly explicit gendered construction of these applications, either in the development of the application itself (as with MamaBear) or the positioning of the applications by media reports and advertisements. Busy working mothers confronted with the challenges of monitoring their children simultaneously in the virtual and real worlds feel that they must turn to leverage information technologies to be good parents. Nancy Willard (2008) provides a critical caricature of this approach to surveillance:

> Digi-Parent sits by a child's computer screen so it can conveniently look over the shoulder of its child. … It will review the profiles of all of its child's friends to make sure they are safe, as well as the material posted by its child and its child's friends. It has been programmed to recognize all of the possible words and phrases that could be used to sexually solicit or cyberbully a child. … The advanced model can be used with "at risk" youth. This model will be programmed to say things like "I love you" "How was your day? "How are you feeling?" "You look a bit sad, is anything wrong?" "You know you can come to me if you have any problems."

Perhaps unsurprisingly, what was once a caricature is becoming a reality, as predictive analytics are increasingly mobilized to identify and intervene in the lives of at-risk youth.

The move away from Web-based applications and toward mobile-based applications allows parents to establish continuous lines of monitoring regardless of location. This form of monitoring generates a tremendous amount of data—status updates, pictures, chats, browsing history, and geographic location. Monitoring applications are marketed through claims that a given service provides the best possible means by which to manage the constant stream of data—increasingly referenced in terms of the dashboard. Parental monitoring applications can be considered are part of a broader set of technologies which have long since been leveraged in other institutions and organizations, including finance, law enforcement, and the military. Dashboards are composed of user interface elements that provide users with a means to monitor and process otherwise unmanageable flows of data. Those familiar with a "war room" type display, in which flows of incoming data are algorithmically processed into statistics and graphical elements, are familiar with this form of technology. This is a necessity in the control society. Dashboards rely on reductive and analytic techniques— in this case, gauges that indicate the level of risk a child is currently exposed to at a glance.

These technologies instrumentalize relationships between youth and adults by producing alerts and warnings and inducing a need for location-based and information-based check-ins at regular intervals. They both support and configure what Raiford Guins (2009, 10) describes as the "parent function," in which "family is … a strategy of rule that operates through culture to further an ethos of security that instrumentalizes cultural practices as they flow freely as solutions to the problematic of securitization." Through the enhanced technologies that support the parent function, family "becomes the normative basis for 'goodness' and the administration of ways of being 'good' through the surveillance, perfection, and maintenance of disciplined freedom" (Guins 2009, 10). Parental monitoring technologies operate as a way of articulating and engendering a particular form of social life, instilling within parents what Campbell (2000) describes as governing mentalities through everyday use. Just as Twitter users increasingly think through the frame of the hashtag, so too have heavy users of parental monitoring applications begun to think through the frame of the alert and the check-in.

Conclusion

Youth Internet safety curricula establish the position of the trusted adult, a position from which truth claims about youth social activities can be made. They provide a conceptual framework that is based on ongoing media coverage of youth Internet safety incidents. By repositioning social networks as surveillance technologies, youth Internet safety discourses act as a pedagogy of surveillance, providing a conceptual frame through which youth Internet safety incidents can be constructed and acted on. Through the position of the trusted adult, the everyday dramas of young people who are living their social lives online become visible as incidents of cyberbullying, inappropriate content, and online predation. These modes of interpreting the data collected through the surveillance of youth further become visible in scientific studies of youth Internet safety, where terms such as *cyberbullying* are prevalent, even though young people tend to understand potentially abusive online behavior very differently than youth Internet safety discourses do (Fisk 2011). After data are stabilized through the concepts of youth Internet safety, they can be mobilized to underwrite various forms of intervention in the forms of policies, modes of technological regulation, and curricula.

As social networking platforms are mobilized and appropriated as tools by adults who are responsible for youth, they are transformed into surveillance mechanisms through pedagogies of surveillance, providing a conceptual frame through which youth Internet safety incidents can be constructed and acted on. Such shifts establish a relationship of suspicion, in terms of both adult constructions of childhood and young people's constructions of adulthood. Children and teenagers who are subjects of surveillance are rendered as untrustworthy and unable to conceptualize the truth of any given situation appropriately. Young people must be placed under continued surveillance, and anyone who is charged with their care has a responsibility to surveil them. Parents who are perceived to be either unable or unwilling to monitor their children online are seen as irresponsible and as one of the primary causes of problems involving youth Internet use.

Research examining the production and circulation of institutional pedagogies of surveillance is relatively scant, and so is research on the everyday work of surveillance, including the training, technologies, and practice of surveillers (Smith 2012). As I argue here, further research in these areas will provide necessary insights into the formation of surveillant subjectivities and the mechanisms by which institutional logics and power penetrate everyday social life.

5 Cyberbullies and Cybercitizens

In this chapter, I examine the youth Internet safety curricula and concepts provided to youth themselves. As Allison James, Chris Jenks, and Alan Prout (1998, 41–42) describe:

Curricula … are more than the description of content. They are spatial theories of cognitive and bodily development and, as such, they contain world-views which are never accidental and are certainly not arbitrary. They involve selections, choices, rules and conventions, all of which relate to questions of power, issues of personal identity and philosophies of human nature and potential, all of which are focused specifically on the child. … Thus, analysis of the school curriculum allows us to initiate our exploration of issues of control within the social space of childhood.

Although it is unlikely that the authors were attempting to link the development of curricula to the transition to a society of control, that is my intent here. As I argue in chapter 3, the various "moral panics" of youth Internet safety can be read as part of a broader transition from a disciplinary society to a control society (Deleuze 1992a), and through youth Internet safety curricula, the logics and mechanisms of control are further dispersed. Nikolas Rose (2000, 324) provides a means for conceptualizing control technologies, explaining that, "A whole range of new technologies—'technologies of freedom'—have been invented that seek to 'govern at a distance' through, though not in spite of, the autonomous choices of relatively independent entities." Outlining the strategic coherence of these "technologies of freedom," Rose (2000, 324) suggests that they can be divided into two categories—"those that seek to regulate conduct by enmeshing individuals within circuits of inclusion and those that seek to act upon pathologies through … circuits of exclusion." These circuits of control appear throughout youth Internet safety curricula, providing youth with the freedom to engage productively with information technologies and enrolling them in the broader effort of securing society through their online choices.

The emergence of cyberbullying as a public health issue that requires cultural intervention within schools and bystander intervention training marks a transition to the "governing at a distance" of control technologies. I initially approach the analysis of youth Internet safety curricula through cyberbullying before moving on to newer concepts that have emerged from youth Internet safety discourses—those of online reputation management and the digital citizen. The chapter concludes by focusing on a recent trend in youth Internet safety curricula—away from a crime-oriented framework and toward a framework that fosters appropriate behavior and digital citizenry.

"Like, uh, through technology": Constructing Cyberbullying

Today it is somewhat commonplace to note that young people remark on the relative lack a of salience conceptual awareness s of the online/offline divide (Ito et al. 2009). As Susan C. Herring (2008, 77) notes, "many of what we consider new technologies (instant messaging, blogs, chat rooms, email, cell phones, search engines, etc.) are 'transparent' to young users—they do not consider them to be technologies, except in the broadest sense." As young people and adults adopt social media as part of everyday practices and terms such as *digital native* (Prensky 2001a, 2001b) proliferate within educational discourses, understanding online life as an extension or facet of traditional sociality has become conceptually possible for adults as well. The idea that youth "do not see" information technologies retains some of its transgressive, exotic element to the extent that the everyday online social practices of young people and adults differ. Even today, statements such as "There is no difference between online and offline for kids" ("Your Child's D.I.G.I.T.A.L. Life" 2010) are common in Internet safety presentations and materials for adults, and they typically are framed in a way that elicits shock among the audience and servers to position children and teenagers as technologically exotic others.

The quoted statement emerges from the digital native discourse, again pointing out that for digital natives, the distinction between communication online and offline is as unremarkable as communication on and off the telephone is for previous generations. The Internet and the mobile phone have, as Rich S. Ling (2012, xi) has suggested, "become woven into [kids'] expectations of one another." The same can be said of adult populations as well, although the drivers of adoption are somewhat different for the two age groups. Adults adopted information technologies primarily through their business uses rather than as social platforms. For generations of adults, computers were first a feature of work life, rather than that of leisure time or intimate communication. "I look at a computer screen all day at work, why would I want to look at one at home?" remains a common refrain among these generations of adults, often in ignorance of the fact that nearly everything is some form of computer screen today. As such, computers have appeared to many as an anti-social technology, as an intrusion of instrumental work life into the home. The early language and concepts of Internet safety—and the problematization of Internet safety as something distinct from safety in general—emerge from a historical moment in which adults found it difficult to imagine an unremarkable transition between online life and offline life. Through this conceptual framing, the online activities of youth are made newly visible and separate from their offline lives, appearing as technologically produced risks that were in need of immediate intervention. These concepts, developed from the privileged perspective of adults without any meaningful inclusion of youth voices, then failed to connect to the lives of the very populations of young people they intended to protect. The separation between online and offline, then, marks out the adult strategic production of power and knowledge, through which everyday youth lives are opened to more productive modes of governance.

Cyberbullying is one of many Internet safety concepts that marks out forms of technological violence and abuse as separate from the offline, local contexts that produce forms of violence among youth. The term has largely been attributed to Canadian educator Bill Belsey (2003), who defines it as "the use of information and communication technologies to support deliberate, repeated, and hostile behaviour by an individual or group, that is intended to harm others." As a broader explanation of youth social life, the term connotes the well-established narrative of bullying, which is made inescapable, painfully public, and rapidly paced by the adoption of technology. As one early report describes (Paulson 2003):

While in some ways it's no worse than old-fashioned bullying, cyberbullying has a few idiosyncrasies. Websites and screen names give bullies a mask of anonymity if they wish it, making them difficult to trace. The pressure for kids to be always on-line means bullies can extend their harassment into their victims' homes. And the miracle of the Web means that sharing an embarrassing photo or private note—with thousands of people—requires little more than the click of a key.

The term rapidly gained acceptance in both media reports (Hayasaki and Chong 2003; Simmons 2003) and the academic literature on youth and violence (Bauman and Bellmore 2014), which quickly placed cyber-bullying into a developmental framework (Berson and Berson 2005). As cellular phones, social networking sites, and gossip sites (precursors to the mobile applications available to youth today) grew in popularity, cyber-bullying drew the concerned attention of schools and parents but was largely eclipsed by the ongoing panic over online predation (discussed in chapter 3).

In 2007, NetSmartz—an Internet safety program developed by the National Center for Missing and Exploited Children (NCMEC)—released a video entitled "Teens Talk Back: Cyberbullying" on its Web site (NetSmartz 2007). Aimed primarily at junior high and high school audiences, the video provides small clips of interviews with young people, framed by a male nar-rator who poses questions about cyberbullying. In one section, the narrator asks "What is cyberbullying?," and the text of his question is displayed on the screen, overlaid with streaming binary code. In individual video clips, three high school–aged students define the word. The first student states that it is "Threats made through the Internet—you know, by e-mail, comments"; the second states that "Cyberbullying is when anyone tries to contact you in a mean way"; and the third student, leaning casually against a locker, states that "It's just basically, like, trash talk—like, uh, through technology." The reaction, while minor, demonstrates the lack of salience that such concepts have for youth. The third student initially uses common slang to define the term and tacks on "through technology" seemingly as an afterthought. Most students in the video appear to resist a definition (a topic that I return to in chapter 7). This said, it is the fact that technology would be an afterthought, that it would only be something mentioned to an adult audience looking for a specific answer that is of importance here. While appearing to provide young people with a voice, these videos instead are designed to instill upon youth the adult concepts of Internet safety—in this case, a concept of technological bullying distinct from local contexts and social relations.

Through videos, handouts, and assemblies, young people are taught to recognize cyberbullying, ignore or block online bullies when possible, and collect digital evidence to show a trusted adult in particularly severe cases (NetSmartz 2007). Relatively few materials mention youth perpetrators of bullying, although educators are instructed to address the issue. Where potential bullying behavior is addressed directly by NetSmartz materials, it is only through the accidental or unintentional actions of a student. In the single video devoted to addressing would-be cyberbullies, a teen soberly explains that he was invited to participate in what he considered to be a private "rating" Web site where he and his male friends rated and joked about female students (NetSmartz 2006c). It is only after his friend "Pat" opens the site to the public that the student is regretfully positioned as an accidental cyberbully, and even then only due to the actions of the unheard from "Pat." Cyberbullying, then, was originally conceptualized in much the same ways that previous forms of youth Internet safety risks were—as a form of harassment that happens *to* youth and that constructs an anonymous cyberbully who commits the offense. This is perhaps unsurprising given that the materials originate from an organization that focuses primarily on youth victimization by adults, at a moment in history when predators retained the focus of the media and legislators. The true work of cyberbullying intervention, then, comes from a vigilant parent who monitors youth online and off, seeking to detect the signs of social isolation and depression that mark a victim of online bullies. In other words, this disciplinary response to cyberbullying actively enrolled parents to surveil youth online (as described in the previous chapter).

In the early 2000s, a number of widely reported suicides (including those of Ryan Halligan, Megan Meier, and Phoebe Prince) drew increased attention to bullying and cyberbullying ("Cyberbullying Suicides" 2012). Responding to the suicide of Justin Aaberg, a gay teenager, in the wake of extensive in-school bullying, columnist Dan Savage and his partner Terry Miller launched the It Gets Better Project on September 21, 2010, by posting a video to YouTube ("What Is the It Gets Better Project?" 2010). In the video, Savage and Miller describe their own experiences with bullying in their respective high schools, which encompassed physical and relational violence. The central message of the video (as the name of the project suggests) is that life after high school has been significantly better for both men. As Miller notes, "Honestly, things got better the day I left high school.

I didn't see the bullies every day, I didn't see the people who harassed me every day, I didn't have to see the school administrators who did nothing about it every day. Life instantly got better" ("It Gets Better" 2010). One day later, Rutgers University student Tyler Clementi committed suicide, after his roommate streamed online video of Clementi kissing another man. The It Gets Better Project immediately gained media attention, and celebrities, public figures, and everyday Internet users began posting their own versions of the "It Gets Better" video and describing their own stories of life after childhood. The campaign rapidly became so popular that President Barack Obama (2010) made his own version of an "It Gets Better" video statement stating, "there is a whole world waiting for you, filled with possibilities. … You'll look back on the struggles you faced with compassion, and wisdom."

Through the It Gets Better campaign, the structural conditions of violence are made visible—although not explicitly so. The everyday experiences of physical and relational violence are inescapable, not because technology allows bullies to reach into the homes of families but because the social worlds of young people are shrinking within the confines of childhood spaces and institutions. Only after "sticking out the bullying and the pain" ("It Gets Better" 2010) and escaping the boundaries of childhood can young people (who are then legally adults) live their lives relatively free of everyday violence. These videos point to the boundaries constituted by particular modes of conceptualizing youth, the boundaries between childhood and "the real world" that highly constrain young people's autonomy and mobility. For children, there is no escape. Even here, these boundaries are assumed to be natural and unmalleable. The ways in which youth are constrained are not considered to be problematic: the "unnatural" behavior of "bullies" is the problem. On the one hand, these boundaries and the way that they circumscribe youth social life allow everyday violence to be inescapable. On the other hand, this inescapable element arguably plays a key role in violent behavior among youth. As the independent mobility of children and teenagers is increasingly constrained and as discourses of safety and developmental psychology are mobilized as rationales for further policing and surveillance, perhaps it is not surprising that disillusioned and disenfranchised young people increasingly act like prisoners.

This form of carceral logic is one of caring and good intentions. Teachers, principals, and parents all want young people to succeed, and in the process of doing whatever is necessary to protect and guide them, they create conditions that fundamentally disempower them. One teacher I spoke with was responsible for in-school detention and explained the recidivism of some students:

Being in in-school [detention], obviously I have my frequent fliers. And it just—you know, the assistant principal is talking to them, the social worker or the psychologist talks to them, I see them one-on-one. They have to fill out a form why they're there, what they did, how things could be different. And yet they're continually coming back, so nothing is changing. You know, obviously not every incident is a bullying incident, but it's the mentality of they're stuck. They're stuck in behaving a certain way, and it doesn't seem like there's anything that anybody's come up with to change that behavior. It's certainly not lack of caring individuals. I love our school. I can't think of one teacher that doesn't really care about the kids, and I think it definitely shows.

Explaining the phenomenon of cyberbullying as a product of technology and developmental limits to cognition fails to consider structural conditions as a possible factor in the production of violent or antisocial behavior among youth. By drawing attention to the new features of seemingly socially distancing information technology and implicating them in a historically established narrative of bullying, existing institutions and power relations are shielded from criticism. Established constructions of childhood, adulthood, and the school as institution are taken as unproblematic through the frames provided by bullying and cyberbullying, excluding them as possible points of intervention.

The increased visibility of bullying behavior made possible through the adoption of information technologies by youth has placed pressure on schools and responsible adults to manage the "growing" problem of bullying. This problem increasingly is framed in terms of culture and public health. As one anonymous op-ed piece in the *Wall Street Journal* noted ("Internet 'Virus'" 2010):

before we get federal authorities involved in fixing the online problem, it's worth noting that hostility and incivility now are ingrained in our broader culture and the online community merely reflects that coarsening of discourse (perhaps cheapened a bit further by anonymity and profanity).

As both bullying and cyberbullying became framed as a broader cultural crisis, intervention strategies began to incorporate a third position within the bullying discourse beyond those of the bully and victim—that of the bystander. Previously excluded from bullying discourses, bystanders are individuals who watch harassment or other violence taking place, whether online or off. Identifying the bystander marks the beginning of a shift toward enrolling all youth in the "battle" against cyberbullying and "empowering" students to make the "choice" to intervene when they see inappropriate behavior. This discourse of empowerment resonates with many young people, who have been increasingly disempowered through the expansion of childhood. This form of empowerment positions those who intervene or otherwise choose to "be positive" in everyday conflicts above those who "choose" to be negative, again masking the social contexts and conditions that structure and produce such conflicts. A high school junior, Lamia Abukhadra (2013), wrote about Rachel's Challenge (an antibullying program for students in one of the school districts in my study) in a letter to the editor of her school newspaper:

The presentation trivialized the hard work of active students that results in tangible community changes such as: composting, community meetings, education about culture, and more. These active community changes don't just grow from kindness, they grow from hard work, communication, planning, and people overcoming differences such as race, gender, or culture. ... The message was very white centric. She was white, the high school she attended was largely white, the people she actually affected were white, and the suburb in which they all lived is rich and white. ...

Rachel's Challenge tells students that if you're really nice and you believe in your hopes and dreams that you can achieve anything and fix the social problems at school. These are not proper tools that students should use to help tackle and talk about the social issues in our school. Dialogue, education about others, and student motivated movements to alleviate tension and change [in] our community are the tools South [High School] needs.

Through the bystander narrative, cyberbullying more clearly becomes what Nikolas Rose (2000) describes as a "circuit of inclusion" in which control is dispersed among students, allowing for a constant modulation of behavior under continuous social surveillance. Youth are directed to "choose" to interpret social situations through the frames of positivity and cyberbullying rather than through their own situated knowledges. This discourse renders students incapable of structural change because it allows them only the "choice" of responding positively in the face of abuse and violence rather than opportunities for meaningful change.

Within the NetSmartz curricula, this dilemma becomes visible through a series of revised tip sheets aimed at teenage audiences and released in 2012.

The sheets provide a range of youth Internet safety tips and announce that "BYSTANDERS ARE GUILTY TOO. If your friends are cyberbullying some-one and you stay silent, you're just as guilty as they are. Speak up and keep your friends in check" (NetSmartz 2012a). This is further explained in a later NetSmartz publication that again emphasizes "empowerment" and "choice," further distributing the responsibility of safety down to the daily actions and behaviors of children and teenagers themselves (NetSmartz 2013c):

Empowering bystanders: When children witness bullying, they may feel like there's nothing they can do. But bystanders' choices can help set the tone for their online environments. If they join in or support the bullying, they are showing that it's OK to be cruel. But if they stand up for the victim and report the bullying, they are send-ing a clear signal that cyberbullying is not cool.

The bystander model of cyberbullying education was built into inter-active comics and games aimed at student audiences. For NetSmartz, the first of these came in the form of an interactive comic entitled "Stand by or Stand Up?" (NetSmartz 2014). In the comic, teenage characters Carlos and John use a mobile application that places animal heads on photos of people, and student participants make a series of decisions about whether Carlos should initially share an embarassing image, contact administrators after it goes viral, or choose to help the main victim (a girl named Katie) toward the end of the story. Although the app seems to offer a range of options at each stage in the decision tree, the decisions do not change the story: the act of taking the picture triggers a chain of events that invariably leads to its viral spread and Katie's harassment. The only significant change is that Carlos can be either punished by administrators or thanked by Katie. Even in the best-case outcome—where Carlos refuses to share the doctored photos, reports the photos to online hosts, and contacts school administra-tors to tell them that harassment is taking place—the principal sternly tells him, "THANK YOU FOR TELLING US THE TRUTH. ... BUT YOU SHOULD HAVE TOLD US ABOUT THIS EARLIER" (NetSmartz 2014). Regardless of his choices, Carlos ends up in the principal's office facing judgment by the authorities. When Katie later thanks him online, he apologizes for failing to report the episode earlier. Empowered to choose, the behavior of young people must be continuously modulated through the anticipation of future consequences that structure the choices of the present.

Managing Reputations

Over the past five years, youth Internet safety education has turned to the concept of online reputation management. Historically, this turn represents an intersection between existing youth Internet safety (centered on the concept of "offline consequences" or inappropriate content) and the rise of online reputation management as a tool in brand management and public relations. This intersection is a subset of the concept of the "personal brand" (Lair, Sullivan, and Cheney 2005), which initially referred to job seekers' use of marketing techniques to structure their increasingly visible online identities. The concerns about online reputation management are unlike youth Internet safety concerns of the past—no one is lurking in the shadows, threatening young people—and represent a new means of conceptualizing online risk. The central mechanism of online reputation management is the gaze of the future admissions board, recruiter, and employer. Through this mechanism and concerns about inappropriate content, previous youth Internet safety concerns are reinterpreted. The threat of cyberbullying is expanded: "Drunk driving literally ends lives. But digital drama can potentially end a bright future for your child and their dreams" (Scheff 2013). Teenagers themselves must choose not to engage in the practices of drama: they must choose not to post pictures of themselves drinking.

One early example of this transition can be seen in Project Privacy and Reputation Online (Project PRO), sponsored by Internet safety curricula provider Internet Keep Safe (iKeepSafe) Coalition and funded in part by AT&T (Internet Keep Safe Coalition 2009b). The iKeepSafe group provides videos on online reputation management, one each for parents, educators, and students. The videos aimed at adults include additional material from psychologists. All three versions of the video provide two short vignettes—one on "The Realities of Negative Digital Reputation" and one on "Digital Reputation … for Positive Outcomes." In the following section, I briefly analyze the content of the video and accompany quotes with discussion and overlapping materials from other curricula. The video provides a structure for thinking about various online safety issues and is an intersection where many key themes discussed throughout this book converge. I use the parent version of the video (Internet Keep Safe Coalition 2009a) for analysis because all of the material is transferred from the student version, with added clips providing parents with expert discussion.

The iKeepSafe video opens with an introduction from one of the directors of iKeepSafe, who summarizes the issue of online reputation management by stating that "I think, more importantly, it's understanding the consequences down the road." The word *consequences* appears frequently in the video and in other youth Internet safety curricula. In the NetSmartz curricula, most of the educational materials aimed at teens focus on the concept of consequences for online activity, with one video entitled simply "Offline Consequences" (NetSmartz n.d.-a). Of the fifteen videos hosted on the NetSmartz site, five focus on the consequences of posting materials to a profile site, and two describe the dangers of viral information spread.

The student version of the iKeepSafe "Privacy and Reputation" (iKeepSafe 2009a) video opens as a young hispanic man in his late teens or early twenties swings a baseball bat alone in a lit field. "Everybody has a dream. I had mine," he says. He explains that he accomplished his dream of going to a college on a baseball scholarship but that his scholarship was taken away after photos were posted online that showed him drinking at an undergraduate college party. "Scholarship gone. Baseball gone. School gone. My dream gone. All because of some picture on a camera phone." NetSmartz (2012b) hosts a similar video entitled "Two Kinds of Stupid" in which Eduardo, a fictional male student, loses his swimming scholarship after posting pictures of himself drinking at a party. A now iconic red Solo cup features prominently in both videos. As Eduardo, the NetSmartz teen, explains: "It was really all me. I was the one who broke the rules, and then I posted the pictures online. … I used to be this [scholarship] kid, and now I'm this [normal] kid." In this video, it is clear that responsibility for the problem lies in the choices that Eduardo was free to make for himself.

These two videos available through NetSmartz and iKeepSafe focus on male athletes who either lost or were seeking college scholarships. In the NetSmartz curricula, female students are portrayed as being concerned with the unwanted visibility of their posts to boys or with the spread of information about the boys they like—and in neither case is this presented as a form of reputation management. Online reputation management content in this way contrasts with earlier videos about inappropriate materials that centered on the sexuality of female students—notably the videos from NetSmartz's parent organization, the National Center for Missing and Exploited Children (NCMEC) that show female students frantically tearing photos off a school bulletin board (NCMEC 2008), being asked "What color underwear today?" by older men in public (NCMEC 2007), or otherwise having nude photos uncontrollably shared by male students (NCMEC 2011). Male students are not portrayed as sharing nude photos or otherwise concerning themselves with relationships, although NetSmartz (2006b) provides a video that demonstrates that they too can be sexually victimized.

Returning again to the iKeepSafe "Privacy and Reputation" video (Internet Keep Safe Coalition 2009a), it suggests that even one misstep can destroy dreams and careers. The baseball player goes to his first college party, drinks his first college beer, and makes the horrible mistake of enjoying it with his new friends and teammates. As he explains, "Everyone has seen it—baseball friends, my coach. I even think my mom saw it. So here I am—poof—everything taken away." Perhaps athletic scholarships are a common theme in these videos because they often have zero tolerance policies for infractions of team rules. In this way, the training materials can provide young people with an image of what the curricula developers want them to see—in this case, the career-ending consequences of a single image—without technically being dishonest. The next segment in the video (which is available only in the parent version) opens with an iKeepSafe representative speaking: "underage drinking? That's actually illegal, and those types of images, those types of comments will follow them and their many jobs that they will not have the opportunity to have because this online reputation could potentially follow them."

However, as the iKeepSafe representative continues to explain to parents,

the reverse is [also] true. If I put things up or I help my child put up information that helps them be recognized as a thought leader, as a community participant, as someone who is articulate ... who is reaching out to the international community through the World Wide Web—that will help them with all of their opportunities.

Although actively posting materials for children is not a common suggestion in the other online safety curricula I have sampled, it is a logical extension of the concept of online reputation management. After all, if adults actively engage in carefully manipulating their own professional brands and young people are expected to do the same, then parents are expected to model those behaviors. What better way to model the behavior of reputation management than by demonstrating to young people the ways that their own image might be turned and manipulated to ensure competitiveness? Indeed, the range of online reputation management services, both for individuals and large organizations, suggests that this practice could be considered good—or at least advantageous—parenting.

Following the brief piece from the iKeepSafe representative, the "Privacy and Reputation" video moves back into material that is provided to youth with a second conversation with a former student named Greg. Greg is presented to the audience against a black background. He is a clean-shaven, white, eighteen- to twenty-five-year-old wearing a casual button-down shirt and jeans—the very image of the young Internet professional. As he goes on to explain:

I started this blog. ... A lot of my friends were posting pictures of them chugging beers and hanging out with friends partying and stuff [on their blogs]. I kind of wanted to make mine more personal. So I started posting things that I thought people cared about. ... Positive stuff. I just wanted to make it influential, innovative. ... Fun stuff. Positive things. ... I was contacted by an industry leader. He said, "I'll pay for all your college." And now I have a direction, I know what I'm going to do, and I've got help along the way, and it's awesome.

The video cuts to a scene of Greg on a couch between two male friends. Greg is working busily on his laptop, while his two friends appear to be playing a video game. A young woman comes up from behind him on the couch and playfully covers his eyes before leaving the frame. Greg closes the segment, explaining that he is a success—a young success. "So blog about positive things, positive things happen."

In Greg's story, the careful curation of an image is "more personal" than the everyday activities of youth life, and such curated identities are far more likely to be paid attention to by the community and the world at large. This sentiment also is echoed in the video "Profile Penalty" (NetSmartz 2006a), in which an animated white, male high school athlete cleans up his online profile before a school visit from a college football recruiter. The athlete removes all of the photos and discussions of pranks he played and replaces them with gym photos and football-related materials. Even his username changes from "ratherbesleepin" to "GRIDIRONMAN." Conceptualized through the frame of online reputation management, youth identities must be carefully constructed in ways that make them appealing to future recruiters and employers. Throughout these materials, young people are told that a single deviation will lead to far-ranging consequences that can never be erased and will follow them for life. These kinds of warning also were found in previous versions of Internet safety curricula, but the frame of online reputation management extends the concept of inappropriate content to include innocuous posts in addition to risky materials with sexual, violent, or drug-related content. In the "Profile Penalty" video, GRIDIRONMAN is worried when a friend reminds him that a blog post describing "twinkies and coke as the perfect meal" remained online, and he hurries to delete the post before the recruiter finds the site.

In the parent version of the "Privacy and Reputation" video, the iKeepSafe representative returns. She explains:

Something that every parent needs to remember is that their child, no matter how smart or wonderful they are—their frontal lobe is not developed until they're somewhere between twenty-two and twenty-five. Which means you can have a very functional child who might not be thinking "What will happen if I ... " and that CEO part of the brain that helps them make really good decisions isn't yet developed. ... This is where [even] a nontechnical parent can actually be very helpful for a technical child.

Although this again is significantly more extreme than the material provided by NetSmartz, it represents a trend toward extending childhood into the early twenties by constructing a new developmental phase. Twenty-four-year-old people may appear to be "functional," but they still require parental guidance and monitoring to assist them with interpreting the appropriateness of online content. Within this phase, youth actively develop the "CEO part of the brain" within their "frontal lobe," allowing them to anticipate the interpretive gaze of the future employer and shape their online personas accordingly. Through such comments developmental and corporate logics are made continuous, wiring the circuits of corporate success to the appropriate development of young people. Youth have the freedom to choose, but they lack the brain capacity—the internal corporate structure—to choose appropriately and must instead be guided by fully developed adult experts.

The video then closes, with light guitar music playing in the background as a list of sponsors is shown. Included in the list are the computer security company Symantec, the American School Counselor Association, Neumont University, Yahoo!, AT&T, and Reputation Defender (now called ReputationDefender, a subsidiary of Reputation.com). ReputationDefender offers online reputation management services to individuals and claims to now have over one million users worldwide (ReputationDefender 2015). In the closing credits of the video, we see the relationships that create these new forms of youth Internet safety videos—developmental psychologists, Internet service providers, and the providers of security software and services.

"Te(a)chInCtrl": The Transition to Digital Citizenship

In January 2015, NetSmartz hosted a webinar entitled "Why We're Moving from Online Safety to Digital Citizenship … and You Should Too" (Nathan and Gallagher 2015). The webinar described a transition away from focusing on online crime and victimization and toward fostering the development of "digital citizens." Describing the transition, the deputy director of the National Center for Missing and Exploited Children (NCMEC), Laurie Nathan, presented images of one child seated before a darkened computer and a smiling child holding a mobile phone. She explained that technology was being positioned more positively and that the emphasis was shifting from protection to a new form of productive freedom. Frank Gallagher, vice president of education for the Cable Impacts Foundation, explained: "There was some concern that in an effort to keep everything safe for students, we'd overreact, or block, or prohibit so much that we would kind of negate the potential benefits."

According to Gallagher, technological adoption and use patterns are moving away from models of media consumption and toward more participatory models (Nathan and Gallagher 2015):

you're able to reach and engage with a global audience, but you don't have the safeguards that the *New York Times* or a CBS has … to make sure that what you put out is safe, accurate, or ethical. … The new technology allows you to post immediately, anywhere, without having to stop and think, or run it by anybody else. It makes a lot of the old advice we used to give to parents obsolete. Like keeping the computer … this big clunky thing—where we used to tell people to keep it in the family room, so mom and dad could monitor it. Well, you can't do that with a smartphone. … Schools, the Internet safety community—all of us have struggled to keep up with those changes.

As is discussed in chapter 3, shifts in technology and young people's patterns of adoption have further problematized the "patches" to the disciplinary technology of the home. Because many children and teenagers now use mobile technologies and smartphones, their access to the Internet can no longer be spatially contained and monitored in place. Instead, they move about freely inside the home or (less frequently) outside of the home, bringing access to the Internet with them into potentially unmonitored spaces. There is, it seems, no other recourse other than to enroll youth themselves in the process of producing the effects of governance, to develop and distribute codes of behavior that guide but do not constrain.

According to the Nathan and Gallagher webinar (2015), the three key elements of the digital citizenship approach are positivity, a holistic interpretation of safety issues, and an understanding of youth agency. Rather than blocking, filtering, and occasionally punishing people for participating in online spaces, the new approach provides a set of "behavioral codes" that give young people the freedom to make their own decisions, relying on adults only when necessary. This form of citizenship also allows them to play an active role in the development of both school policies and curricula. Nathan compares the old messages delivered under the Internet safety framework with the new messages provided through the concept of digital citizenship. "Predators can track children to their homes" becomes "Most solicitation is done by peers"; "Communicating with strangers is bad" becomes "Everyone is responsible for creating a positive online experience"; and "The Internet is like the Wild, Wild, West" becomes "Most kids are not cyberbullying and sexting." Repeatedly emphasized is that everyone needs to take a role in creating the new, positive online environment: "If one teen acts poorly, how is that going to impact another teen? So it's really about everyone sharing that responsibility." The presentation demonstrates the shift from disciplinary to control technologies and the extension of disciplined freedoms to youth. Through the discourse of empowerment, children and teenagers are placed on the new information highway (in a Deleuzian rather Clintonian sense) and are free to roam the now colonized frontier.

At the end of the presentation, Nathan announces a new online educator training program that is aimed at any "trusted adult" who provides digital citizen education. The program (called Teaching Digital Citizenship) is sponsored by Disney's Club Penguin (which is described in detail in the next chapter) and repackages NetSmartz's presenter training to reflect a shift to digital citizenry while not abandoning the concept of Internet Safety. Nathan says, "It's always a challenge to revolutionize years' worth of resources, but we're certainly making good headway." After making the NetSmartz announcement, Gallagher shows a slide that misspells the URL for a digital citizenry resource for educators. The slide reads http://www.techInCtrl.com (instead of the correct URL, http://www.teachInCtrl.com). Gallagher suddenly notes the typographical error: "Cable Impacts ... has created something we call 'TeachInCtrl,' and, um, I appear to have misspelled that. The URL is 'teach': 'T-E-A-C-H-In-Ctrl-dot-org.' ... Ah, well, 'teach,' 'tech.' It's all the same thing, right? (laughter)."

The online educator training program is one of many transitional steps that NetSmartz is taking to revise its curricula to focus on digital citizenship. The Teaching Digital Citizenship program includes several short videos that provide new conceptual categories of online participation. Many of the goals of this transition to digital citizenship as the framework for media educators are undoubtedly positive—regardless of how they might be theorized as part of a potentially disturbing shift toward societies of control. I imagine that young people would vastly prefer (and feel more respected within) the disciplined freedoms of control technologies to the overt boundaries and surveillance of disciplinary governance. The ease with which most children and teenagers have taken to social networking services and applications in many ways confirms this. Further, this turn to digital citizenship and the positive conceptualization of youth technology use is, after all, the very approach championed by many of the other authors in this book series, including myself (Ito et al. 2009; Ito et al. 2013). Youth *should* be treated with a level of respect and authority in discussions of online life that are intended to protect and provide them with critical resources, and the positive elements of networked communication far outweigh the potential risks of porn, predators, bullies, and bad reputations.

The videos show, however, that it is no simple task to rework "years of resources" and sunk costs around a more positive message. To date, many of the previous NetSmartz materials have simply been recycled into the new educator framework. Further, the new framework hides much in the concepts that it promotes, and it constructs a form of digital literacy, ethics, and citizenship that largely lacks a critical understanding of online participation or the technologies that support it. In the next section of the chapter, I provide an analysis of NetSmartz and Club Penguin's Teaching Digital Citizenship online educator training program (NetSmartz 2015), examining some of the "positive" elements of the curricula. I will note that this new online educator training program will undoubtedly be revised as NetSmartz adds additional materials that provide more details about the group's vision for digital citizenry.

Digital Literacy and Ethics

Digital literacy and ethics are new issues addressed by NetSmartz, and they can be seen as key "positive" elements of the new framework of digital citizenship. Critical media literacy has long been considered a necessary element of educational reform. Mizuko Ito and colleagues (2009, xii) consider the concept to be a central issue in their groundbreaking work, *Hanging Out, Messing Around, and Geeking Out: Kids Living and Learning with New Media*, where they define *media literacy* as

ways of understanding, interpreting, and critiquing media, but also the means for creative and social expression, online search and navigation, and a host of new technical skills. The potential gap in literacies and participation skills creates new challenges for educators who struggle to bridge media engagement inside and outside the classroom.

The text describes genres of media participation among young people and grounds media literacy practices in extensive anthropological research. Participation is a key component of media literacy, so students need to be taught to both critically consume and also produce texts in various formats, learning how the production of a piece is inherently tied to its message (Kellner and Share 2005, 2007). Media literacy emphasizes youth access to the tools of media production, allowing them to actively generate, reinterpret, and disseminate content grounded in their own perspectives and encouraging critical engagement with dominant media messages. Lawrence Lessig (2008) describes this form of participatory media production as readwrite (RW) culture, made possible through the accessibility of inexpensive tools for creating, editing, and publishing in a broad range of digital formats. Frequently drawing on the work of Paolo Freire (1968), advocates of critical media literacy argue that by encouraging participation in RW culture, we encourage the development of a citizenry who is capable of more than the uncritical consumption and reproduction of media content provided by the global elite.

The Teaching Digital Citizenship online educator training program, however, defines *digital literacy* and *digital ethics* as follows: "Digital literacy is being able to discern trustworthy information online. Digital ethics is not pirating online material or using technology to cheat." The presenter then explains that "Cheating and piracy can be so easy that children may not consider the consequences." Digital literacy is defined only in terms of media consumption—being able to determine which sources are trustworthy. In this case, trustworthy URLs are located at .edu or .gov domains, and other sites require additional research to determine validity. This appears to be the extent of critical engagement with media. Young people also are told that they should "not pirate" or "use technology to cheat," once again ensuring that dominant intellectual property rights are secured. Indeed, the only other participatory element of the curriculum appears to be a brief mention of teaching youth to share copyrighted material legally—again positioning children and teenagers not as producers of content but rather as distributors of the content developed by others.

The presenter ends the segment by saying, "Making them aware that piracy is wrong and that you can't trust everything online is a great place to start." This is arguably a negative point from which to begin a conversation with young people about participatory digital citizenship, again refocusing the message on the risky potentials of information technology. The program provides a core message reinforcing the principles of what Lessig (2008) describes as read-only (RO) culture—in which media is produced and protected by small groups of intellectual property holders, at the cost of more participatory modes of engaging with culture—wrapped in the language of RW culture. Accordingly, *citizenship* is again defined in terms that closely match the definition provided by Nikolas Rose (2000, 327), who describes the "inclusive identities" of circuits of inclusion, in which

Citizenship is not primarily realized in a relation with the state, nor does it involve participation in a uniform public sphere; citizenship, rather, entails active engagement in a diversified and dispersed variety of private, corporate, and quasi-corporate practices, of which working and shopping are paradigmatic.

Thus, rather than the critical, engaged citizenship that might be fostered by unprecedented access to information resources and tools of media manipulation, instead we have a subject of control who is free to choose from and (legally) redistribute any of the materials made available to them.

Inappropriate Content

In the Teaching Digital Citizenship online educator training program, "inappropriate content" is established as the umbrella concept that encompasses a broad range of content issues, including exposure to pornographic or violent content, exposure to advertising, and reputation management—although cyberbullying and sexting are excluded and provided with their own top-level categories. As the video narrator explains, "There was a time when parents and teachers were able to choose the content appropriate for children, but on the Internet all the content is equally accessible. Websites about ponies and websites about pornography are both just a click away." Perhaps influenced by the work of Sonia Livingstone (2009), the program suggests providing resources to younger children who have encountered material that they themselves have defined as troubling, and to otherwise avoid penalizing youth for doing so. The presenter explains that children and teenagers should be taught that they can disengage from content by using the Back button or simply shutting off the screen. Adults are positioned as resources for cases where young people require additional assistance and should explain to them that online materials can be disturbing but that the Internet is otherwise a valuable "tool."

The concept of content is not limited to materials that children and teenagers are exposed to, however, and also covers content that they choose to post. In this regard, inappropriate content again covers online reputation management, and educators are instructed to provide students with access to the resources described in the previous section. Again, the "Profile Penalty" and "Two Kinds of Stupid" videos are provided as key resources for teaching about the consequences of posting materials that may be perceived as inappropriate. As is often repeated throughout various online safety materials, the lesson is that "Once a child puts something online, they can't take it back." In this section of the program, the language of digital citizenship and participation again masks a return to Internet safety messages. Rather than encouraging youth to create and share media, they are instead encouraged to think carefully about how the media they create and share might someday hurt them. This places a secondary layer of restrictions on the forms of media that youth might produce, in addition to that of strong copyright protection, and outlining media production in terms of risk rather than possibility.

Young people are again asked to consider the consequences of their actions through the view of an imagined parent, school administrator, law enforcement officer, or employer, leaving no space for mistakes in a persistent digital world of media that can never "be taken back." No mention is made of practical steps which might be taken should children or adults want to remove content from various online spaces. It is simply assumed that any content posted online for any period of time must remain in place, a course of action that ensures no content can ever actually be taken back, even in cases where it would be trivial to do so. Trusted adults are instead told to focus youth attention on the consequences of posting inappropriate content, ranging from parental discipline to criminal charges.

Cyberbullying

The content on cyberbullying offered by the Teaching Digital Citizenship online educator training program is similar to that provided previously by the NetSmartz materials, with no substantial change in the content but some slight shifts in delivery. As previously mentioned, a narrative of cyberbullying is presented in which online forms of harassment become functionally inescapable. The narrative of bullies, victims, and "the bystanders who watch, but do nothing" remains consistent with the more recently released materials provided by NetSmartz described previously. One notable change is the connection between online and offline forms of bullying— although online and offline bullying remain distinct forms of behavior. As the presenter describes: "cyberbullies are usually peers they know. They don't feel safe at school because the bully is there, but now they don't feel safe at home either because the bullying is happening 24/7 online."

Regardless of how youth Internet safety materials are theorized from an academic standpoint, NetSmartz promotes a level of respect among children and teenagers online through this new direction. Although the distribution of responsibility is a form of governance, it also is a means by which young people gain some degree of agency. The message that "One of the most important things for any digital citizen to understand is that everyone deserves respect" is a positive shift from the former youth-as-victim model previously held by NetSmartz and most other safety curricula.

Online Privacy

In the Teaching Digital Citizenship online educator training program, privacy is constituted in relation to the online criminal, the scammer, the predator, and the bully. Privacy becomes an act of restraint. Young people are encouraged to avoid posting personal information and to allow only people who know them offline to view their posts and online content.

Further, the concept of privacy aligns with that provided by social networking services and Web sites. The platform itself is never called into question; only the other, risky individuals who share the space are potentially dangerous. The often repeated refrain again appears relative to online privacy concerns: "Think about the consequences." The consequences are the ways that sharing personal or private information might lead to victimization rather than the ways that large-scale data collection and analysis might shape students' futures.

The information provided to youth on protecting their online privacy comes in the form of basic computer security tips. As the presenter explains, privacy can be protected by knowing "tips on protecting their personal information. Basic rules like how to make a strong password and what information they should never post go a long way." In this way again, the sexual predator is used to create a particular understanding of what privacy is (kids don't want adults creeping around their profiles), and the construction of this particular form of outsider then leads young people to ignore the technologies themselves. Trusted adults and trusted systems can, by their very nature, be trusted to protect the privacy of youth.

Other forms of safety curricula are available to educators, and they provide differently conceptualized forms of materials and resources around the issues of safety and citizenship. The Digital Bytes program offered by Common Sense Media (2014) breaks down the boundaries between safety and citizenship through a series of videos and exercises. Children and teenagers are provided with options to direct their own study, presented with questions and materials that reflect contemporary digital issues, and encouraged to respond by producing their own materials and posting them online. On many levels, the program accomplishes the goals set forth by NetSmartz, including a positive, productive stance toward using information technologies and providing routes for critical engagement. In the Digital Bytes framework, for example, the definition of *privacy* includes "freedom from corporate tracking and data collection." Although Digital Bytes provides a more positive, respectful safety curriculum for youth, it is not as well positioned as NetSmartz. Law enforcement officials know the National Center for Missing and Exploited Children and understand the ways in which NCMEC conceptualizes online activity in terms of risk and safety. Ultimately, law enforcement officials will provide a significant amount of youth Internet safety materials—if not directly to students, then to the "trusted adults" who will.

Internet Safety in Practice

Although the content of youth Internet safety curricula has changed over time and continues to do so, the presentation of the material arguably has failed to transition as quickly. In this sense, the transition from discipline to control is not easy. In school districts with shrinking budgets and restrictive filters, youth Internet safety education in practice falls short of the practices recommended by curricula made available through providers such as NetSmartz. One focus group conversation between a librarian and teacher made this clear:

Librarian: [Students] want to do something about it. I just don't know if they know what to do. My perspective is that if we taught them, if everything wasn't so blocked at school, and just let them have a little more freedom, and taught them more online etiquette (and "how to be better digital citizens" is a big buzzword in library science), then maybe this wouldn't be such an issue. I mean, maybe it would. Kids are still going to be mean whether you teach them this or not. But I know that they've had an eye towards trying to deal with it, but it doesn't seem to have gotten any better. ...
Teacher: I kind of like your comment of feeling so filtered that we can't really educate because we can't get anywhere to try to show them anything. You know, I can tell the kids, especially with my special ed. kids, "If you go on Facebook." But I can't go on there and show them. I can't show them how to set up the privacy settings or to be able to take a post off that they can't believe they just put on ... because you can't show them how it would look. ... So when I talk about Facebook, I don't know that they're even picturing the screen in their mind the way they would if it was in front of them.

Additionally, although youth Internet safety curricula usually are oriented toward opening lines of communication and empowering young people to make their own choices, they lose that emphasis when they are reinterpreted through the disciplinary frame of law enforcement. Law enforcement officials commonly teach about youth Internet safety and provide their services to school districts in a mutually beneficial exchange. Because schools often face unfunded mandates to provide youth Internet safety education to their students, they reach out to law enforcement officials, who frequently use videos or other resources from NetSmartz in their presentations. In these presentations, the sense of a real and looming threat is reinforced when the presenter provides examples of the disastrous consequences of inappropriate youth Internet use. Although law enforcement professionals provide many valuable services to communities, their perspectives on Internet safety are shaped by their frequent exposure to highly disturbing crimes and are not always the most appropriate for children and teenagers who have little or no experience with victimization online.

In 2010, I was invited to attend two youth Internet safety presentations put on by the New York State Police Computer Crime Unit. As I sat in the audience of students waiting for the first presentation to begin, I heard someone exclaim, "I'm almost eighteen. I don't need to know about Internet safety awareness!" One disruptive student was removed from the audience by the principal, and when questioned about her behavior, she shouted, "I don't fuckin' want to be here!" Three boys discussed the title slide:

Student A: This is going to be fuckin' hysterical.
Student B: Look what it's called!
Student C (laughing):   It's hysterical, right!

After the students settled into their seats, the presenter said, "Teens online: this is you guys. You are perpetrators, and you are victims," which left little room for safe, legal Internet use by youth. This was a theme throughout the presentation as the state trooper explained how easily investigators could track and monitor youth online, particularly those engaged in illegal activities. As with most presentations by law enforcement, the presenter showed a slideshow based on NetSmartz materials and other outside resources and added anecdotes from his own experiences. Such presentations are often somewhat unpolished, and officers (working at no cost to the school district) make do with the materials available to them. In this case, the slideshow contained materials that seemed to be repurposed from presentations originally provided to parents and law enforcement audiences. In addition to the usual NetSmartz materials, the presenter included content covering child pornography and hacking of school systems. The presenter pointed at the screen when first of the slides on child pornography appeared and said, "What takes up 90 percent of my time these days? Child pornography." Each time he covered many of the central youth Internet safety issues of the time—including online predators, inappropriate content, piracy, and cyberbullying—he framed them in terms of the ease with which law enforcement agents could identify and track perpetrators of such crimes, often explicitly describing the process of digital evidence collection. By the end of the presentation, I was left with two clear messages: "We can find you, and we will arrest you," and "The people who say something are typically the ones who don't get in trouble."

The students in the audience with me appeared to be surprised that they were not anonymous online, which in both of the two sessions I attended led to questions about punishment and consequences. Based on these questions (primarily about whether various online activities would lead to their arrest), many students seemed to have only a superficial understanding of the justice system. This lack of understanding was used by the presenter to reinforce the specter of punishment for youth Internet users. In his discussion of file sharing, the presenter mentioned students who had been arrested through an FBI crackdown and the "Hundreds of thousands of dollars in civil penalties in the industry crackdown per person," leaving some students in the audience noticeably concerned. Because the presenter did not say that individuals would have to engage in large-scale digital piracy operations before they would draw attention from law enforcement, students were led to believe that they could be criminally prosecuted for their file-sharing activities.

In a later interview with an information technology director of a different school district, I asked about his experiences with youth Internet safety presentations. In this district, presentations by law enforcement officers to students were common. He explained his experiences at such assemblies:

I can say that I have been to several workshops where they've had state police just put the fear of God into some of these people, and I think it loses the kids. It's almost like you have to mentor them [more] than intimidate them. ... [The state police] said, "If you do this you're going to go to jail." When you look at the audience and the kids are snickering, they're not taking it seriously. I think it's that power of authority that's trying to clamp down on students' rights. ... When you use a threatening approach, it really puts up a wall with a lot of kids.

This director's observations resonated with my own experiences at youth Internet safety presentations targeted at both young people and adults. Kids laugh at the youth Internet safety education they receive from adults, and as someone who has largely "grown up" with the Internet, I frequently find myself laughing along with them. Despite the seriousness of the risks represented by the cyberbully and online predator, there is something humorous about the ways they are presented through Internet safety curricula, in the well-meaning but often misguided attempts by adults to tell kids how it really is out there in what they see as the wild west of cyberspace.

Even attempts by adults to provide space for youth perspectives can fail to grasp the power relations that structure such interactions. Incorporating youth perspectives into discussions of online safety and risk is not simple. The interests and experiences of actual young people frequently are dismissed or unheard by adults in positions of power. The people who are invited to participate in presentations are typically victims of online crimes who understand their experiences largely through the contexts and language provided by adults (Deleting Online Predators Act 2006). When adult presenters ask nonvictims to provide their perspectives, they usually ignore the young people who try to discuss the problem critically. In a 2010 cyberbullying discussion at a local school district that included law enforcement officers, school administrators, and psychological and legal experts, the student body president was asked to provide his perspective. He was the sole youth representative on the panel. In his statement to the panel and audience, he said the following ("Cyberbullying: Responding to the Challenges" 2010):

I think the level of abstraction and anonymity on the Internet causes a lack of social grace. Many teenagers—I'm probably privy to this myself—I think a lot of what we write, we might not think it has meaning. I think if you scroll down comments on any Web site or blog, you'll find, uh, a lot of meaningless dreck. ... I would never advocate for, you know, censoring or monitoring someone's use of the Internet as a free speech thing. I think that we need to, perhaps, take it upon ourselves to teach kids about civility online. I think that when people write in all caps or, you know, a thousand exclamation points, it just shows a lack of maturity that (laughs) is probably, probably, found among a lot of teenagers. I myself have never seen or been the victim or perpetrated cyberbullying. I don't think I've ever perpetrated cyberbullying, and of my friends who I've asked this week, none of them could tell me any examples that they themselves have seen, so maybe I'm just a skewed sample. But I imagine that a lot of it does go unreported because a lot of what we see on the Internet seems harmless and empty. (laughs) ... We should try to do better. (laughs)

Throughout the remainder of the discussion, the student's statements went largely undiscussed by the other panel members and the audience. Seeking to bring the student back into the conversation, the moderator, a local news anchor, asked him the following ("Cyberbullying: Responding to the Challenges" 2010):

Jason, I wonder if anything has changed for you sitting here this evening. Any perspective on how many people see this or how far your words can go? Granted you say you haven't been a victim of or your friends haven't been. Has this changed your perspective on the vast reach of virtual words. ... Do you think that kids realize the tone that their words can take and how far their words can travel?

To this, the student body president responded by saying, "I'm kind of worried that I'm like hopelessly out of touch. There are kids jumping on others, as described. I don't think I've seen anything like that. ... I guess they must not [realize], if this is a problem" ("Cyberbullying: Responding to the Challenges" 2010). In this situation, even a positive move to engage a student in a discussion of a topic of adult concern becomes part of the mechanism by which youth knowledge and context are subjugated to adults' interpretations of youth sociality online—that it is inappropriate at best, dangerous at worse, and in need of continuous surveillance.

6   Parents, Nonparents, and School Administrators

As is shown in the previous chapters, parents and other adults who are charged with protecting youth online have been variously positioned—as overwhelmed by a ceaseless barrage of obscene content and shadowy predators, as left behind by neurologically flexible and technically adept children, and, properly trained, as the trusted enforcers of the online world. Because parents and school administrators are vested in the authority of the family and the school, they are key agents in the larger apparatus of youth Internet safety. However, as media, legislative, and curricular representatives have moved to position and govern parents and administrators, they have developed their own practices and techniques for supervising youth that are grounded in their own concerns. These everyday practices of adults connect to, draw on, or resist the dominant strategies of youth Internet safety discourses. Examining adult monitoring practices "on the ground" demonstrates the ways that adults, as much as young people, are constituted and positioned by youth Internet safety discourses.

Jacques Donzelot's (1979) work again becomes relevant for connecting the parenting practices of today to the pedagogies developed to align parenting practices to the needs of the state in the eighteenth century. Donzelot called attention to the historical construction of the modern family through the production of once novel pedagogies and images that provided parents with a diagram for family life. These technologies of the family have long since vanished into the everyday practice of being a "good parent." Parents' efforts to protect youth online move to reconstitute spheres of protected development within or layered on online spaces, again making visible and problematizing the naturalized technologies of the modern family. Inherent to the power relations established by surveillance practices are contested ontologies—struggles over who "knows better." As parents and administrators figure youth and the Internet, they draw on developmental psychology and strategically aligned concepts of technology in ways that make monitoring and policing youth online both possible and necessary.

Unlike media reports, Internet safety presenters, and legislators, the parents, teachers, and school administrators I spoke with in focus groups rarely exoticized youth engagement with information technologies. Despite media and policy discourses, few interviewees seemed to be alarmed about Internet safety issues. Their concerns over these issues were not presented as overwhelming or surprising. In general, parents and administrators were confident in their ability to supervise youth online and enjoyed trading stories of how they successfully kept their kids "out of trouble." Even those who felt they needed to develop a deeper understanding of the technology to supervise their children were in no particular hurry to do so. Additionally, nothing seemed particularly out of the ordinary as they described their experiences with monitoring the children they were responsible for, contrary to discourses that position them as out of touch and in desperate need of assistance. Further, the issues they raised during focus group sessions rarely were about Internet safety incidents and more frequently were about offline problems that were in some way touched by information technology. An assistant principal in one district stated, "I would say the Internet piece of my job is minimal. Typically, it's behaviors within the building itself, and it's not computer-related or technology-related. It's, you know, just kids being kids, basically." Even so, the strategies mobilized by parents and administrators to supervise youth online—and the ways in which they conceptualized youth social lives through such strategies— continued to "work with" the larger strategies embedded in youth Internet safety discourses.

Who Knows Better?

For both young people and adults, at the core of Internet safety issues are problems of expertise. Exactly who "knows better" in terms of how to stay safe online is of concern for various reasons. Although the portrayal of young people online has shifted slightly within the past few years, their technical skills are perceived to be superior to those of the adults who are charged with protecting them, but they are viewed as lacking the necessary wisdom to protect themselves from potential threats online. Beyond these general perceptions, figuring the relative expertise of youth and adults is key in youth Internet safety discourses, and struggles over expertise are fundamentally struggles over power. I frequently heard both parents and young people discussing the extent to which each other understood what was happening online and by extension who had the power to tell the truth of youth practice.

These struggles often took place around the framing of various forms of social interactions as benign or malicious, appropriate or inappropriate, or safe or risky. Parents often stated that they do "know better" despite also acknowledging that they had relatively little experience with information technologies and knew little about the social practices that took place online. One mother stated: "I hear that all the time! 'You have no idea, Mom!' But I *do*! I'm sure I don't know the full extent of everything that's said, but I feel like I have a handle." From the parental and administrative perspective, this sense of having "a handle" or "getting it" means understanding enough of youth Internet practices to effectively surveil and police. The "handle" allows the adult to operate unilaterally on youth Internet practice. In this way, youth perspectives on Internet practice are easily and frequently dismissed by parents:

My son made the comment to me, "I don't understand why they're just getting on this bullying stuff now. It's been going on forever. But they're making a big deal out of it just because of." And he's like, "They think that because a couple of kids." And he didn't take it lightly. He took it very seriously. But he's like, "Because a couple of kids from wherever committed suicide, now all of a sudden we're getting hammered with this cyberbullying and this bullying, and it's not that predominant in the school system." I was like, "Is it? And you just don't know it."

Similarly another parent mentioned that her daughter

said when she took the survey [administered by this study], "I just hit no or negative on all of them because none of that stuff has ever happened here or to me." I go, "Well, it might have happened to someone else," and she said "Not in our school!" And I go, "Honey, trust me. It happens. You just don't know it." So she's just clueless when it comes to that.

These dismissals frequently relied on the assumptions and logics of developmental psychology. Biologically underdeveloped children and teenagers are not and cannot be positioned in a way that provides them with primary responsibility for their own safety online. One principal stated that youth Internet safety problems—and youth behavioral problems more generally—were "a developmental thing." As another administrator described:

They don't look at it the same way we do. They're just vomiting at the mouth, and they're not looking at it. ... It's kind of like, "Think before you click" and all those other little catchphrases out there, and kids aren't wired to do that at that age.

A parent invoked a slightly softer version of the developmental discourse in a focus group session:

So there are some positive things. A lot of it's positive. But we do need to train our parents. ... I think that we can make a pretty good judgment about whether it's appropriate or not, but [kids]—they're learning, they're growing, they're not able to do that in some situations.

These types of comments were common in discussions with parents, teachers, and administrators, as is demonstrated in a number of other quotes throughout the chapter. Young people are framed as not being able to make decisions in the same way as an adult might because the ability to do so is attained at a later stage of development. Their risky behaviors were explained in terms of a lack of developmental "filters" or as problems with information technology "getting in the way" of social development. Beyond explicit developmental claims, many other references to irrational or unreasonable behavior, stupidity, or an inability to process information also were grounded in developmental assumptions (Gabriel 2013). Developmental logics have become so commonplace that they now are all but invisible in everyday conversations concerning youth and supervision. In the focus group and interview sessions with adults, these logics performed a particular kind of work, again placing adults into positions of authority and expertise where they could pass judgment on the appropriateness of youth behavior online.

Some parents and administrators I spoke with acknowledged the expertise of young people, who were seen to have a contextualized understanding of cyberspaces and years of experience with information technologies that allowed them to outperform their parents in such spaces. A minority of parents empowered young people and trusted them to handle potential problems online themselves:

Parent A: I think my kids are right on about the dangers that are out there. I think they're aware. Fully aware. And that's by allowing them to have the computer and trusting them.

Parent B: I don't think mine does because she's too trusting. She scares me.

Another parent had presented herself as a technological optimist and stated, "I think kids do know a lot more than what the parents think they know. I really think they do. I just feel like there's a lot more going on electronically than we really realize." This type of parent was consistently in the minority in focus groups and frequently was responded to negatively by other parents. The possibility that kids "might know more" was positioned as a failure of parenting. One parent described the ways in which learning from her children how to stay safe online made her feel as if she was inadequate and was not doing enough to protect her children:

My kids will say to me, though—like on Facebook, if somebody pops up and wants to be your friend, and they'll say to me, "You don't know that name. Don't do it." But they have to tell me what to do, and that makes me a little uncomfortable. Because I don't know. You know what I mean? They know so much more than I do. Not just that but everything. How do I protect them? It goes back to trust. I feel like I should know more—that I'm really not doing my job as a parent because I don't know more.

Another parent elaborated:

I don't like Facebook. My children are very well versed with computers, and that is a concern because they know more than I do. Obviously, as a parent you want to be on top of things, and when you have to go to them for help, then you know you're not on top of it. ... They just are well versed because they were brought up in a computer generation.

In these cases, despite the fact that the parent was open to learning from her children about social networking platforms, that was not enough to "do her job as a parent." She felt that she needed to establish a position of expertise over her children and to become the one who "knows better." A failure to be "on top of things" was therefore a failure in the ability to supervise their children, with seemingly complex technologies creating a gap in relative expertise between parents and young people. An inability to access or read the actions of youth online translates into an inability to judge the appropriateness of those actions.

One of the less overt struggles over the conceptualization of online communication is over the information technologies themselves. For many of the adults I spoke with, the Internet was conceived of not as a complex and heterogeneous social space but rather as a tool with proper and improper uses. It is overly simplistic to label the "television generation" as having a largely passive understanding of technology, contrasted with the more participatory understanding of the "Internet generation" (Herring 2008). However, it would be equally problematic to ignore the ways in which the ways of life of a generation were shaped by the passive consumption engendered by many forms of mass media. It is somewhat unsurprising, therefore, that adults in the study explained information technologies as passive tools with appropriate and inappropriate uses. One principal (and parent) explained the conceptualization of information technology relative to youth, again raising the issue of developmental capacity:

In my opinion, it is almost an adult tool that we've put into children's hands, and they don't know how to handle it. You know, it was something that was really meant for business but became a real social thing. And children are social by nature, and they have not developed the filters they need to make adult decisions.

Another parent was more explicit in a focus group session, briefly dominating the discussion while the other participants nodded heads and murmured in agreement:

It's a tool. ... I use it as a tool. I try to teach my son, as a tool. They play games, they get on to some mindless games and stuff, but if he wants to use it: "What are you using it for?" He uses it as research. He's just not on there aimlessly looking at nothing. That's what I think Facebook, MySpace has become. ... The younger generation coming in—it's like, "Hey, man. You may not want to be doing this stuff out there in public. It will be misinterpreted. You may think it's harmless, but someone may use it against you, against me. You're part of an organization." That's why I say it's a tool. It should be used as a tool. Some people use it as mindless, air-out everything. That's why I look at it as a tool. That's how I use it. It's how I want to teach my kids what it is. The consequence is when you use a tool wrong, bad things can happen. When you use a torch to thaw out pipes and set your house on fire, you didn't do it right. There's a way to do it right and a way to do it wrong. Similar to how you use the Internet: for a wrong thing, ... there's a consequence. I took my son off the computer Saturday and said, "Go outside and do something."

Conceptualized as a tool rather than as a social space, the actions of youth online are easily placed within the adult frame of judgment. Children and teenagers are "using" the tool properly or improperly, and given their developmental inability to make "adult decisions" about an "adult tool," only adults have the necessary biology and expertise to determine what constitutes proper and improper use. Tools in this sense lack a social context of their own. Instead, a social context is brought to them by their users through their appropriate or inappropriate use (Poster 2001). As Raiford Guins (2008, 66) describes, "The 'tool' metaphor for administering our relationship to the Internet is disconcerting when it precludes other possible ways to conceive of social relations to technology and our place within networked computing." This construction of information technology bolsters the ability of adults to establish their conceptual frame as the dominant conceptual frame and further distances them from the social context within which youth Internet practices could be considered meaningful or appropriate. Engaged in various acts of parental supervision online, adults entering into online spaces are then merely using technology in appropriate ways rather than abruptly walking into a private social gathering to which they were not invited.

Strategies and Publics

Overall, the strategies for monitoring children and teenagers and keeping them safe online described to me by parents largely mirrored those described by Margaret K. Nelson (2010): parents were engaged in surveillance practices, frequently were reluctant to do so, and largely were willing to use information technologies to support those practices. Parents who participated in the focus group sessions wanted to keep their children out of trouble, representing something of a shift from the more protective discourses offered by youth Internet safety curricula. In my discussions with adults, young people were assumed to be capable of and engaged in various forms of inappropriate behavior both online and off. Protecting young people from harm forms part of their rationale because much of the trouble they might find themselves is seen to have lasting effects, but the emphasis is on maintaining a specific kind of appropriate sociality regardless of context. Youth were broadly perceived to be "up to something" inappropriate, regardless of the evidence. One exchange between parents in a focus group demonstrates the ongoing suspicion:

Parent A: … But it's just trying to stay on top of it. Like you said, I don't know most of what the stuff is all, kids—
Parent B: Yeah, because they delete their history.
Parent A: They delete their history. They're not honest.
Parent C: They're not honest.
Parent A: And again they establish filters [to circumvent parent supervision].

These statements suggest that parents are suspicious of their children's behaviors online, but they also displayed excitement and humor, suggesting

that parents enjoyed the challenge of uncovering or preventing inappropriate activities. Introducing themselves to one focus group, two parents
joked that they were, "The meanest parents in [the school district]" to the
laughter and approval of the other participants. Another parent provided
an exchange between herself and her daughter as an example (and again
demonstrating the role of knowledge in these exchanges):

[My daughter] the other night had her phone and made a smart comment to me, so
I made her—"Well, it's time for you to go to bed. Put your phone down." She said,
"But I haven't said good night to my friends!" So I said, "Say goodnight." She goes, "I
don't want to leave my phone down here. I don't want it down on the table. I want
it in my room!" I go, "You realize I can just call Verizon and have them print all your
text messages, right?" I don't know if I can, but she didn't know. The look on her
face was priceless. She says, "You can? All right. ..."

Stories of this kind were common throughout the focus group sessions,
and participants proudly described their parental successes. This pleasure
in catching youth was not derived from arbitrarily imposing parental order
on the lives of their children but rather from feeling that by becoming "the
meanest parents" they were becoming the safest parents. Arguably, the pressure to perform good parenthood was heightened within focus group sessions because parent participants actively monitored and openly supported
the surveillance strategies of other participants (Henderson, Harmon, and
Houser 2010; Knowles 1996). Strategies for parental "meanness" invariably
centered on access limitations and surveillance, and those who failed to
engage in such practices were positioned as bad, disinterested parents (as is
detailed later in this chapter).

Many parents outright denied or placed heavy restrictions on access to
technologies, including cell phones, computers, and social networking sites.
These parents were more likely to have children in elementary and middle
school. One particularly restrictive parent stated: "You can have a Facebook
when you no longer live in my house. And that's my rule ... because I
don't want them to get hurt online." Another restricted access to both cell
phones and social networking: "No cell phones, no Facebook. They use the
computer to play games. That's usually supervised. I know where they've
been and have parental controls on it." For some of the more restrictive parents, preventing access to these technologies was a way to extend a period
of innocence and childhood. Restricting access to technologies was seen

as restricting access to inappropriate content and modes of communication perceived as rude or otherwise problematic (as described later in this chapter). In this sense, communication technologies are positioned as adult technologies that interfere with young people's ability to "be kids." As one parent explained: "It's a new toy. Very distracting, you know. It opens them up. [By limiting access, you] keep them being a kid a little bit longer." This parent described the ways in which he was constantly connected to work and other people through his own cell phone. His attempt to prevent his children from having access to a phone was less to keep them out of danger and more to delay their entry into the hyperconnected adult world.

The most commonly described surveillance strategies included requiring their children to access the family's computer in an easily visible space, having them provide passwords for their online accounts, and monitoring their children's messages on social networking sites and cell phones and their Web browser histories. Parents legitimized engaging in such forms of surveillance as their parental responsibility and their right to search and monitor the property that they paid for and supported:

We have told the kids, "I want your passwords. Write your passwords down." And with their cellphones as well: "At any time, I may ask for your cell phone, and let me see what's up with you. Let me see what you're texting your friends. That's my responsibility as a parent. We bought the phone for you, and we can do that." They were all very put off with that at first, but they kind of got used to that idea.

Such statements ignored the fact that few children—particularly those who are under the legal working age—are able to obtain or afford cell phones, computers, and high-speed Internet access without adult assistance.

This said, many parents hesitated to monitor their children online, not wanting to violate their privacy and not wanting to find anything that might incriminate them:

You know, it does feel like it's an invasion of their privacy, but I say, "You know, we're paying that phone bill, so it's not really your phone. It's our phone." ... They live in your house. This is how you know it. I guess my Mom was right because she kept saying, "If you don't check their things, you're not going to know what was going on." Like I said, sometimes I checked and found things I didn't want to know about, but if I hadn't, I wouldn't have known. I don't do it all the time. They think I can go online and check their texts. You can tell who they text and who texted them, but you do have to get a court order to actually see the text. But they don't know that.

When asked what made the Internet different from the "real" space of the bedroom, another parent responded:

It's a combination, in terms of things. I guess, it's like, I don't—there are just things I don't want to see, that they shouldn't be doing. I think it's a reflection on how they're perceived. Their room—I don't go in their room because it is, it's private. Whereas the Internet is a public thing. Especially if I find stuff on my laptop. Guess what? "It's my property you decided to do something stupid on." And there's going to be a lot more consequences. But again, people have mentioned trust is earned, and if I have a reason to think that there's something, red flags are going off.

Note the references to things that the participants "don't want to see" and "don't want to know about." In this way, many of the parents I spoke with framed surveillance as a productive necessity. Although these parents were hesitant to engage in surveillance practices, they explained them as inescapable elements of good parenting that often resulted in necessarily actionable data. Further, the problem of not wanting to see was not one of the content itself but rather that it was made visible to the parents. One parent with a relatively relaxed approach to parental controls and monitoring stated the following:

I have a Facebook, and I'm friends with them, so I can see it. And I peruse it pretty often just to see what's going on. And I peruse their friends' Facebooks as well. I have to say it's pretty amazing to me how dumb some of those kids are—really, no. The pictures that their parents aren't seeing with them with open beer cans, you know. It's pretty amazing to me.

Here it is not the open beer cans that are the problem. It is the readily available photos of the beer cans, necessitating a parental response. Inherent in the statement is an acknowledgment that kids frequently experiment with or regularly drink alcohol but that parents cannot openly support (at worst) or ignore (at best) publicly inappropriate behavior. As is discussed later in the chapter, the statement also is a judgment against other parents who "aren't seeing" the photos of open beer cans.

This concept of necessarily actionable information was also a key theme for school administrators. Again, these groups of adults did not necessarily "want" to find incriminating information, but the availability of the information led it to be collected and acted on. In one interview, an assistant principle described the ways that these incidents occur from a school policy perspective:

Especially kids who are plugged into something here at school, whether it's athletics or drama or theater or anything extracurricular. The posting of pictures, things that we can see if we choose to that are on there that are incriminating. I mean, they find themselves in a position sometimes where they're violating our code of ethics or our code of conduct for athletes and extracurricular activities, and we have to hold them accountable for that. It's amazing how many kids don't understand that—that we can reach out and touch that like anyone else can. ... What we tell them is, "It's there. Not only can I see it, but everyone else can see it. If I can see it, I have the right to hold you accountable for it. So you can decide whether or not you're going to pull it down, but I'm going to pick up the phone and call your parents and let them know it's on there.

Beyond demonstrating the accessibility of information, this quote indicates an approach to policy that is common in school districts. School administrators saw policies addressing online behavioral problems to be unnecessary, given existing codes of conduct that guided student behavior outside of school. These codes of conduct allowed school administrators to address perceived problems with posted content online and remain within the "jurisdiction" of the school district, positioned between the home and the judicial system and further tightening ties between the family and the school.

The adults I spoke with constituted networked publics (boyd 2007) not in terms of small, interest bounded groups, but rather as the broadest possible audience now and into the future. Such concepts of the circulation of online content conflate the possibility of viral spread with the reality of viral spread. There is no difference between content that could be viewed by anyone and content that will be viewed by anyone. As such, online content of any type was fair game for adult collection and reinterpretation. One parent remarked: "They're finite, and the Internet is endless." Speaking about the perceived persistence of online material, an administrator said, "What's funny now may not be funny twenty-two years from now. You can twist things or statements out of context." Many images of teens holding up signs displaying variations of "This message will not go far. My parents say otherwise. Like and share" have become viral phenomena on social networks (regretfully for my news feed, Facebook among them). One such image has had over three million shares on Facebook since December 2013 (*Being Mommy* 2013) and are pointed to as evidence that adults "know better." I would argue that such statements are akin to telling youth that they should be cautious about getting into cars with friends, given the reality that "Roads can go anywhere." Parents must adopt the worst-case frame to maintain their status as effective parents—made all the more pressing because material posted by youth is perceived to be accessible to other parents who are dutifully monitoring their own children's online activities. Further, this construction of networked publics allows parents and adults to rationalize the ongoing and increasingly intrusive surveillance into the lives of youth. Although many parents I spoke with would hesitate to search a child's bedroom or read a private diary, they were comfortable with the idea of monitoring the online activities of youth. By framing the audience of all online content in terms of the broadest possible audience, all online content becomes "public." The material posted online by youth can be considered private like a diary to the same extent that it can be considered public like the front page of a newspaper—what matters most is context. Choosing to position online communication as public, parents need not concern themselves with issues of privacy, although they often feel discomfort in seeing what they "don't want to see" as they move uninvited through the online social spaces of youth.

As with the Internet safety curricula discussed in the previous chapter, the dominant interpretive context in this case becomes that of the imagined future employer or recruiter. Perhaps best representing this context, another parent who also owned and operated a summer camp for youth described how she monitored both her own children and her teenage employees:

I'm not [just] monitoring my own children. I'm monitoring thirty staff for the summer. I'll put on there [on the Facebook wall], "Naughty word alert!" They'll come back and say, "What did I say?" I'll say, "The P-I-S-S-E-D word is not socially acceptable, even though you think it is." … As we tell them, that what you write, anything you write, is a reflection of you. So if you're going for that job and that person happens to be a friend, then you've got to remember that they cannot say about hiring you because of— But I have had people who I have not hired back because of their behavior on Facebook. So I think kids need to be aware, to be reminded that is a reflection on them even though it is just something they're typing on.

For this parent and the others who described the ways that they required their children to remove online content, monitoring youth online involves monitoring the ways in which they constitute themselves as individuals. There is only one social context for good parents: the "appropriate" context which is reconstituted as they enter an online space, where appropriateness is derived from the combined gaze of other vigilant parents collectively envisioning the needs of future employers. From their privileged position as adults, imposing this context onto an online social space occurs naturally and invisibly. As with a number of other quotes throughout this chapter, this notion of appropriateness is implicit in the participants references to the inability of youth to make "adult" decisions. In this sense, adult decisions are those that best match the anticipated image of the ideal worker throughout the lifespan of an individual, maximizing opportunities for development and economic growth.

Some parents used the indeterminacy of online identity to rationalize their surveilling and policing of online activities. Two parents in a discussion expressed their concern that predators could develop false identities:

Parent A: She's seventeen. How do you not know it's a forty-year-old man? You don't!
Parent B: Anyone can impersonate anyone. ... It's scary!

One parent who had worked for several years in law enforcement described being shocked at the construction of identities in virtual worlds:

Well, you have all this virtual, virtual worlds. They develop their own avatar, and they can make themselves look however they want! And they can do whatever they want in those virtual worlds. I think that's a little messed up, quite honestly. So you're pretending to be something that you're not, and you're doing things that you would never, probably never even think about doing as your real person. But yet, the sky's the limit.

Many parents and administrators simply refused to engage with social networking platforms as social spaces and instead use them solely for surveillance purposes. When asked about his online activities, dismissing social networking activity as "stuff," one principal stated:

I'm not on Facebook. I'm not on social networking stuff. I'm not a part of that. In my position, I feel for me personally, it's a bad decision for me to be involved in those type of things, but I do have access to my kids. Both my kids are on it.

Another principal described the potential pitfalls of engaging with social media in legal but potentially inappropriate ways as a faculty member and public persona:

Just because of the positions we're in—it's a public, you're in a public person. The public is paying for your position, and there's a certain rules and expectations of you, that, you can't be, unfortunately be doing. So we had board members in [the school district] doing the ice luge [drinking] a few years back. There were pictures.

And they're adults. They're over the age of twenty-one. And just because of their role in that district and that. There's an example of that.

A parent found it difficult to describe what made social networks seem problematic and said simply: "I don't like Facebook myself because I don't know about it. And I think that there's stuff on there that's just, like, bad. People talk about people and stuff, so I don't like Facebook."

Adults who did use social networking sites—specifically Facebook—frequently described their use of the space to monitor youth online. Parents were more likely to engage in such behaviors than administrators, teachers, and other adults I spoke with, and many parents created accounts solely for that purpose. By demanding that their children "friend" them through the service, they are then able to view all of the comments made by the friended account. As one parent described:

I have a MySpace, and the only reason I have a MySpace is because my daughter has one. So she had to up my MySpace and add me as a friend, or she couldn't have a MySpace. So I go on every so often and check her status. If I don't like anything, I'm like, "Take it off, or I close it." Period. I monitor, but you still— That's only Facebook and MySpace. There's a whole big other Web out there that I'm missing, I'm sure, that I'm a little uncomfortable about.

Both young people and adults referred to this form of constant, unwanted surveillance as "creeping." Some adults took this to an extreme by setting up their account to send text message updates to their phone every time their child posted a status update. Given that Facebook and other social networks allow users to "defriend" other accounts without notifying the defriended user, such parents became suspicious when long periods passed without any visible activity. This practice of monitoring youth through social networks has been bolstered by various third-party applications that can access social networking data, facilitating the development of automated monitoring systems. By further requesting that their children allow these applications access to their social networking profile (typically Facebook), parents can receive automated alerts of potentially risky behaviors.

One school resource officer (a police officer assigned to a school district) that I spoke with saw the accessibility of youth online in social networks as an excellent resource. Rather than fearing the relative expertise of youth online, he used it to his advantage to gain information and engage with young people in his district. Discussing the students in his district, he stated, "They live this technology every day. ... I struggle with it a little. ...

[I ask students,] 'You're a tech junkie. What does this mean?'" Engaging with students in such a way allowed the officer to surveil online spaces, including social networking sites and confiscated cell phones, more effectively. Further, he indicated that young people were seemingly happy to assist him and provide their expertise, a common statement among parents and administrators. Youth, eager to have a brief opportunity to be taken seriously and demonstrate their expertise, are more than happy to show provide adult authority figures with access to their social worlds.

Not all parents, however, felt strongly enough about the risks involved in Internet use to violate their children's privacy. Many parents considered reading online material and texts to be similar to searching a bedroom or reading a diary, although in one case other parents stated that those were acceptable practices. At least one or two parents in each focus group session said that they trusted their children until given a reason not to. One simply stated, "I always trust until they break it." These parents seemed to believe that the general guidance they had provided to their children and the basic moral principles by which they lived their lives would prove sufficient to keep their children out of trouble. In this sense, the extent of surveillance necessary to meet parental responsibilities was a controversial topic, and these parents defended themselves against other participants who actively monitored their children online and off. In the focus group session described above, where parents joked about being the "meanest" in the district, the one participant who did not use strict parental controls on the family computer began to change her stance under the perceived pressure from the other parents. Among the last to describe the kinds of protections and supervisory measures that her family used, she said, "But probably we need to do a little bit more about patrolling it better. I never really thought I needed to. But maybe I need to think again."

Similarly, not all parents and administrators I spoke with saw engagement with social networking sites solely as a method for surveilling youth. Some registered for accounts to keep in touch with family and friends and foster community ties. The summer camp operator spoke positively about her online experiences, which were not solely for surveillance. Instead, the supervisory elements of her experiences online were embedded in the everyday practices of social life. This mode of parental and adult supervision might be considered to be participatory surveillance (Albrechtslund 2008) or social surveillance, which Alice E. Marwick (2012) describes as seeing "what friends, family, and acquaintances are 'up to'" (378) via social media and being "characterized by both watching and a high awareness of being watched" (379). However, this mode of surveillance depends highly on the interpretation of the technology, the relationship between the adult and youth being monitored, and the content being observed. Parental surveillance can fluidly shift between social surveillance and instrumental/traditional modes of surveillance, producing different kinds of relationships with young people at different moments. However, adults who actively participate in the lives of youth online undoubtedly have a clearer understanding of the languages and practices of online spaces. They understand social networking platforms not as a tool but as social spaces, each with their own practices, languages, and contexts.

Nonparents

Among parents, there was an underlying sense that the actions of youth online reflected poorly on parents poorly and exposed them to being perceived irresponsibility. It was not simply that parents who fail to supervise their children are bad parents but that these parents could be implicated in the production of youth Internet safety problems. In this sense, both young people and parents are under suspicion. One parent described the ways in which the behavior of youth online was linked to the parent's reputation:

I check their pages just to be sure they aren't cursing or saying anything inappropriate—because that's a reflection on me, you know, as well of their safety. It's a reflection on me.

Even when parents might support or otherwise understand youth behaviors online, they still must restrain the perceived inappropriateness of youth behavior out of concern that such inappropriateness would be linked back to them. The possibility that young people's online behaviors might appear to others as inappropriate drives parents' monitoring behavior, as the materials posted by their children are seen as part of the constructed online identity of the adults themselves. As young people "write themselves into being" (boyd 2008) online, they also write their parents into being, and the perceived inappropriateness of young people's postings signal the effectiveness or ineffectiveness of parental monitoring strategies to other parents. This heightens visibility around parenting practices and allows the surveillant gaze to penetrate further into the home, even for parents and other adults who do not participate in online communications. The ways that young people use information technologies to communicate with one another make both their own private practices and their guardians' parenting practices visible and available to the surveillant gaze.

Accordingly, parents of children and teenagers who engaged in inappropriate behavior were cited as a primary factor contributing to the behavior itself:

That's a family issue as well. I can't imagine—I can't imagine my twelve-year-old picking up her shirt. There's a parental problem going on there.

These adults were assigned to a category of parents—those who through a lack of supervision or caring had effectively become nonparents, constituted in ways which stripped them of their authority to delineate between appropriate and inappropriate actions. This categorization was particularly prominent in one suburban district where parents in both the middle school and high school focus groups discussed the role played by nonparents in Internet safety and bullying incidents. Two parents of high school students began a discussion about such nonparents and actively positioned themselves as "parents who care" in relation to these other nonparticipant parents:

Parent A: Parents are a big part of it, though. All of us here show that we're parents that care. There's a lot of parents out there that don't. They don't monitor. They don't care what their kids are watching or whatever at what age.

Parent B: There's a much smaller subgroup. My son got into a fight with a whole bunch of other kids last year, and I immediately called. I wanted to know exactly what happened. They're like, "Mr. [parent], you don't have to worry about [student]. What you did—you talked to him. You're good. He's not the problem. But some parents I've tried to talk to don't care. They can't be bothered."

School administrators, particularly principals, frequently described the differences between parents and nonparents by comparing levels of participation and willingness to attend school events. One assistant principal described the audience at an Internet safety presentation he developed and presented with local law enforcement officers:

It was a nice turnout. You know, you always get concerned because you don't necessarily get the right parents. Um, but in this presentation, I felt pretty good about my audience. I felt like there was a nice percentage of parents that really needed to hear the information.

Similarly, a principal in another district indicated that some parents behaved inappropriately alongside their children:

Last year, we had some issues with cyberbullying. ... We're trying to solicit some help from parents in the community. That's slowly coming around because we had some parents that were actively involved in that mess last year. It's amazing the things parents will allow their kids to do with their consent and help sometimes.

Other parents were less critical of such nonparents and cited societal changes and economic pressures as major reasons for a lack of supervision:

I think society has changed. I think kids don't have as much supervision. I think two parents work in a family, and that's not the way it used to be. I think a lot of things have changed. We see more and more kids go home without parents home. It's just the way it is. It has to be that way. There's more chance for them to do things without parents being aware.

The parents, teachers, and administrators I spoke with throughout this study were primarily white, middle-class parents in rural and suburban school districts. Most participants self-selected to participate in the focus group sessions, which were perceived as the actions of "parents who care." In the one participating urban school district, only one parent attended the focus group session, and she was accompanied by a school staff member (whose children formerly attended the school) who was concerned about the lack of participation in the study. This mode of surveillance (monitoring the practices of other parents) is "assumed to be most common among middle- and upper-class" parents (Henderson et al. 2010, 234). Implicit in parent' statements is the delineation of class boundaries: the middle- and upper-income parents were "parents who care," while "some parents" who are absent from their family homes due to economic constraints fall into the category of the nonparent. As Demie Kurz (2009, 260–261) describes, "The assumptions are that monitoring is a top-down, straightforward task that parents either do or don't do, and that parents entirely control whether or not monitoring takes place. 'Good parents' monitor their children well, while 'bad parents' do not." Constructions of the nonparent make invisible distinctions in access to information technology between working-class and upper-middle-class youth (Clark 2009; Ito et al. 2009; Livingstone and Helsper 2007), assuming similar forms, spaces, and motivations for access. Further, financial inequality structures both young people's access to information technology and also parents' access to monitoring tools: "Less flexible jobs and lesser financial resources circumscribe the style of parenting that can be adopted" (Nelson 2010, 165). Although the parents and administrators who participated in the study probably would resist stating that the construction of nonparents was grounded largely in socioeconomic class, it was clear throughout the discussion that was the case.

In their discussions about the role played by nonparents in Internet safety incidents, parents and administrators are constructing disciplinary gaps between the institutions of the family and the school. Here we can see elements of the pedagogical models that Jacques Donzelot (1979, 47) outlines in his work—namely, that of supervised freedom:

The problem in regard to the working-class child was not so much the weight of obsolescent constraints as it was excessive freedom—being left to the streets—and the techniques employed consisted in limiting this freedom, in shepherding the child back to spaces where he could be more closely watched: the school or the family dwelling.

This mode of pedagogy was aimed at the working class because the children of the elite were not commonly "left to the streets." The pedagogy of supervised freedom is arguably commonplace today and remains woven into the dominant construction of the contemporary family as a technology of governance. Similarly, Annette Lareau (2003) has examined the ways that contemporary working-class parents tend to work toward what she describes as the accomplishment of natural growth by providing their children with higher levels of independent mobility and reducing monitoring and developmental regulation. Under the logic of supervised freedom, "everyone" knows that leaving your child unsupervised, whether out in the world or out on the Internet, is unacceptably risky. Discussions about parents who fail to supervise their children operate as a means to categorize groups of parents as lower class, in need of further support and education by the state and parenting experts. Although working-class nonparents who allow their children to roam unsupervised on the streets received the most criticism in focus groups, nonparents who allow unsupervised access to the virtual streets—the information superhighway (to borrow from earlier policy discourses) were also criticized. The failure to supervise youth, whether online or off, was seen to be the driving force behind bullying, oversharing, and posting otherwise inappropriate content.

These nonparents were used as a rationale for furthering ties between the family and the school. At a strategic level, this discursively establishes support for a control form of surveillance through the continuous monitoring of youth online regardless of their institutional location. Lareau (2003, 3) notes the ways in which "the cultural logic of [the accomplishment of natural growth] is out of synch with the standards of institutions," and according to this logic, parents who failed surveil or discipline their children were positioned as needing further assistance or governance by the school district. As one administrator described:

I do think that if they were just using these things in school, we would be okay. ... I am seeing everyday schools take on more social responsibility, whether it's feeding children, immunizing—whatever it is. I think it's, in my opinion, one of those social responsibilities we need to take on because it's more interesting to the students than it is to their parents. And the students are the IT people in their homes, and they can pull the wool over their parents' eyes. ... I do think we need to take on more responsibility of educating them about it. ... Anytime we can keep children safe, we need to.

This was echoed by one high school parent who noted: "Well, that would be good if the school did step in for the kids that are not parented at home and monitored at that home. They'd have to come up with a way to do it. That's the problem." Another parent participating in the conversation noted that nonparents expect schools to monitor their children and yet will resist efforts to do so: "A lot of parents expect these schools to take on the role of a parent. To a certain point. Then they're like, 'Oh, no, no, no, no! Don't do that!'" Preventing the school from further extending its reach into their homes was seen as yet another strike against nonparents.

Media and Development

Throughout the focus group sessions with parents and teachers, the most commonly voiced concern was the social development of children and teenagers. Participants spent little time discussing cyberbullying, online sexual predators, pornography, piracy, or sexting—although changing modes of sociality were seen to be contributing factors to nearly all other youth Internet safety problems. Changing modes of sociality were attributed to two central forces—youth exposure to media content and the increasing mediation of communication. Concerns over exposure to media content were less frequently discussed by focus group participants, perhaps because it appears to have less direct relevance to youth Internet safety issues, but when the topic did arise, participants spoke passionately about it. After being asked to explain a statement made concerning the "crap" that young people were exposed to online, one parent responded:

Information about drugs, sex, language, violence. ... My son was twelve at the time, and he went over to a friend's house. ... The parents asked if he could watch *XXX* [a Vin Diesel action film]. ... We could debate the effect of those movies, the games, on kids, but for me it was like, "No!" It's everything across the board from—as a society, the Internet has allowed people to become a lot more open and talk about different things. People talk about all sorts of things on the Internet that as a parent, I don't want my kids exposed to.

The topic repeatedly arose in the teacher focus group, where one participant stated:

through the media ... they're just inundated. You know, they all watch *Jersey Shore*, and if they look at that and they think that that's normal, then that's what they should strive to be like. Whereas my generation grew up with *Full House*.

This can be tied to concerns about exposure to content labeled as "adult" because young people are understood to lack the developmental ability to make sense of such materials. The appropriateness of content and the biological inability of youth to "filter" or make sense of such material were also common concerns that often were referenced by school staff and parents: "That's what worries me—that they might see something and I might not be there to help them process that."

When young people are exposed to such content (the concern is rarely that youth might actively seek it out), their developmentally incapable minds incorrectly process it and create a problematic model for social behavior. This pattern was discussed frequently by parents and administrators. Participants felt that the mediation of communication allowed for by information technologies was hindering the natural development of social skills through face-to-face interactions. Given the enormous amount of texting, instant messaging, and posting that youth engage in, they are seen to have a reduced understanding of nonverbal interactions. In face-to-face social situations, youth are seen by adults to be nervous, have poor etiquette, and are unable to maintain appropriate eye contact with others. As summarized by an exchange between three parents in one district:

Parent A: So my daughter had a new roommate who came to our house for dinner. And the entire—it was a barbecue, it was casual. But she sat across the picnic table, texting and doing Facebook the whole time! Which—I'm from the generation ... I mean, that's rude! She's having a conversation with people who knows where, and we're face to face! And that bugs me. I don't think there's enough etiquette. It's so new, and they're so used to it.

Parent B: I have kids who come over and do that. They can't even give you eye contact to carry on a conversation. I think when they're nervous, the phone comes out. So yeah.

Parent C: I think that's a problem there. No boundaries. We are not teaching boundaries.

In another district, one parent described this issue as her primary concern regarding Internet safety issues, to widespread agreement with the other focus group participants:

I worry about this generation's social skills and business life and when they get out of school, because you're in a whole different world then. And you have to communicate with your peers and people you work with. And I just worry about it all the time. That's my biggest concern.

Similar conversations were conducted in other focus groups with parents and teachers. Young people were seen as increasingly unable to socialize with adults or one another properly, leading to a general lack of respect and an inability to empathize with others. For some, youth are seen to be possibly "addicted" to using information technologies and to prefer to communicate with them over face-to-face methods. As one teacher/parent remarked: "It's so interesting to me how addicted they are. They just can't control themselves."

Similarly, the pace of communication is seen to have changed, with information technologies allowing faster response times and encouraging less thought and reflection. The medium is seen to afford more damaging types of communication. The teacher focus group participants explained this new phenomenon:

Teacher A: I think that's the immediacy factor, too. Ten years ago, you couldn't do that. ... You might be really pissed, and then you get through your day, and it's said and done, and you kind of forget about it. Now you just—they pull out their phone, and they can text, or they can post a message, cause everybody has a smartphone now, and they do it without thinking. ...

Teacher B: Yeah, there's no wait time.

Teacher A: ... I mean, studies show there's no developed prefrontal cortex here. There's no thinking about consequences.

Teacher B: Well, and also think about when you're angry. You're not even adults with a prefrontal cortex. When you get angry, when you can immediately say what's on your mind.

Here, the perceived affordances of the technology are linked with the developmental capacity of young people. Lacking a "prefrontal cortex," they immediately type things that are on their mind, failing to process and forecast the potential consequences of their actions. Further, the "speed" of communication made possible by information technologies allows those communications to be sent faster and spread further. This sentiment was commonly expressed by the adults I spoke with, and few acknowledged that the technologies facilitating these fast-paced communications allowed for forms of asynchronous communication. The social platforms most commonly used by youth, including text messaging, social networks, and various forms of microblogging all afford (if not encourage) slower, more thoughtful messaging when compared to face-to-face communication, a point that is overlooked by the narrative of underdeveloped brains in a fast-paced world of technology.

This uncontrollable, fast-paced addiction that facilitates a lack of boundaries and social skills is described as a major contributing factor in cyberbullying incidents, sexting, and a general inattentiveness in the classroom and home. Parents explain the perceived generation gap by a combination of developmental level and technological effects as part of what Gill Valentine and Sarah L. Holloway (2002) call a debunker discourse—roughly analogous to a negative myth of the digital native. On one register, this operates as a discursive mechanism that shifts blame away from families in cases of perceived inappropriate youth Internet practices, allows for easy problematization, subjugates youth agency, and provides a means for parents to publicly save face. On another, such discourses make visible the construction of the family itself and the ways in which the family is constructed as a technology. Similar to concerns over the nonparent, concerns over particular forms of youth sociality can be linked to historical discourses of the family. In addition to describing a pedagogical model that operated on the working class, Donzelot (1979, 47) outlined a model that operated on the bourgeoisie:

What of childhood? … the solicitude of which it was the object took the form of a protected liberation, a freeing of children from vulgar fears and constraints. The bourgeois family drew a sanitary cordon around the child which delimited his sphere of development: inside this perimeter the growth of his body and mind would be encouraged by enlisting all the contributions of psychopedagogy in its service and controlled by means of a discreet observation.

In this instance, the goal was to reconfigure the family in a way that pro-
tects/frees children and teenagers from inappropriate influences—namely,
the vulgar influences of the working-class servants who worked within the
bourgeois home. Such influences were seen to produce young people who
were unfit for work or social life among adults, in spite coming from seemingly strong genetic material. Mothers were given responsibility for raising children in the home, excluding servants and ensuring access to only
the most developmentally appropriate content and activities. Although full
access to the unattended streets was seen as a problem, so too was the lack
of experience gained in the sheltered bourgeois home. Affluent youth were
liberated from the home in a controlled manner by providing access to
the experiences of the street while limiting vulgar influences. Again indirectly building on Donzelot's work on protected liberation, Annette Lareau (2003) develops the concept of concerted cultivation to describe the
practices of working-class families. Through concerted cultivation, parents
closely monitor and manage the lives of young people while seeking to
cultivate talents, skills, experiences, and knowledges for optimal developmental growth.

Although domestic servants and restrictive practices have ceased to
threaten the modern family, information technologies now pose a similar
threat in the form of excessive "screen time." According to a policy statement from the American Academy of Pediatrics (Strasburger et al. 2003),

Media … are a dominant force in children's lives. Although media are not the leading cause of any major health problem in the United States, the evidence is now clear
that they can and do contribute substantially to many different risks and health
problems. … However, media literacy and prosocial uses of media may enhance
knowledge, connectedness, and health. The overwhelming penetration of media
into children's and teenagers' lives necessitates a renewed commitment to changing the way pediatricians, parents, teachers, and society address the use of media to
mitigate potential health risks and foster appropriate media use.

In effect, the "penetration of media into children's and teenagers' lives
necessitates" the penetration of the adult gaze made possible by those
media. Here, the oversheltering of young people within the family home
has been supplanted by their ability to engage in excessive screen time,
which is seen to impede traditionally developmental activities, including
exercise, spending time outside, and socializing (face-to-face) with peers
and family. As one focus group parent described:

I think the time they spend on it, too, bothers me. We have to set limits in our house. There's so many other educational things—reading a book, going for a run, going to visit your grandparents. You know. And I think that the computer use gets in the way of developing in certain areas.

Similarly, taking the place of domestic servants are various providers of adult content, discussion forums, and other young people, all exposing kids to what the parent quoted previously in this section described as mediated "crap." As an extension of the pedagogy of protected liberation, concerns about excessive screen time are seen primarily in affluent parents whose children have significantly more and more consistent access to a broad range of devices and content options compared to children in lower-income families—what Lareau (2003, 184) describes as the "cluttered comfort" of affluent families. Through this developmental logic, primarily affluent youth are turned away from one another as the seemingly vulgar interactions of youth are made visible through information technologies and bounded off. Establishing the "real world" as the primary site of development, however, demonstrates the invisibility of a generational loss of independent mobility. Encouraging youth to "go outside" and "do something" provides few developmental benefits as the range of mobility of youth outside of adult supervision diminishes and Western society becomes more highly individualized. In this sense, youth Internet safety discourses extend beyond the Internet and information technologies to locate the collapse of community and social graces in excessive screen time—rather than perceiving screen time as a function of the collapse of community. Extensive studies have been performed on the relationships between the independent mobility of young people and physical activity (Schoeppe et al. 2014) and on the relationships between screen time and physical activity (Maitland et al. 2013), but none have examined a possible relationship between independent mobility and screen time.

Constructing the Incident

In nearly every focus group that I held with parents, they told me victimization stories. These stories were always described seriously and were of significant concern to the adults involved. These parents were doing their best to ensure the safety of their children. These stories further demonstrate the ways that parents use Internet safety discourses to interpret and frame their children's online experiences. It is through the telling of these stories that parents and other responsible adults construct delineated Internet safety or cybersecurity "incidents" from the smooth, everyday social lives of youth. The term *incident* is used by network security, information assurance, and law enforcement professionals to describe breaches of information security policies, and the parents and administrators I spoke with rarely used the term. Incidents are the translation of everyday youth practices online through the frame of the trusted adult into discrete, intervenable narratives. From the parental perspective, such incidents occur without warning and with relatively little context to make sense of what is happening. Here I present two such incidents and provide alternate readings to examine the ways that youth Internet safety discourses—rearticulated by parents—frame youth activity.

In the first incident, a mother explained how her fifth-grade daughter read inappropriate sexual language while on the Disney-run children's social site Club Penguin. Club Penguin allows youth to chat and play games in a relatively secure virtual space. As the mother described,

when our daughter was in fifth grade, we kind of had a scary experience where I think she innocently was on one of these—it was a game that you get on and play? But on the game, there's a place you can go on and chat, and she used a different name—user name or whatever. And apparently there was a man who kept talking to her. And I don't know why she kept talking back to him, but he said some very inappropriate, very sexual things to her—things he was going to do to her. And she was mortified. I think she was scared. I feel very badly she didn't feel comfortable coming to me about it. But she wrote it down on a piece of paper to show one of her friends, and the friend's parent found it in the book bag and told. I feel fortunate that happened because then the parent called the principal, the principal called me, said, "Come in. We need to talk." And that's how I found out about it. ... I feel very badly because as a fifth grader, she was exposed to a lot of stuff that you protect your children from, and I felt like I wasn't doing my job. That's when we got the laptop to stay in the living room or in the dining room.

As the focus group parents continued their conversation, someone mentioned that similar incidents could easily take place right in front of parents under the guise of "cute little penguins." The mother in the above example and other focus group participants went on to discuss what I later identified as Disney's Club Penguin. The focus group parents lacked detail in their knowledge of the site and were unaware of the name of the site or that it was run by Disney.

The parents also were unaware that Club Penguin is designed to be a safe site for youth. The site's information page assures parents that "Intuitive safe chat helps kids talk to friends by suggesting phrases, while blocking inappropriate language" (Club Penguin n.d.). The site also suggests that engaging with the activities and social life of the site will help children achieve developmental milestones, from motor skills to money management. Because Club Penguin has built safety measures into the design of the site, it makes a relatively poor platform for predators, although the high concentration of children undoubtedly attracts predators who attempt to engage with young visitors. Language filters and automatic banning make sustained inappropriate conversations, such as forms of "grooming" necessary to gain the trust of youth online, difficult. In addition to the automated filters, youth can and are encouraged to report inappropriate language and behavior to the site administrators. Even so, there are ways to circumvent the language filters until such activities are reported or otherwise noticed by the site. One youth survey participant referenced the site and an experience on it by saying that "When I was on Club Penguin, this 'penguin' asked for my address."

Although extended grooming is not possible through the site, it makes an ideal target for online "trolling"—where users attempt to elicit strong reactions from others for amusement. Many Internet trolls have attempted to annoy or harass Club Penguin users, and numerous YouTube videos show (clearly older) users logging on and "shouting" statements such as "KILL YOUR PARENTS" and "HAVE S E X WITH DEAD CORPSES," using spaces between letters to mask the word *sex* from the automated filters (Club Penguin 2010). Trolling attempts often deliberately try to disrupt an online space and are performed in the spirit of a prank—although an offensive one. Although the troll's intent would not change the fact that a fifth-grade student was exposed to offensive and inappropriate language, it would reduce the severity of the incident and the adult reaction to the incident. In this case, the absence of an attempt to lure or sexually victimize a child is significant. The status of the child as victim in this case also seems unclear although by no means dismissible. The parent in this case mentions the "fear" that her child felt, although it is unclear whether the child was afraid that her parents would ban her from Club Penguin or whether she was afraid of the content of the messages. The mortification she experienced could have been caused by having her backpack searched by an adult and having private material shared with the principal and her parents. In this case, it is easier for a child to block or report an online predator than it is to manage the consequences of a parent "seeing something."

A second incident was told by a parent in different focus group. This parent said that her fourteen-year-old daughter had an online exchange with someone, which resulted in a telephone call to the girl from a man:

When she was littler, she was going on to something—probably when she was in middle school. I got a phone call one night at home, and they were like, "Hello, is [daughter's name] there?" I was like, "Yeah?" It sounded like an older guy. I asked, "Can I ask who is calling?" He goes, "Well, she'll know." I was like, "Okay … ." And I said, "[Daughter' name], phone!" And I stayed on the phone. She got on, and he goes, "You don't sound like you're eighteen!" And I go, "That's cause she's not. Can I ask who is calling?" He said that she went on for, like, a home business. So I'm like—I freaked out. I said, "She's not eighteen. She's fourteen. You need to hang up." And, um, actually, she was younger. I yelled at her, and we cut her off the computer for, like, a year. I'm like, "You can't do that. If your phone number is out there, they can easily have tracked you." So that right there has made me step up my security of her. But with the phone, with the iPod, with the friends, it's very hard.

Although there was little discussion of this incident among the other participants, the fact that the call was unexpected, the "freaking out," and the suspicions over the stated purpose of the call might indicate a certain level of misunderstanding on the part of the caller.

This second incident can be reread by taking the statements of the anonymous caller at face value. His surprise that the girl did not "sound eighteen" is likely enough to discount the possibility that a predator was on the line. Potential employers need to discern the ages of applicants just as much as a potential predator does, and there are numerous "work from home" or "secret shopper" organizations online—even if many of them deceptive or outright fraudulent (Blake 2009). Such a scheme might be attractive to a tween or teen who is looking for work and lacks access to a car or legal working status. It is unclear to what extent this incident involved information technologies, if it did at all, and yet the parent's immediate explanation was that an Internet predator had called her fourteen-year-old daughter, resulting in "like a year" of restricted computer and mobile device access for the girl.

Regardless of the ways that events played out in these two incidents, the parents demonstrated a lack of a situated expertise concerning youth Internet practices. In place of understanding, the discourse of the Internet predator was mobilized to fill in and make sense of the situation. The uncertainty built into the Internet predator narrative allows it to be used to reposition the elements of many such online incidents. Internet trolls and work recruiters are fit into the subject position of the predator, tweens and teenagers are fit into that of unwitting victims in need of protection, and the Internet is recast as a dangerous and risky space for young people. Such interpretations of youth Internet practices can lead to increased surveillance and protective measures, which make it less likely that young people will go to parents when they genuinely need help, further reinforcing and perpetuating the need for increased surveillance and protective measures by parents.

This is not to say that all parents are clueless about the practices of youth online but rather to note that when parents are uncertain about the details of a situation, they are provided with worst-case conceptual resources by the media's coverage and Internet safety curricula. Youth Internet practices can appear quite risky from the social distance constructed by generational divides. Allowing even the smallest possibility that their children might be victimized if they interpret their own social experiences would be considered bad parenting. Despite the visibility offered to parents through information technologies, parents are left feeling that they could have done better and that "their suspicions were not sufficiently strong" (Foucault 1978). Even parents who do not view their children as having been victims of a youth Internet safety incident feel that they are not doing enough and that the protections they have in place are too weak. Even after collecting all of her children's online credentials and using them to monitor their online presence, one parent continued to view her efforts as insufficient: "But I don't know. I still feel like I could be doing more to protect them."

7 "IT'S ALL COMMON SENSE!": Kids, Drama, and Internet Safety

In this chapter, I move to "the ground" of youth Internet safety discourses and examine the practices and discourses of children, tweens, and teenagers. The chapter is organized along the lines of youth Internet safety discourse, based largely on my experiences as a presenter at numerous Internet safety events. These presentations (like the one provided to adults in chapter 3) always begin with less troubling material—concerns about young people's technical expertise and brief discussions of their everyday lives and the technologies that support them. After providing this background, presenters then reveal the "shocking truth" about youth and the Internet by providing statistics on online victimization and risky behaviors and explaining the current technology-driven safety risk (such as predators and cyberbullies). Finally, the presentation ends with a return to adults and their own practices around youth Internet safety issues.

A central theme of this chapter is the lack of salience that Internet safety concepts hold for both young people and adults in everyday life. The typologies and languages of youth Internet safety do not synch with the ways that young people explain their concerns and experiences with the Internet. Kids do not talk about predators and cyberbullies as much as they talk about creeps and drama, particularly among themselves. Further, the different terms do not simply represent different ways of saying the same thing. They conceptualize the actions of youth online and off in fundamentally different ways, making visible or hidden various elements of practice and technology. I focus here on the latest form of Internet safety panic, cyberbullying, and look at the differences between concepts of cyberbullying and drama. Drama and bullying operate as different but overlapping concepts for youth and adults, providing tactical options for the framing and positioning of children and teenagers who are engaged in various forms of conflict and social interaction. In this sense, cyberbullying as part of a broader youth Internet safety discourse does not simply operate on youth and adults: both groups use the discourse in various contexts for specific purposes.

Although the concepts of youth Internet safety—particularly cyberbullying—may not be the ones that young people use regularly to explain their own experiences, this in no way reduces the actual risks and harms faced by youth online. Children, tweens, and teenagers are engaged in a range of problematic social activities, and information technologies variously facilitate, extend, or modify these activities in ways that deserve attention. Further, kids do understand what cyberbullying is, and many have personally witnessed or experienced forms of relational violence online that they would describe as cyberbullying. In this chapter, I do not dismiss the concepts of Internet safety and the underlying behavioral phenomena they seek to address but rather examine and unpack the concepts that are provided to young people as if they were self-evident. I seek to answer this question: if young people are considered experts and do not use these concepts to navigate and make sense of the everyday, why are the concepts of Internet safety widely used in curricula and by policymakers?

Some methodological points need to be noted prior to continuing with the chapter. First, I maintain the original formatting of student responses to qualitative survey items. Beyond ellipses and bracketed text, all spelling, grammar, punctuation, and slang are taken directly from the raw survey data. Second, the qualitative items on the survey were designed to induce young people to respond in open-ended ways so that I could examine the ways they conceptualize risk and abuse in their everyday lives. As such, my analysis takes the entire data set as a corpus and frequently makes connections between responses to different questions The corpus was analyzed using IBM SPSS Text Analytics for Surveys software, and any number of discrete "concepts" could appear in any given response—yielding many of the counts found in this chapter.

Young People, Adults, and Technical Expertise

It is not news that most young people have not mastered all computer and information technologies and further that they approach those technologies for widely different purposes (Ito et al. 2009; Livingstone 2009; Montgomery 2007). However, youth Internet safety discourses position children and teenagers as if they were universally raised in close, nurturing proximity to information technologies. In my own discussions with young people in focus group sessions, they described varying degrees of access to and engagement with information technologies. Some survey respondents wrote about their frequent use of information technologies: "In school, im on the internet to do school work, or find things out for the next history club meeting. At home im on facebook, aim, and other sites, with iTunes blareing." But many participants noted that they rarely went online other than for school work and preferred to avoid social networking sites. Some, particularly in rural districts, noted that they either had no computer at home or lacked access to high-speed Internet connections. This often set up frustrating situations for rural youth. One survey respondent wrote this: "at home, my internet is very slow and very annoying. at school we are not allowed to get on Myspace or Facebook."

Yet others seemed to avoid the Internet and information technologies wherever they could. In fact, before the start of one focus group session, I received a surprising telephone call from a parent who wanted to warn me that her son might "bias" my study given his lack of interest in computers or the Internet. I was, of course, happy to have him participate. The focus group sessions included a significant number of these low-interest participants, but they were not in the majority. In the online survey results, students also described varying interest in information technologies and the Internet. One survey respondent wrote, "come on this is me were talking about here! i do homework. occasionally check email. the last time i checked my email i had stuff from july unopened in there." Another wrote, "well i dont use the internet only for education and i dont plan to use the internet that much either i just rather use it for Homework and projects."

Somewhat surprisingly, young people and adults made similar comments in focus group discussions of information technology and in their qualitative survey responses. Both groups seemed to be doing what they could with the tools and conceptual resources they had access to and were trying to make sense of life online with other priorities and concerns in mind. Although most survey participants stated that they were "highly skilled" with information technology (46 percent, $n = 3,104$), statements by participants in both the survey and focus groups were full of technical inaccuracies. Young people rarely seemed fully confident in their knowledge of information technologies, in the ways the technologies worked, and in the policies that regulated them in and out of school. The lack of technical knowledge became particularly clear in the descriptions of viruses and malware by survey participants. Students mentioned viruses regularly throughout the responses and their virus-related concerns, risky behaviors, and general thoughts on Internet safety. Many referenced "viruses" as a motivation for avoiding particular behaviors online, and others explained that viruses were an Internet safety concern and that students needed to know more about them. The responses made clear that most young respondents knew little about malware, their attack vectors, or their payloads. They wrote survey responses that referenced viruses: "facebook and myspace because i guess they can spread viruses to you computer," "videos there migh be a virus," and "runescape because it can give out virusis." None of the adults I spoke with as part of the study mentioned viruses or malware, but the myth of the virus resonates with my experiences as a former information technology help desk employee, where users would explain any and all potential technical problems as a "virus."

Unsurprisingly, youth frequently rely on adults for guidance when they work and play using information technologies. According to Henry Jenkins of the University of Southern California (Online Safety and Technology Working Group 2010, 2),

most young people are trying to make the right choices in a world that most of us don't fully understand yet, a world where they can't get good advice from the adults around them, where they are moving into new activities that were not part of the life of their parents growing up—very capable young people who are doing responsible things, taking advantage of the technologies that are around them.

Children and teenagers are susceptible to the lies, half truths, and inaccuracies told to them by law enforcement officers and parents. One middle-school survey participant demonstrated a somewhat panicked understanding of location data that are embedded in photos:

Somtimes i get very scared aftter i go online and im near people I dont know. My mother told me everything on how people can find you after talking to them on the internet and how they can find u off your cell phones if u post a pic using ur cell phone! so ive been really concernd about all tht stuff..like when ppl come my direction i feel so scared untill they pass i also dont know if thts a bad thing or a good thing!

Other students explained that they stopped engaging in various online activities after hearing about dangers from their parents: "i dont go on youtube much any more because my dad said that it can cause virusis!" and "World of Warcraft has many gateways for viruses, dad thinks it's risky." The survey responses suggest that many adults use the threat of computer viruses to prevent youth from engaging in some online behaviors, further contributing to the myth of the virus. Although "who knows better" remains a contested issue for young people, they do not universally claim to know more than their parents about the technologies or the risks that might be associated with them and often seek out assistance from adults. Even those who do not actively seek assistance are nonetheless provided advice, guidance, and technologically grounded narratives by adults, and many accept what is provided as truth.

Just as the parents and administrators I spoke with constructed the figure of the child online, so too did young people construct the figure of the concerned adult. Most of the discussions with and written survey responses from the young people in my study described supportive and helpful parents, family members, and school employees, even though they also frequently questioned the technical ability of their parents and other adults. In focus group sessions, young participants explained: "I don't think they would understand what I was doing if I told them. 'What do you mean you can talk to everybody at one time?,'" and "She was yelling because the computer wouldn't turn off. 'Press the button!' 'Oh.'" Others acknowledged that their parents had a basic level of technical ability but had yet to fully engage with social networking platforms and spaces:

Um, I don't know. My mom has a Facebook, but she doesn't really know how to do anything. My dad, he's like a caveman. So it's like—I don't know. ... they understand, but they don't get the point. They're like, "Why do you waste your time online?"

Less frequently but not uncommonly, students described parents with high levels of technical skill. One described her parents as "Facebook addict[s]," and another noted that "My dad ... he knows a lot about things that we use. He just wants to know what we're doing."

Over half (56 percent, $n = 3,062$) of the student survey respondents reported that they had engaged in what adults would view as risky behavior online, and of those who responded that they do engage in risky online behaviors, most (84 percent, *n* = 1,705) reported that they engaged in these behaviors primarily at home rather than at school. This is somewhat unsurprising given the filters that restrict Internet access within school buildings. When young survey respondents were asked to name the forms of risky behaviors they engaged in, however (focusing on activities that they thought adults would consider risky), over six hundred wrote one word: "facebook." Even in more lengthy answers, using Facebook was overwhelmingly mentioned as something that adults thought was risky behavior. Facebook emerged from the data as the most mentioned form of "risky behavior" (*p* = 858), and it was followed by "myspace" (*p* = 225). Other common online activities that adults might perceive as risky included streaming video, chatting, shopping, gaming, and viewing pornography. Linking this sense of riskiness to the adults' construction of networked publics, a survey respondent explained:

Facebook … but it's only because they [adults] think that it's completely open and that you're automatically friends with everyone else. But as long as you don't have information showing to the world, and don't add/accept people you don't know (basically just be smart online) then it's not a risk

Answering the same question, another described: "the activites are that i engage in is twitter my mother really thinks it is risky and she thinks im to young." Another said simply: "my dad thinks just being on the computer is risky." For some students, the message from adults that social networking itself was risky was accepted as truth. One survey respondent wrote: "I used to really want a Facebook, then I found out how dangerous it is." These responses support the arguments put forth by Valerie Steeves (2009) and Torin Monahan (2006)—namely, that online surveillance of young people instills in them a sense that they are under suspicion and prevents them from openly using relatively safe information technologies. As another survey respondent noted:

I have never had a bad experience using the internet up to now. I think that teachers and people are making kids paranoid, and making parents trust their kids less. Despite what people may think, were smart thease days

Survey Responses of Young People Who Gave Up Activities Because They Were Risky

Using game cheat codes; most sites usually ask you for your name, number, date of birth, and home address. …

youtube, facebook

talking to people on facebook.

talking to friends online, i use the phone more often

something inappropriate, but luckily my parents stopped me. (i was so embarrased)

runescape because it can give out virusis

really nothing i dont go on youtube much any more because my dad said that it can cause virusis!

porn cetain games, certain social networks

None, i have no idea what i would be doing that is so risky.

None casue u wanna no why i do not stop them cause they are not risky i am old aenough to take care of my self and my mom will help me through things i can't handle even thiough i am not a mammas boy

Myspace because it's more risky than Facebook.

I have stopped talking to people i don't know. I have also stopped talking to my friends online unless i was 100% sure it was them i was talking to.

i have stopped accepting everyone as friends on facebook and now i actually look at who they are and what mutural friends there are and if i dont know who they are i contact a mutrual friend and if they dont know i tell my parents that someone i do not know is trying to befriend me so they can take care of it and/or be aware of it

I got off deviantart.com because some of the artwork was a bit inappropriate.

Going on youtube, going on myspace, using unsecure emails, and going on any site not yet approved by my mom, when shes not home, or not within a few feet in case of emergency.

facebook because they have viruses on the website.

downloading games on to my computer because i think they can come with viruses

club penguin becuse people can stalk you

arguing and rumering i said "the rumor you guys do to other people will end at you again"

Any time that I am prompted to download something from a suspicious website, I close it. If I click into any website, and it looks like pornography, I exit out of the page and check to see if my computer security has been breached.

adult content (kept getting grounded for it)

a 1 gb game that took up to much space

This sense of being under suspicion also provides young people with a tool for resistance, however, because the ability to predict how adults will respond to particular forms of behavior allows children and teenagers to have a level of control. In focus group sessions and the survey data (particularly the survey data where responses were anonymous), young people routinely made light of Internet safety issues, reflecting a critical knowledge about the relationship between youth, Internet safety, and adults. They indicated an understanding of the stereotypical online risks and the terms one might use to provoke an emotional response from adults seeking to protect their children online. These statements appeared most frequently in response to a question on the kinds of risky online behaviors they engage in. For example, participants wrote various types of responses: "Nothing, i live on the edge everyday. i love being friends wit 50 year old men on facebook."; "Setting up sexual meetings with middle aged men"; and "pedo . com is not a foot fetish site!!!!" Another wrote, "Don't talk to strangers. If they talk to you yell 'STRANGER DANGER!!!! STRANGER DANGER!!!!!' Then go away from the compter." Finally, one respondent wrote, "I LOVE MY EXPERIENCES ONLINE. THEY ARE FILLED WITH EXCITING PORN FILLED ACTIVITIES." Although these comments are undoubtedly "inappropriate" for young people in grades six to twelve, they demonstrate that young people understand the dangers from predators and sexting and that they feel that engaging in such behavior is ridiculous. Most kids are not interested in engaging with people they think are creepy, but they are willing to provoke those who would make the misguided assumption that they would so easily be creeped on. Even the humorous statements show an understanding of the ways that adults who are responsible for the protection of youth are positioned and required to act.

Context and Content: Internet Safety Concerns

To understand how young people rank Internet safety among their other priorities, I asked student survey participants to describe their major concerns for the current school year. Most topics in their responses referenced issues like grades and schoolwork ($p = 1,718$), extracurricular activities ($p = 202$), and social status ($p = 129$; "I am concerned that people might think I am a loser. That Im not cool"). Many respondents lacked major concerns ($p = 604$). References to information technologies were rare. Only two responses mentioned online problems—"online bullying" ($p = 1$) and "cyborg bullying" ($p = 1$). In the latter case, it is unclear whether or not the response was another attempt at survey trolling. Participants did note concerns with bullying ($p = 87$), relational violence ($p = 66$), and physical violence ($p = 39$), but again in relatively small numbers. The focus group conversations were similar and often followed the patterns that were found in the parent focus groups and interviews with administrators. Although young people referred to information technologies, few of their problems or concerns were easily categorized into the typologies of risk offered by Internet safety discourses.

Young people's concerns regarding safety and information technology often centered on issues of context. They were concerned that statements taken out of context would result in arguments with their peers that would be carried over to school or otherwise produce or reproduce "drama" (this is discussed later in the chapter). Similarly, they were concerned that the adults who monitored their online activities would take their or their friends' statements out of context. Many students were particularly concerned that the inappropriate nature of such interactions would lead to punishment, further restriction of access to information technology, or heightened monitoring by adults. Beyond concerns over context, young people described two primary Internet safety concerns—filtering at school and difficulties with malware and advertising at home.

The most frequently referenced Internet safety issue that young people mentioned in the focus groups and the surveys was the expansion of online arguments and their transition to school, which the respondents commonly referred to as *drama*. They explained how changes in status updates and other social networking activities could expand into large conflicts between multiple opposing groups. As one group of high school focus group participants explained:

Student A: Just posting something and having it come back at you. Like, just saying something stupid and having someone use it.

Student B: Like, people starting stupid drama over things that happen on Facebook. That sucks.

Student C: Acting hardcore at the keyboard.

Student B: People have no fear when you cannot see them over the Internet. ...

Student A: People say a lot of dumb things on Facebook. ...

Student B: ... and then you get to school.

Occasionally, these confrontations were described as having fizzled out after they were brought to school where students had to meet face to face: "Mostly people just want to run their mouths. When they confront them, they don't do anything." At other times, problems at school became disruptive and major points of difficulty for youth. Again, these forms of conflict were the main concerns that young people had in terms of online risk. They worried that online statements would be taken out of context, be deliberately misread, be responded to negatively by others, and spark widespread furor on social networks and in school. Approximately one in five students who answered the survey (21 percent, n = 3,102) reported having had an argument in school due to online activity.

This concern was confirmed by school administrators, who repeatedly mentioned having to deal with small arguments that began (or moved) online and quickly grew into issues that had the potential to disrupt entire schools. Described by one middle school principal,

"She put this on Facebook about me, and I'm going to kick her ass!" I think we deal with a lot of the backlash of what's written on Facebook the night before.

An assistant principal who had worked in both a middle school and a high school explained this as the "social network dilemma":

The other part of the Internet that reaches my desk is the social network dilemma. … With kids having problems on social networks with each other and then bringing it into the school and having problems with their fellow classmates. We've been dealing with that more this year than before.

Further, in-school problems with online drama require administrators to expand their jurisdiction through expansive school policies (described in previous chapters). One administrator described this expansion of school power in a community panel on cyberbullying ("Cyberbullying: Responding to the Challenges" 2010):

Ten years ago, if we got a call from a parent about something that happened online or over the phone, we would pretty much say, "Well, that happened out of the school, and I'm going to refer you our school resource officer." And that's just no longer the case anymore because anything that happens outside school is brought into school.

Beyond perceived problems with the increasing visibility and scope of online arguments that transition into schools, young people frequently described their concerns about blocked Internet content at school, both in focus group sessions and in survey responses:

Everything is blocked on the school server, i'm not even sure why we have internet at the high school. There's absolutely no freedom. They say you can surf the web if you have free time. ... too bad there's nothing to surf.

Young people regularly mentioned the difficulties that their school's Web filtering caused when they tried to do research projects and when teachers were unable to access blocked resources to supplement classroom discussions. Common resources that were blocked by school filtering systems included *Wikipedia* (focus group: "Oh, look. *Wikipedia* is blocked as a forum") and Google Images (survey: "At home you can use websites that may be blocked at school, such as google images"). Although some students said that they could ask their school's technology services department to unblock particular sites, this method was viewed as clumsy and time consuming—suggesting that they rarely used this approach. In a teacher focus group, a participant expressed frustration that the school's filters limited her ability to provide her students with personalized Internet safety lessons:

... we can't really educate because we can't get anywhere to try to show them anything. You know, I can tell the kids, especially with my special ed. kids, "If you go on Facebook." But I can't go on there and show them. I can't show them how to set up the privacy settings or to be able to take a post off that they can't believe they just put on. Or model that when they put up a really bad post that they weren't thinking, to go back on and say, "I completely apologize for what I just wrote. I wasn't thinking"—because you can't show them how it would look. And especially for my population, they don't think abstractly. So when I talk about Facebook, I don't know that they're even picturing the screen in their mind the way they would if it was in front of them.

A small group of student survey respondents noted primary concerns related to their general lack of freedom and autonomy. These responses ranged from the short ("to much restriction," "No fun or freedoms," and "We have like zero freedom") to longer descriptions of the problem:

I am most concerned about us being treated like we are elementary school kids, and having no freedom, such as to walk around the hallways during extended period and having to have a pass to leave the school.

These responses were primarily located in a district that installed an extensive surveillance system to monitor and restrict the activities of students throughout the school day. Security cameras monitored the school buildings, and off-the-shelf audio monitors in the bathrooms and locker rooms reportedly allowed school administrators to monitor activities without violating the visual privacy of students. Online, students accessed the

Web through a highly restrictive filter and were prevented from cell phone use on school grounds by district policy. The unintended consequence of these two policies, as described by middle schoolers, was to convert bathrooms and locker rooms into zones of unmonitored text communication. Cell phones were typically hidden in pockets and were used to send text messages to other students within such spaces outside of adult surveillance. Students felt that these rules were ineffective, particularly because they were unevenly enforced by faculty members.

In other major studies of youth Internet safety, young people stated that they were concerned about being exposed to obscene or otherwise unwanted content (Livingstone et al. 2011; Mitchell, Finkelhor, and Wolak 2003; Wolak, Mitchell, and Finkelhor 2007). Some participants in this study referred to concerns over unwanted/unblocked advertising and inappropriate content. In one high school focus group, students said the following:

Student A: The more information you put on Facebook, the more they steal it … to sell you stuff.
Student B: If you go on certain sites, they automatically have your ID and send crap to your email!
Student C: I know my cousin—every pop-up he gets is, like, "Free iPod!" and he'll click on it. I'm, like, "You're an idiot. They're not going to give you a free iPod!"

Survey respondents said, "I hate pop up ads," and "beachball popups are dangerous." Only two survey respondents mentioned having been unwillingly exposed to pornographic content: "we should not have any things popping up in the screen because theres pictures of peoplenaked sometimes and it disgusting," and "one time i got sent a picture of a huge penis"

Finally, young people rarely referred to adult predators in focus group conversations, although this might be because such discussions make participants feel uncomfortable. Within the survey data, however, there were a number of references to pedophiles and "creeps." The word *predator* was not frequently used ($p = 22$) across the survey corpus and was used only in responses that explained key Internet safety concepts. The word *creep* was relatively more common ($p = 49$), but again it was used primarily to explain key safety tips ("um playing games is fun but never go into chat roooms with creepy men bc they will rape u!!! h"). Some survey responses described concerns over adult predators online. One respondent described what appeared to be a false alarm:

a couple of years ago this girl liked me in are school and aim me and was lke hey and i didnt no who it was and i thought it was a friend from my basketball camp but it wasnt and she was asking me out when she waas acting as a guy and it was scary. i thought it was some creep. it was scary but its fine now

Similarly, another respondent, in a slightly more serious situation explained:

I have been stalked i gave a guy my cell number he wouldlint stop talking to me in nasty ways he sed he was 16 he turnd out to be 47 year old who hadd raped a12 yearold girl and woudint stop talikng about it so i called the cops

Most survey respondents (with one notable exception discussed later in the chapter) seemed to be wary of but usually (not always) capable of avoiding and managing the threats posed by online predators.

Common Sense and the Lack Thereof: Protection and Risky Behavior Online

Most of the young people that I spoke with and surveyed expressed a need for Internet safety education. Despite laughing about the materials presented to them, they recognized that risks were involved with online communication and that they required some guidance to recognize and navigate those risks. Only 62 percent (n = 3,084) of the survey respondents reported having seen Internet safety materials at school (22 percent were unsure if they had). It was clear that many of the key concepts provided by youth Internet safety curricula had reached students and that they were relatively comfortable with those concepts. Focus group participants described common strategies for protecting themselves online ("Don't post personal information"; "Block some sites"; "Firewalls up at all times"). The survey data similarly showed an awareness of basic Internet safety practices, with most respondents stating that keeping personal information private and avoiding strangers were the two main principles that children and teenagers should be taught in school.

In focus groups, responses to questions about staying safe online were usually voiced in an extremely disinterested and rehearsed manner. In their written survey responses, students said that being safe online was generally an issue of "common sense" and not "being stupid," and their tone often seemed frustrated. In every focus group, at least one student noted how simple the concepts of avoiding strangers, protecting personal information, and avoiding trouble were, and in the online survey responses, these statements were frequently capitalized and followed by several exclamation points. As one survey participant exclaimed, "don't be stupid, stupid!" This was a common theme in the survey data. One student wrote, "It's all common sense. I use my judgement on what to do or what not to do on the internet. I have not yet had any problems." Another wrote, "IT'S ALL COMMON SENSE!!!!!!!!!!!!!!! THE ONLY WAY BAD THINGS HAPPEN IS IF YOU DO SOMETHING STUPID OR IF YOU PUT YOURSELF OUT THERE FOR PEOPLE TO FIND YOU!!!!!!!!!!!!!!!!!!!!!!!!!!" In part, these judgments on how to stay safe online were supported by young people's sense that they could easily manage online problems. One stated that, "It's really kind of a joke. You can just log off. You can do all kinds of things to stop it, including just telling someone." Another student wrote, "There's generally always a way to get out of it. You can always just block or X out of your computer window."

Other participants seemed to understand that not all young people followed either the prescribed rules of Internet safety or the informal guidelines of common sense. One student noted that "You do have a group of kids who have the common sense, but not all of them do." Others said that staying safe online was a matter of common sense but that youth frequently took risks regardless:

Student A: It [the presentation by the district attorney] was common sense!
Student B: The common sense that everyone breaks. ...

A survey respondent noted that "A lot of people are going to meet others that they have only talked to once. They share almost anything with them." Others directly referenced themselves, noting that, "im not gonna stop doing something online because its not safe imean if it can hurt me in any way then ill stop but other than that im not gonna stop." Many survey participants noted that they engaged in risky behaviors that violated the "common sense" of Internet safety, including "Talking to strangers on chat rooms," "Chatlines, giving phone numbers out, or where i live," and "sending sexual pictures."

The most disturbing report of victimization to emerge from the survey data involved a sixth-grade boy. When he was asked if he wanted to add anything at the end of the survey, he wrote the following:

Once i was online and this guy would keep messageing me over and over i had told him once i didnt want to talk but he kept doing it. I had finally said okay and started talking to him, he told me he was a younger man but ended up being a very older man. He keept telling me he wanted to met and that he would pay me to have sex with him. … i kept saying no and every time i did he would rasie the price. i knew something was wrong and i new if i really di d this it would be bad, after the men got to 6,000 dollars i almost considerd going but then i said no and got off.i felt very violated and wrong and never went on that sight again.

This response was easily the most concerning, but other survey respondents also described experiences with various forms of relational violence, physical violence, and sexual solicitation. With these cases (particularly within the quantitative survey data), it was not always clear that these experiences made young people feel uncomfortable or otherwise victimized. The survey was designed to avoid asking them to describe or otherwise recall such experiences. It is clear from the responses in the accompanying box that students, even under the best of conditions, require some degree of adult guidance and monitoring, whether online or off. Youth resistance to such necessary guidance and monitoring is a response not to the guidance itself but to the form it takes.

Young people found value in the forms of Internet safety education they received, and many wanted to learn more about staying safe beyond the information their schools had already provided to them. When asked if their school required more Internet safety education, only 12 percent (*n* = 2,916) responded no. However, students felt that their school's curricula were outdated, provided generic information, and did not explain specific methods for using and configuring online spaces. When asked how relevant Internet safety materials were to their lives, responses varied. Many described a significant disconnect from the materials and their experiences online: "We always hear this one story about this girl who got a text message and killed herself. Is that how it really is? No." One student expressed his frustration at the fixation on cyberbullying, stating that "I think that they're focusing on the wrong type of bullying. … The school talks a lot about cyberbullying. I'm sick of it. I'm not listening anymore."

A survey participant wrote that Internet safety materials were

Not really very [relatable]. They focus on the "big risks" and most students aren't doing really risky things. They do things that aren't the most safe, like posting a million pictures of themselves or advertising their whereabouts on their facebook status.

When i had a Facebook account someone hacked it.

Welll. … .My dad's friend Thomas is telling me to talk to this girl [NAME REMOVED] and I don't know her and he gave her my phone # which I don't know how he knows it but he keeps tellin' me to talk to her and no one knows if she's real..it's scary

well im online constently and iv never had a problem with it befor besides my stalker ingame

well i do not want anyone to talk about me or my friend and i need to know if they are talking about me thier is a fried who id being to me and my friend so i need to find out if she ia talikng about or not becouse people are meaning mean to me and my friend sometimes:)

… theres pictures of peoplenaked sometimes and it disgusting

Sometimes students will look up something of personal interest and ads will pop up and students will get in trouble and are accused of looking something up inappropiatly. We aren't looking anything up that is inappropiate it is the ads that come up and take us away to different web pages.

People asking you what your name is and how old you are, and telling you your sexy and that they wanna date you when they don't even know you. ! It's pretty creepy.

people are stupid because they make fun of me because my brother is gay and it ticks me off

one time at band camp i was searching the Internet and a man disguesied as beatful girl talk to me

One time my mom kept on getting chatted to by some lady who was saying inappropriate things. We would try to ask her who she was and she would ignore our questions and keep harrasing us!

ok so one time i downloded a hack pack for one of my online games and when i clicked on one of the bottons something came up with nakid pics … :(

Not much. I have a lot of friends online and only 2 know my first name. We talk a lot and I used to be a big risk taker when I was younger and that was when they got my name. It was only my first and nothing has happened and I'm glad. I've had an experience with a friend on a kid site where this girl kept asking us our names and where we lived and our numbers. We didn't tell her anything. If it even was a her.

No I'm not aloud to have a cell phone, Facebook, or and other account so i don't think I don't have to worry about it.

my friend just met a boy online and she thought that he hated her, it was really a hacker who hacked into her boyfriends account.

My experiences are that i go online on facebook everyday but i just might delete it because to has too much drama

look up the video 2 guys 1 hammer its a murder video showing 3 friends killing a man this is wrong yes in everyway yet it is still on the Internet you except us to answer if theres anything wrong with the Internet yes everything it helps and wrongs in the same time people are cynical mynical and do what they want free will look into it

I've never had any trouble with anything on the Internet, no matter what i do

i once had a friend,a close friend actual and she was being very bad on the computer and she gave away her real name and my real name and her real picture to this boy and my real picture to this guy after i told the conciler she stoppped talking to him for 4 months but then started talking to him again and then i told my resource room teacher and she brought in [a local law enforcement officer] and hes now looking for the guy and my friend is perfectly safe

i loveeeee porn! even though its dangerous, i dont care. … i use skype to expose my body to people i dont know, and it is awsome!!!!:D

I have safe experiences on the Internet. Most social networking sites have very high privacy standards and I fell extremely safe on them. Adults don't always understand how safety is increasing on the Internet and can sometimes say things out of hand and false about Internet safety

I have have people on Myspace that are much older than me IM me and call me names like sweatheart or gorgeous. It made me feel a little uncomfortable.

anything from being cussed at getting yelled at getting told to f off and just having people start drama.

Others felt that the materials they received reflected the ways they understood the Internet but that they were growing weary of the materials: "Quite [relevant], but the majority of it is common sense," and "Pretty [relevant]. helpful but I feel its brought up too much." They commonly expressed fatigue after receiving the same materials year after year with little variation. From the survey results:

we're smart kids and the schools dont give us enough credit because they shove all of this internet safety down our throats, when we already know everything they're telling us. this makes us not want to listen.

In a focus group, a high school student noted that "By second grade, you know everything." This was reinforced by the quantitative data from the survey. Of the survey respondents who reported having had some form of Internet safety education at their school, 79 percent ($n = 1,753$) reported that they already knew most or all of the information provided to them. Further, there is some evidence to suggest that the relevance of youth Internet safety materials correlates with grade level, with younger students being more likely to find the materials relevant (partial $\eta2$ (6) = 0.019, $p = 0.002$). Put simply, middle school and high school students are tired of youth Internet safety. They are tired of being provided with the same, generic materials year after year—and this fatigue can easily lose youth who otherwise want and need the guidance of adults.

Bullying—Online and Off

Young people do not discuss the Internet or Internet safety issues in the same way that adults do. Perhaps more accurately, they do not mobilize the institutional discourses of youth Internet safety with the same frequency that adults do. Slippage and issues with dual consciousness (Herring 2008) are certainly far from uncommon—as one survey respondent wrote:

The internet is everywhere around the world, and is a big aspect in our global society. when somebody bully's online its called "cyber-bullying" and everybody can see it if they wanted to all they have to do is log online. as opposed to bullying in person which may be equally or less embarassing.

By adopting the languages of youth Internet safety, young people can appear knowledgeable and secure, soothing adult anxieties around online risks and allowing them some level of control over a situation. Otherwise, most young people rarely speak in terms of predators or cyberporn, and at the time this research was conducted (at the height of concerns over youth suicides connected to online harassment), they do not use the term *cyberbullying*.

Toward the end of my research in schools, I held several focus groups with students, and although they discussed harassment and other forms of violence, they failed to use the term *cyberbullying* without first being prompted by an adult. In one middle school session, students were asked if *cyberbullying* was a term they used in conversations with each other and if they did not use it, then who did? When I asked the first question to a group of high schoolers, they answered, "No." When asked who did use the word, they responded loudly, and in unison: "Teachers, adults." Similarly, students in a middle school focus group said, "Nobody uses it." One middle school girl sitting next to me rolled her eyes and said under her breath, "It's an old lady word." Various other participants commented by stating that "It just sounds, like, weird" and "We don't really talk about it."

As I continued my research with young people in focus groups and with the online survey, responses were much the same. Similarly, the term was absent from my conversations with school administrators, parents, and other adults. They rarely, if ever, used the word unprompted—although parents were more likely than administrators to do so. I asked a principal why she had not used the word at the end of our conversation, and she said, "Bullying is bullying is bullying." When I did not introduce the term as part of my questions about online safety, research participants—both youth and adults—described "drama," "creepers," and even the broader category of bullying but rarely discussed cyberbullying as something separate or distinct until otherwise prompted to do so. As with the youth participants, cyberbullying also was of limited concern to the administrators I spoke with. One principal mentioned that

As far as bullying, cyberbullying—I am not spending the bulk of my time addressing bullying issues. I have a bully in my office once a week. I have a student that lacks the basic skills to function in school five times a day.

It was not that drama was more frequently discussed than bullying but rather that most participants felt that it was unnecessary to distinguish between online and offline bullying. Regardless of the language used to explain the problem, violence in a number of forms was certainly a concern for young people. They were concerned about relational violence ("Like going to the other clases and not doing anything right being a big fatty and people callung me names and stuff like that"), physical violence ("Many people hear about weapons in school but do nothing about it! What if that person with the knife or blade or even gun hurt or KILLED someone!!!"), and suicide ("I was most concerned about people calling other people names. Also, some people would talk about commiting suicide"). They discussed their concerns with these forms of violence in a variety of ways and rarely distinguished between online and offline forms of violence. I carefully use the word *violence* here because young people occasionally objected to how the word *bullying* was used. They felt that bullying and drama represented specific forms of behaviors and relations. Young people also frequently used offline consequences as a rationale for blurring distinctions between online and offline bullying. Survey participants wrote that "if people fight on Facebook, its more then likely to continue at school" and "tha online thing gets into school andand then tha drama begins."

When survey participants were asked about the differences between bullying and online bullying, responses varied. The most significant category of response was, simply, that there was no difference between the two ($p = 689$), and responses that mentioned a difference usually began with some form of "there is no difference but." This was closely followed by responses that mentioned physical violence ($p = 636$) or physical presence ($p = 504$) as distinguishing elements of offline bullying ("I cant get punched in the face online," and "bullying in person is right to their face"). Other commonly referenced concepts also appeared in definitions provided by participants, including cowardice ($p = 181$), anonymity ($p = 161$), the ability to "say more" online ($p = 146$), and a wider audience ($p = 100$). Responses that stated that one form of bullying was worse than the other were nearly evenly split, with slightly more references to offline bullying being worse ($p = 198$) than references to online bullying being worse ($p = 129$). A small number of survey responders wrote that online bullying was a positive ($p = 36$) because it allowed students to notify parents and school administrators and provided evidence of abusive behavior. A survey respondent wrote that "on line they can say something to you and you can get them in trouble by showing your parents." Another described online bullying as far easier to handle, noting that "because bullying on the computer you could tell your mom or parents and bullying in person the bully wont let you tell on them or trhey will beat you up." Other participants disagreed and said that the lack of immediate adult supervision combined with anonymity problematized efforts to track down bullies.

Dan Olweus's (2012, 4) definition of *bullying* includes three central criteria: "intentionality, some repetitiveness, and a power imbalance between perpetrators and target." In the modified definition provided to student participants in his study, he says, "But we don't call it bullying when the teasing is done in a friendly and playful way. Also, it is not bullying when two students of about the same strength or power argue or fight" (4). When asked to define bullying, most students in the study touched on the key

Survey Responses of Young People about the Differences between Online and Offline Bullying

youre not face to face online and it isnt as easy to face somone you cant see.

you push and say gimme yo money in person and online you could just harass them.

you cant prove if someone is bullying you in school. online or over text messages you can print off or save and show someone

You are more open on line because the other person does not know who you are so you can say any thing and mostly not get in trouble.

Yes, online bullying is a load of shit

when u do it in person u beat them up or stop it but only it keeps going and going on till someone snaps

when people bully online it stays up for everyone to see

Well i guess its less harmful on line because you can' with the technology now a days' block people from your pages and all that stuff. Up front bullying is more harmful because if you get abused physically you cant just block them. They will just keep coming back no matter what you do.

They are both bad things to do but the one difference between the two is that it's harder to bully a person upfront while it's not as hard to bully online. It seems to me like their is more bulling online then there is when a person bullies someone upfront.

There is not too much of a difference but while bullying in person could harm the person and spread through gossip, bullying online never goes away. If a post was put online it will never go away. It can always be found.

There is no difference at all. Bullying is bullying.

there arent really that many differences but bullying in person people talk about it for a while but after a while everyone forgets about it (sometimes, depending on how bad it was) and bullying online everyone can read it and add to and it never goes away its and it always seems bigger than what it really was

The differences are you can say whatever you want online but everyone can find out exactly what you said and you can hide yourself in your house or whereever you are. Bullying in person you can't get much proof and still can hurt someone

the difference is u cant see the person and you don't know how they feel

The difference between bullying online and bullying in person is that the person who bully online is more of a coward because they hide behind a computer and a keyboard. Whatever they put on the Internet is going to be there forever and everyone can see it

(continued)

The Bullying IN PERSON IS MORE SERIOUS IN PERSON BECAUSE THEY KNOW YOU AND THEY CAN DO IT EVERY DAY ONLINE IS NOT A BIG CONCERN BECAUSE U CAN STOP GETTIN ONLINE I WATCHED THE NEWS AND A GIRL COMMITED SUICIDESO MAYBE MAYBE NOT

in my eyes, there is no difference . bullying is bullying no matter where you are . if youre online, you are still saying hurtful things to someone . but online may be worse because people can make up lies and just like that, the whole school will know about it . rather then someone goes up to you in school and calls you a name not everyone in the school will know unless you tell them . and plus online you never really know who you are talking too . people could say they are you and embarress you.

if you are being "bullied online, obviously the person has no balls and cant say anything to your face and should be shut down from all contact online and faced in real life where things actualy mater. and then destroyed

Online Bullying Is Most Likely Trash Talkingg And In Perons Bullying Is More Likely To Get Physical And Mentally But Both Are Physical At Times

Online its more rougher but in person people are just pussys

Online bullying is not quite as bad as in person bullying because with online people might just be saying they are gunna do something when they really probably wont do anything when with in person bullying they might accually do something.

Bullying online is worse, because you don't know who it could be on the computer talking to you, and they could say more worse things than they can in person or to someone else. It's easier to prove that they said stuff, though.

Bullying online is more mentally straining because people will say anything over the Internet and not in person, so it is extremely hurtful. Bullying in person as shown in movies and such, is physically painful but happens less and less as electronics become more appliable to the situation.

Bullying online involes with people typing mean things and lately I've seen people from Newspaper die because of it. And Bulling in person well i have'nt seen so it's not affecting everyone in my school elements of the definition. A survey participant wrote about the concept of bullying:

To me, bullying means that you are harassing other people that are below you, teasing them, and making fun and picking on other people. Also, when most people bully others, they do it just to make themselves feel good or just to show off for their friends.

Their responses diverged from Olweus's definition by identifying bullying as something that "troubled" kids or kids who otherwise feel inadequate engage in:

Bullying means that someone is being hurt because they are different or the person doing the bullying is troubled and uses it to lash out at the world. Bullying is a horrible thing that shouldn't happen to anyone.

Another survey respondent wrote: "Bullying means that kids are insecure so they are mean to other kids." These descriptions of bullies frequently tied these "troubles" and "insecurities" to socioeconomic status: "bullying is mostly when kids that have a hard life at home with their family and take out their anger on others." Another student gave this definition of bullies: "Big tough pieces of shit that would become regulars at a gas station there whole life, while the kids they picked on make 4x their salary." These additions to Olweus's definition expand on the discursive work of the term and allow students to use it to conceptualize the practices of others. Bullying becomes a practice of the insecure, troubled, the poor, and people from unstable families, and framing another person as a "bully" provides students with a positional tool in the ongoing dramas of everyday life.

"DRAMAAAAAAAAAAAAA[tic]" Tactics

When I expected to read or hear discussions of cyberbullying, I often instead encountered discussions of drama. Responding to a survey question on important Internet safety concepts, one student wrote, "Don't talk to anyone that you don't know. Be nice to people. Don't start drama." Drama appeared to be a major concern for survey participants:

Grades and fitting in, my goal last year was basically to stay out of all the drama, so when I did get pulled in, I tried to keep my opinions out of the way and never took sides, I also worry about keeping people safe and preventing fights, I am a girl who enjoys peace, friendship, and safety.

One student respondent wrote that she had similar concerns "about my friends being hurt DRAMA," and another respondent wrote about the effects of drama on the school environment: "There is way too much drama in the school and it sometimes interferes with the learning part of school." Many students wrote short answers to some open survey questions: "drama" or variations on "DRAMAAAAAAAA" with varying numbers of the letter A.

Survey Responses of Young People about Online Drama

Fights and Drama, Interfering with my school work

the drama going on in the high school is the thing i'm most concerned about

My most concerns are the test, how the other kids in school are and the big one drama.

i was mostly concerened about drama and problems at school. The most thing was failing.

Last year I was concerned about other peoples drama and didnt want it to affect my school work.

Mostly grades and drama. The drama was a big concern because there was always some kind going on!

Kowing all the teachers to a certain extent and getting to class on time ! Also drama because not only do u have to worry about the kids you np but the kids u dont no!

To stay away from all the bullying and Drama.

There was a lot of drama and drugs.

rumors, drama,. … being bashed on for my lifestyle.

DRAMAAAAAAAAAAAAAAAAAA

I was concerned about drama, so many kids were talking about eachother, some kids were starting it online. Not at school,I dont think.

I was worried about my friends being hurt DRAMA

since school started this year i am most concerned about losing friends i had last year and past tensions coming back and bringing drama with them.

Drama among tweens and teenagers is a fluid concept that everyone seems to be able to recognize when they see it. At a local conference for school administrators, I asked a school superintendent what her definition of *drama* was, given the frequency with which the word appeared in my data. As she described it, drama was the intentional performance of attention-drawing conflicts that passed through family and friendship ties and often was grounded in old grudges—a description that shares much with Cindy D. Ness's (2010) work on inner-city violence among youth. Drama is not merely about putting someone down or getting in a fight. It is about the attention and excitement that such conflicts generate, regardless of who the perceived winner is. Dramas are fundamentally power plays. Through their work with teenage youth, Alice E. Marwick and danah boyd (2014, 5) similarly define *drama* as "performative, interpersonal conflict that takes place in front of an active, engaged audience, often on social media." Drama is mobilized by those who have a sense of the local power relations from which a conflict emerges and the ways that those relations play a role in the production and continuation of conflict. Like a soap opera, it demands and draws an audience that understands those relationships and the historical significance of the conflict. Throughout the performance of drama, there rarely are easily discernible bullies and victims or winners and losers because drama becomes visible as a continuous, self-reinforcing flow that is rarely segmented into discrete incidents with clear beginnings and endings. As such, drama is a highly positional activity that allows people to display conflict and emotion publicly and on a large scale. Drama is a tactical game where young people make interpretive moves and counter moves that reposition themselves and others within networks of power relations.

Social networks allow the performance of drama to take place publicly, incite participation by removing a degree of social context (allowing for multiple interpretations), and provide easy mechanisms by which others may choose to participate. This was made clear in many of the survey responses that referred to drama. One student wrote simply that "Most the drama is over the computer i guess." Others focused on Facebook as a site of drama, writing that "there is saying about facebook. 'stop drama, if you you want to say something say to my face not over facebook.'" One respondent seemed to use the online survey as a generator of drama, stating that

"This Girl [name of another student] she Starts mad drama." A focus group participant similarly described drama in her high school:

So much drama because of online things. ... You can, like, pull all your friends into it. One thing like that happened to me. Where you say something to someone you don't like at all or have no business having comments on something of yours. Then all your friends join in. ... There's this huge thing, and there's no point to it. People that don't talk to you at all or that you don't like comment on your thing.

Despite the anonymity offered by the Internet, young people used local social context to pin down otherwise anonymous or deceptive actors in dramatic conflicts. As one student focus group participant described: "It could also be a Facebook status update saying, 'There was a fight.' ... You don't have to say their name. People already know."

Drama and bullying are highly gendered and also reconstitute gender identities among youth (Marwick and boyd 2014). As described by a middle school focus group participant: "Verbal for the girls and aggressive for the guys. Girls are more sassy and dramatic." Drama is positioned as the more feminine behavior. Females are seen to be more social and are made responsible for the performance of social reproduction: "If people would get over the girl drama and stop fighting over boys, we would be fine!" Survey respondents commonly described fighting in gendered terms: "BOYS BEATING ON BOYS" or "FIGHTS! basically bewteen ALLLLLLLLLLL boys." Another student survey respondent described the differences between boys and girls:

People can be bullying on facebook and probably would never say anything in person and in person it's usually a group of guys picking on one other kid for no reason. Girls bully in person too but probably more online

Online bullying is viewed as a less masculine activity. As survey respondents wrote: "Bullying online means the bully is a pussy and won't say it in person," and "well cyber bullying is worse cuz if ur talkin smack over the computer then ur a pussy and u dont have the balls to say what u want to say to that certain individual." This also was noted by school administrators I spoke with. One described the differences that he observed:

I think girls are generally more apt to gossip, rumor, and drama. I think the vehicle by which they can perform those acts related to drama, gossip, and rumor—the vehicle for doing that is readily available in the palm of their hand. Guys—it's more intimidating. It's not drama. It's toughness, and can you really convey how tough you are with a text message? I don't think you can. That, in my mind, really characterizes the difference. Toughness is easier with face-to-face or with a bump [in the hallway].

The quantitative survey data further demonstrate that there is a significant (if minor) gender difference in experiences with arguments and rumors online. Gender was a significant factor in whether the survey respondent had been in an argument at school as a result of something that happened online (partial $\eta2$ (1) = 0.003, p = 0.002), with females (1.726) more likely than males (1.802) to experience these arguments. Gender was again a significant factor in whether the survey respondents had experienced the spread of rumors about them (partial $\eta2$ (1) = 0.008, $p < 0.001$), with females (1.737) marginally more likely than males (1.856) to have rumors spread about them. This suggests that although gender plays a role in determining the likelihood of having been in an argument in school or having had rumors spread online, it holds relatively little explanatory power compared to other potential forces or variables.

Although drama is constituted as a predominantly feminine activity and bullying is constructed as a predominantly masculine activity, boys also participate in drama, girls also participate in bullying, and both activities interpretively bleed into one another. However, mediated communication allows young people to inflict harm in the absence of many social cues and without physical contact—leading them to perceive online bullying as a less confrontational and therefore less masculine form of bullying. In another survey response that distinguished between online and offline bullying, the student wrote: "Bullying online is agirl way of bullying because they are to afraid to do it in their face. Bullying in person is worse because every one around you can hear what is going on." Through the technical and gendered construction of online bullying, the practice becomes visible for youth as a highly specific and relatively rare practice compared with drama and bullying. As the feminine form of an otherwise masculine behavior, it falls askew of the traditional gender identities intensely policed by youth. As a practice of cowardice for boys, of confrontation for girls, and of low status for all, the discursive barriers to online bullying are curb high. Young people do not use the term *cyberbullying* because they think that it is an "old lady word," and they do not discuss online bullying very often because it is a marginally untenable activity. No one wants to be placed as an online or cyberbully.

Marwick and boyd (2011, 2014) further characterize drama as a key discursive mechanism that allows young people to conceptualize their social lives outside of the victim/perpetrator dichotomy provided by the frame of bullying and to insulate themselves from the psychic costs of inflicting harm on others. If drama operates as a protective mechanism for tweens and teenagers, then bullying (as described in the chapter) operates as an offensive positioning tool within dramatic conflicts. They mobilize the term *bullying* tactically, framing the dramatic performances of others in terms of the troubled, insecure, and low-income bully—allowing themselves (or allied parties) to adopt the position of the victim. Examples of this played out within the survey data itself. One student participant wrote about an interaction between her sister and her best friend:

What bulling means to me is that the person who is bulling people are really childish. And that they dont have a life and would bully other people just so that they could feel bad about themselves just like the person who bullied the peron. theres this one person bulling my sister. She was my bestfriend. Now shes just walking away from it. Shes being the bigger person, and the bully is just a low life loser.

In a similar survey response, another student framed her "frenemy" as a cyberbully before slipping back into the language of drama:

i went through people cyberbullying me last year and i know how it feels to be called a "fat cake" and a "plastic." Im friends with the person till this day and sometimes i wonder if i should be i dont want to cause drama.

Even beyond positioning enemies and frenemies as troubled, mobilizing the discourse of bullying provides dramatic performers with a means to enroll adult institutional support. My own research has shown that young people are able to troll researchers through their highly embellished survey responses, and Kathleen P. Allen's (2014) research has described how young people sometimes manipulate adults as part of a dramatic performance. A drama between friends provides little by way of reaction by adults, but a potential cyberbullying incident commands adult attention. No adult can make light of a claim of bullying, less so as information technologies potentially make such forms of violence inescapable, broad-reaching, and persistent. The worst-case frame must be taken seriously, often to predictable and manageable effect. The dramatic actor who can successfully frame themselves as the victim can socially position their opponent(s) as low-class, psychologically troubled individuals while simultaneously inviting adults to intervene by enacting institutional discipline against the "bully."

Bullying: "an inacurate word used by adults"

One student survey participant wrote about his views on bullying, perhaps reacting to the adult-provided survey itself:

bullying is an annoying, inacurate word used by adults. I would explain this word, "bullying" as someone hurting another person with intent and knowing what they are doing. This textbook version is not what really goes on. It usually begins with a comment or snyde remark that bothers someone who then builds it up to more than it's worth.

This survey participant constructs the everyday practice of drama and criticizes adult attempts to frame dramatic practices in terms of bullying— likely dismissing youth perspectives in the process. Although the concepts of bullying and cyberbullying included in youth Internet safety discourses operate as part of a larger strategic apparatus of state governance, in everyday practice adults tactically mobilize the concept in much the way that young people do. Adults are aware of the concept of drama, particularly as the term has moved into mainstream discourses. Participants in a teacher focus group connected drama with social networking and explained that it is not solely a pattern of youth behavior:

Teacher A: And everybody sees it. What I've seen with [daughter's name's] Facebook is somebody has a problem about something. And then someone comments, and that one comments, and before you know it, there are thirty-six comments, and they're pointing fingers at people. And they don't realize that if you have a personal issue with somebody, you keep it to yourself. Go to that one person. Not every single friend of yours has to see what is going on. You don't have to comment on everybody's. And I see that a lot. Of course, she's in junior high, not middle school, whatever. ...

Teacher B: It's just not kids though. ...

Teacher C: I think it causes more conflict when they come back to school. The drama ... you know.

Teacher B: But adults do that, too. I've got a niece that posts everything, and she's almost thirty. Like, I don't want to know this stuff.

The adults I spoke with also constituted drama as a gendered activity and routinely made the connections between gender, technology, and dramatic behavior. In an interview, two male principals explained:

Principal: I think it's mostly girls. I think because girls are on [Facebook], that gets them revved up. … The drama builds, and then you've got this girl and her little group of friends, and this girl and her little group of friends, and then they get together and cackle and start pulling each other's hair out. Scratching. That's how they fight. … Girls are dramatic.
Assistant principal: On the opposite, boys are more up-front. … If I have an issue with you, I'm just going to say, "I have an issue with you." … They won't use Facebook.

The discursive work of the concept of bullying provides a slightly different array of tactical options for adults in comparison to youth. First, the frame of bullying constructs the clear positions of perpetrator and victim, constructing bounded incidents from otherwise complex relations and the constant flow of drama. This allows young people to position themselves as victims in relation to an aggressor, and it allows adults to position youth for further disciplinary action. By bounding off the complexities of past relationships, conflicts, and political factions, adults can identify troubled bullies and protect innocent victims.

Second, just as the framing of conflict in terms of bullying allows young people to trigger adult disciplinary mechanisms, it similarly allows school administrators and parents to involve law enforcement officers. One assistant principal explained this, again constructing online bullying in terms of cowardice:

I think you see less of the "calling you out on the playground" type bullying. … I've had this conversation with many kids—that when they do this type of thing on the cell phones and Internet, you're doing it because you're a coward. You're a coward. You have not got the intestinal fortitude to look them in the eye and tell them what you think. So you choose to do it namelessly and facelessly. That's what it is. But that doesn't make it any less of a crime or any less of an unacceptable behavior. It's the same thing.

By invoking the participation of law enforcement, adults further call into play the state's legal apparatus. Forty-nine states have passed bullying statutes, and most include cyberbullying and electronic harassment and give schools the ability to impose disciplinary actions beyond their normal jurisdiction (Hinduja and Patchin 2015). Fourteen of these state laws include possible criminal penalties for bullying. As parents' expectations and the laws have expanded the reach of school administrators, youth social interactions are increasingly framed by administrators in terms of bullying as an interventionary strategy. One teacher I spoke with described this shift:

Schools have found themselves having to punish students for bullying, cyberbullying. ... I truly don't think 90 percent of the kids do it to be mean. I think they just do it because they're being stupid. They're not thinking it through. The mom picks it up and reads it and is like, "Oh, my God!" And we're taking it out of context. We didn't necessarily hear the conversation that came before it.

Third, bullying is again constituted as an activity of the working class and socioeconomically disadvantaged— as something that happens in low-income or neglectful families. This allows connections to be made between the figure of the nonparent described in the previous chapter and the figure of the troubled bully. A parent explicitly made this connection:

As parents that are actively paying attention to what their kids are doing, there's a healthy percentage on the other side where they don't. It's like the kid we talked about—like the kids who bully. A lot of the parents can't be bothered. That may be a factor of they can't be bothered because they're stressed out and working two jobs. That's not to be judgmental. It's just a problem when you're trying and you're seeing what other kids are posting.

In this way, bullying acts as a further mechanism for policing the parenting practices of the working class and socioeconomically disadvantaged. By connecting the figure of the nonparent with the frame of bullying, adults can choose to engage in intergenerational dramatic performances by placing (or supporting) their child in the subject position of the victim, by reconfiguring the power relations between the child and her opponent, and by further reconfiguring the power relations between families. Parents of troubled bullies "can't be bothered" and "That's not to be judgmental."

Not all parents are strategizing their use of bullying and drama, which can be demonstrated through their use of the term *cyberbullying*. For adults who rarely if ever used the term, cyberbullying presented itself as an institutional framing of online bullying. For these adults, cyberbullying is a construction of the news media, legislators, and Internet safety curricula and is distanced from the everyday lives of young people and the adults who supervise them. When one teacher was asked why she had not used the term to discuss online violence, she said the following:

I think we usually say *bullying*, and then we specify *online*. And like, we might be talking, discussing a kid, and say, "Well, that kid's a bully," but I've never heard someone say that someone was a cyberbully. You know, I feel like it's more of a group thing online. Like, someone will post something, and other people will join on, but it's not—there's not someone out there who is just a cyberbully.

Online bullying is connected to the identities of known individuals who can be implicated in forms of violence carried out online. Discussing online conflicts in terms of cyberbullying appears to be disconnected from a local context because the lack of social context allows the cyberbully to dissolve into the anonymous online mob. *Cyberbullying* becomes a term used to describe nonlocal conflicts made visible by information technologies or presented by the news media. Similarly, the concept of bullying—and by extension cyberbullying—provides adults with a means to make sense of youth conflict, even when they otherwise lack the social context to determine the power dynamics at play.

As adults move away from the social context of the everyday lives of young people and increasingly interact with the online social spaces of youth as instrumental tools for surveillance, their reliance on the bullying frame increases. Arguably, this is facilitated by youth Internet safety curricula, which move to destabilize existing adult understandings of drama. Conceptualizing drama and bullying in such a way further explains the recent "epidemic" of cyberbullying. The capacity for Internet users to remain anonymous or to adopt the identity of another further strips social situations of easily accessible context. As such, those surveilling online spaces can be left with little or, worse, misleading immediate context with which to make sense of a situation. As a student focus group participant remarked:

People who aren't in close relationship with us every day don't really know what we do on Facebook. So they don't really understand, like, why people are fighting on Facebook. ... I think they should find out more about it. Because if they're not coming up with things that help people ...

Conclusion

Most young people who are active on Internet social media sites require and seek out the guidance of parents, teachers, and school administrators as well as informational resources provided to them as part of a larger Internet safety curriculum. The risks associated with youth social interactions—online or off—are not harmless or otherwise dismissible. And young people and adults are not Machiavellian tacticians. However, for all the risks, conflicts, dramas, and concerns, the everyday practices of youth Internet safety are fundamentally the practices through which power flows and operates.

Youth are not helpless victims of online abuses, and adults are not fascist disciplinarians—but both groups make tactical decisions about how to frame their lives and interactions on an everyday basis, drawing on and contributing to strategic discourses of Internet safety.

Overall, kids seem to be navigating social lives that are layered with online technologies in ways that are relatively safe. Most know the risks and actively seek guidance and mentorship from adults. A real danger, however, lies not in the perceived threats of a life lived with new technologies but rather in the failure to take children and teenagers seriously as they explain the technical and political topologies they navigate every day. Most kids are more at risk from having their views of the world—and the network of everyday concerns contained within—dismissed by well-meaning adults than they are of being victimized by the lurking sexual predator or the anonymous cyberbully. Without respect for youth perspectives, efforts to promote Internet safety and digital citizenship will continue to do more to protect childhood and the adult-child relations that produce forms of victimization than to provide young people with meaningful skills and concepts that allow them to play a role in protecting themselves.

8 Conclusion

My mom and other adults are always so concerned that my friends or I are doing things that are wrong because I don't want her meddling, but it's just my private space where I can be a teenager.

i think that you people over exaggerate and that it not really a big deal that kids go on facebook and post that they got drunk or something. your all hypocrits. we are not children anymore. id rather party it up now while i can until i actually have to settle down and start my life.

—Student survey respondents

There *is* something slightly hypocritical about adults' reactions when young people post content that adults simply "don't want to see." After all, generations of young people have had opportunities to "party it up" or "be a teenager" in their own private spaces. These opportunities have been decreasing as visibility increases through online social networks and as children and teenagers incorporate social networks into their everyday lives. It becomes a question of determining the extent to which we allow space for "just being a teenager" or "partying it up." What kinds of citizens might be produced by various modes of surveillance, spheres of development, and pedagogies of the family? As is discussed in previous chapters, questions relating to structural and institutional changes have been made impossible through the dominant discourses of childhood and safety. In this concluding chapter, I argue that we find ourselves in a position to examine the construction of childhood through the discomfort of youth Internet safety "crashes."

In this chapter, I first connect trends in securing the national infrastructure to trends in protecting youth online, focusing primarily on the ways that partnerships are being forged between private industry and government, while largely excluding families and children. By failing to recognize the ways that concepts of safety and security govern populations, we produce cyberlaborers rather than cyber- or digital citizens. Second, I outline suggestions for moving forward with much-needed efforts to keep youth safe, both online and off, drawing on Julie E. Cohen's (2012) discussion of the "conditions of human flourishing." Finally, I conclude the chapter by developing the concept of the technological "crash" as a means by which we might resist the dominant discourses that shape forms of development, technology, and citizenship.

Cybersecurity and Internet Safety

National cybersecurity again became a national priority after numerous attacks on major American corporations and institutions, perhaps most notably the attacks on Sony Pictures Entertainment in November and December 2014. Significant efforts by the U.S. government are underway to secure cyberspace—a term that seemed to fall out of fashion only to reemerge as the Internet was reconceptualized by the military as the fifth domain of warfare (Lawson 2012). Compared to youth Internet safety discourses, cybersecurity discourses do not easily draw boundaries between online and offline spaces. These discourses make clear that the "space" in this fifth domain is produced by information systems that are run by private corporations and government institutions and now undergird and support the everyday practices of global business. Conceptualizing and securing the fifth domain in this way requires further interlinkages between state and private actors (ignoring the strategic implications of such discourses and the modes of governance they make possible, a topic that is worth exploring but beyond the scope of this book). Since 2013, various standards and resources have been made available through the Department of Homeland Security via a voluntary program known as "C3: Converging, Connecting, Coordinating" (Department of Homeland Security 2015). These programs encourage private industry to establish cohesive data sharing and incident response practices and allow more seamless action by law enforcement and Homeland Security agents where necessary.

The move to secure the national infrastructure comes at the tail end of a conceptual shift in the field of information assurance that repositions the role played by security within an organization in terms of enabling, rather

than preventing, agile business practices. In a move away from security
stances that restrict access or prevent use or activities that might increase
organizational risks, information security officers are being encouraged to
support business practices and allow for more flexible use. The primary
rationale for this has been that highly restrictive controls and security measures simply do not work. Users and employees who feel that they cannot perform their job functions under such measures can and will find
workarounds, often resulting in even more insecure systems. As Donald A.
Norman's cynical slogan says: *"The more secure you make something, the less
secure it becomes"* (2009, emphasis in original). This move toward security as
enabler can be seen as part of a broader turn toward social and human factors in information assurance. Although the idea that social engineering—
exploiting social and organizational weaknesses as part of an attack—can
be more successful than purely technological approaches is not new, it has
seen something of a resurgence of interest as "Bring your own device" and
social media policies have become increasingly commonplace.

Understanding security as an enabler of business—as a process that supports the everyday work of society both online and off—means recognizing
the ways that information technologies have been invisibly woven into
social practices. Without this understanding, organizations find themselves
unable to respond effectively to some forms of attack. All of this, as any
information assurance professional can tell you, is nothing new—and yet
this understanding of the interplay between the social and the technical
in terms of security has yet to be transferred to the spaces of everyday life
beyond the adult world of business. The dominant modes of managing risk
enable business practices, but they disable the practices of everyday life. As
I have argued throughout this book, the apparatus of youth Internet safety
separates online and offline contexts and polices the social lives of youth
by regulating visible online activity. Combined with the shrinking of spaces
within which young people can operate free of adult surveillance or management and the expansion of the developmental/neurobiological categories of childhood, children and teenagers (and arguably many adults) are
left without a space where they can be something other than the representative of an ideal workforce. As predicted by security and usability experts,
these populations look for workarounds or stay away from online spaces to
avoid misunderstandings or further drama.

Young people have long found workarounds for the forms of security imposed on them—particularly when very restrictive practices are in place. Although some engage in technical measures (such as using proxy servers to circumvent filters or disabling monitoring software), the simplest path is to move into online spaces that lack the architecture for tracking or monitoring users. Studies on the demographics of Facebook, a platform that increasingly insists on real names and is populated by adults, suggest that it appears to be losing teenagers and twenty-somethings ("Teens Continue" 2015; Saul 2014). As noted by Mary Madden et al. (2013, 2),

teens ... have waning enthusiasm for Facebook, disliking the increasing adult presence, people sharing excessively, and stressful "drama," but they keep using it because participation is an important part of overall teenage socializing.

Perhaps recognizing this, software developers have recently launched applications and platforms that allow anonymous, temporary, and often location-based messaging between users—and provide technological means for limiting some risky elements of online communication. Snapchat allows for relatively temporary picture and video messaging with limited reach. YikYak provides a location-based anonymous kind of forum. Other apps, such as Kik, provide a popular space that adults are relatively unaware of (and likely have some difficulty navigating). Kik (2015) has claimed that "Over 40% of US teens and young adults use Kik to connect with their friends." As discussed in chapter 7, some young people have decided to avoid all social activities online.

Although it is not clear the extent to which there is an ongoing youth exodus from Facebook, as its adult population grows, its social positioning among young users will undoubtedly continue to change. A site that originally was used only by Harvard University undergraduates (boyd 2012) is increasingly populated by adults. Put differently, Facebook is no longer cool—although it will undoubtedly remain a widely used platform by both teens and adults into the foreseeable future. If the practices of the parents discussed in chapter 6 are any indication, many young people will feel the need to maintain a Facebook presence simply to provide adults with a more public version of themselves to monitor. Coolness itself is a concept that is constructed and expressed relative to generational boundaries, historically as a form of "resistance to subjugation and humiliation" (Pountain and Robins 2000, 12). As such, the cool places for youth to socialize will always be those with relatively less adult surveillance, which drives teenagers to adopt social applications and platforms that provide few, if any, substantially new features—other than freedom from parental surveillance. New applications that are designed to seem youthful and modern both entice youth and limit adoption by older generations, providing a neatly segmented demographic for advertisers and data brokers. The construction of adolescent cool by marketers is no longer simply about positioning youth as consumers who purchase their way to an identity that is separate from adults. It further positions young consumers as generators of valuable data. Websites with social applications and platforms carry more and more placeholders and advertisements—perhaps a sign that mobile applications have become more relevant for many young people than the Web. Indeed, most of the Kik Web site promotes data collection and marketing services to brand managers and developers, and one page on the site suggests that marketers should use the service to "STOP COLLECTING. START CONNECTING" (Kik 2015).

Both the adults and young people who participated in the study agreed that young people require and seek out adult guidance in navigating the challenges of their everyday lives. At issue is the technology that is used to provide this guidance—the mechanisms that we choose to foster and produce new members of society. By restricting and circumscribing young lives, the instrumental relationships of youth Internet safety discourses reproduce the conditions of youth vulnerability and violence. The continued securing of youth and childhood online further constrains the spaces within which youth may occupy free of surveillance, delegitimates situated perspectives and knowledges, and instills suspicion and distrust into family and peer relationships. As childhood is secured, so too does it expand, as developmental categories delay the start of adulthood (Arnett 2000). Emerging adulthood then requires emerging technologies of adult surveillance and supervision (Hofer et al. 2009). The restricting and securing of young people drive their search for workarounds and cool new spaces, identities, and relationships that allow new forms of agency and control. Any visible transgressions of childhood—the risky and violent behaviors of youth—are framed in terms of technologies and underdeveloped brains rather than in terms of structure and power. The children and teenagers who retain a presence on existing "uncool" online spaces are placed under the continuous and anticipatory gaze of future employers, and those who seek out spaces free from adults open their social lives to the predictive analytics of brand managers and marketers. Through the persistent, increasingly penetrating gaze of the future employer, young people lose the capacity for free expression and action. As Jonathan Zittrain (2008, 212) describes:

Today we are all becoming politicians. People in power, whether at parliamentary debates or press conferences, have learned to stick to carefully planned talking points, accepting the drawbacks of appearing stilted and saying little of substance in exchange for the benefits of predictability and stability. Ubiquitous sensors threaten to push everyone toward treating each public encounter as if it were a press conference, creating fewer spaces in which citizens can express their private selves.

This trend toward caution has undoubtedly not been lost on youth, particularly as online reputation management has become more prevalent in Internet safety curricula. As one student survey respondent wrote when responding to the final open-ended question:

The internet is an amazing tool for modern day Americans. It has created a instant access to almost all the information in the world. but at the same time it has exposed most Americans so we as a nation must learn how to control our private lifes on and now off the internet

Regardless of the intent of those working to secure critical national infrastructure, such efforts produce a form of security that emerges from deeper ties between government and private industry and largely excludes families, schools, and youth. Cybersecurity is conceptualized as a force for enabling business practices (Norman 2009) and is not yet one that enables the practice of everyday life for youth. The results are forms of security and safety that do not allow for what Julie E. Cohen (2012, 223) has described as "human flourishing in a networked world." It should be unsurprising, then, that the forms of education provided to parents and young people disconnect online and offline lives in ways that produce observable subjects and largely eschew any critical discussion of mass data collection, advertising practices, digital labor, or alternatives to Western concepts of intellectual property. Although claiming to provide the tools and resources that can develop a generation of engaged twenty-first-century cybercitizens, those who shape youth Internet safety discourses seem intent on producing a generation of compliant twenty-first-century cyberlaborers. Rather than acknowledging that young people engage in behaviors that are irrelevant to their ability to be productive members of society—behaviors that many adults engaged in when they were young—we instead encourage them to avoid improprieties that a future employer might find problematic.

Toward a (Cyber)Safety of Everyday Life

As has been noted throughout this book, children and teenagers both want and need adult guidance in navigating their everyday lives. The question becomes how we might conceptualize a better form of youth (cyber)safety education. First, a (cyber)safety of everyday life must recognize the deep interconnections between online and offline socialities. Attempts to keep young people safe must reconnect cybersafety and offline safety because the two are inseparable. There can be no simple escape from the power relations and subjectivities that condition everyday life. Information technologies provide people with new and extended forms of social interaction that produce new forms of vulnerability and risk, and these risks warrant attention—but in ways that recognize that online sociality is often a result of, contributor to, or otherwise woven throughout offline social problems. Internet safety problems are rarely confined to online social platforms, and the young people who are most at risk offline are also those who are at most risk online (boyd 2014; Congressional Internet Advisory Committee Forum 2007; Internet Safety Technical Task Force 2008). Because of this, fostering relationships and communities that support youth, both online and off, must be a critical component of any form of (cyber)safety education. Citing the work of Jane Jacobs (1961), danah boyd (2014) suggests that a form of community-grounded, social monitoring might be encouraged through the concept of concerned "eyes on the street." For boyd (2014, 127), the online and offline quarantining of youth from adults places young people at risk and widens generational and contextual divides: "Instead of trying to distance ourselves from teens in this new media, we have a unique opportunity to leverage visibility and face the stark and complex dynamics that shape teens' lives head on. … Fear is not the solution, empathy is."

Protecting youth online requires establishing forms of community support through relationships of respect and mutual understanding rather than of instrumental surveillance. Internet safety education for both youth and adults should focus not on risks, vulnerabilities, and crimes but rather on lines of communication between youth and adults. Although youth Internet safety curricula universally provide materials that aim to do this, such materials are quickly pushed aside as fears of bullies, predators, and inappropriate information dominate presentations and videos. Beyond discussions of the materials, there are few opportunities to place both young people and adults in the same room to discuss their perspectives on risk and the Internet.

In her work on the architectures of security and control, Julie E. Cohen (2012, 5), provides a framework for developing information architectures that foster what she describes as the play of everyday life:

Play is related to rule structure in a way that is inverse and inherently interstitial; it is a function of the spaces that the constraints leave unoccupied. Understanding capabilities for human flourishing as inextricably linked to the structural attributes of the networked information environment—to its semantic and physical architectures and particularly to its interstitial structure—points toward three conditions that are necessary to enable their development. Those conditions are access to knowledge, operational transparency, and semantic discontinuity.

For Cohen, play is not simply a form of juvenile activity. It is a critical element of everyday human existence that takes place between the machinations of institutional subjugation and is fundamental to resistance and creativity. The designs of technological systems are key to youth safety— not merely because people require protection from the dark forces of the Internet but because they must be provided with technological tools that allow for "safer" power relations and subjectivities, both online and off. For Cohen, any such system must first provide access to knowledge: a user of the system must have enough information to engage in the critical activity of play. Second, systems must be transparent: they clearly outline surveillance practices, the limits of information flow within the network, and the underlying design principles that allow them to operate. Finally, systems must provide a level of semantic discontinuity: their flexibility and unpredictability must allow creative and critical practices to emerge, while actively widening gaps between social contexts.

Generally, any move to protect youth must maintain these conditions of human flourishing. Most importantly, young people must have access to knowledge. This is certainly the goal of existing youth Internet safety programs, but as I argue in chapter 5, the forms of safety information provided to young people are limited and sometimes distorted. Young Internet users require access to information about the threats posed by predators and bullies and by the posting of inappropriate material online, but they also need information about intellectual property, algorithmic culture, and mass surveillance. Increasing access to knowledge in ways that promote youth safety must involve a variety of pedagogical methods that move past the predictable assemblies provided by law enforcement officials or district attorneys described in chapters 4 and 5. Although law enforcement officers perform an important role in protecting youth online, their role also fosters a view of young people as victims, criminals, and informants, providing them with an often distorted understanding of the law and the everyday risks they face.

The shift from top-down, banking models of safety education then requires a move towards more learner-centered, participatory modes of learning. To produce a form of youth safety that moves beyond concepts which implicitly divide online and offline lives, so too must youth be provided with the tools and resources to critically make sense of their own social contexts. In this regard, media literacy operates only as a means to foster a critical social awareness, providing youth with a range of platforms through which to make sense of their positions through the production of culture. There can be no Internet safety or digital citizenship without critical media literacy. Youth should be provided with the means and opportunity to reinterpret and reimagine safety concepts, and policies from their own situated positions.

Children and teenagers should also be informed of the ways that their lives are shaped by surveillance practices—including the forms of adult supervision that they face and also the data collection done by the applications and networks that they interact with. This is in many ways inseparable from Cohen's insistence upon semantic discontinuity, which here would suggest that young people have spaces, online and off, which are largely free from the threat of adult surveillance. This is not to say that youth should not be monitored or provided with guidance, but rather that youth should have opportunities to make sense of their own lives relatively free from concern that their activities will be reinterpreted through the dual lenses of adult instrumentalism and appropriateness. As mentioned previously, young people are already seeking these spaces out and incorporating them into everyday social life. While platforms such as YikYak, Yeti, and Kik all variously support forms of potentially harmful interactions between youth, as I have argued throughout this book, these forms of violence are symptomatic of much larger social problems—the apps merely make these symptoms more visible.

Beyond mere context collapse, however, the principle of semantic discontinuity suggests that sociotechnical architectures be imperfect and incomplete in ways that afford cultural repurposing and control of personal information. On one hand, this requires that the systems that facilitate social interaction and media production imperfectly protect copyright. On the other, the principle requires that the data collected from children and teens as they use these platforms be shared and circulated among other institutions in limited ways. Compared to other forms of concerns over youth and the Internet, relatively little attention has been paid to the ways data is collected from young people and used in other contexts. Indeed, issues of data collection, privacy, and algorithmic control affect the whole of society, and to date, have gone relatively unnoticed by the news media and policymakers (Pasquale 2015). As discussed previously in the chapter, the online social spaces of youth are increasingly marketed to advertisers as tools for providing critical insight into teenage buying behaviors, anxieties, and social lives. Children and teens are perceived to be incapable of making decisions about who to speak with online, but fully capable of making rational consumer decisions in a predatory, often toxic advertising media landscape.

Related to these efforts is first, the need for adults to take youth perspectives seriously when they develop safety policies and curricula so that these materials respond to safety needs and concerns articulated by young people rather than only the needs of adults. Not only would this approach respond more directly to the problems that young people perceive, but it would incorporate youth concepts and terminology into forms of safety education in ways that better connect to the lives of youth. Similarly, adults must take more seriously the platforms and cultures of youth online. Young people are not simply wasting time online, they are actively engaged in the political struggles and cultural activities that allow them to negotiate their everyday social arenas. If we want youth to take us seriously, we must also take them and the things that they choose to do seriously. Neither adults nor kids universally "know better," but it should be possible to combine youth and adult perspectives to develop safety curricula that youth do not immediately dismiss or otherwise laugh at.

Second, when young people's perspectives are taken seriously, they gain a basic level of power and respect. As I argue in chapter 5, increasing restrictions on tweens and teenagers' access to adult culture and independent mobility have led to feelings of disempowerment and could be a factor in their violent behaviors. Allowing young people to participate in the processes that shape and regulate their lives may rework some of the social conditions that produce violent and otherwise risky behaviors among youth both online and off. This is one of the many goals of critical media literacy, and other forms of digitally supported learning which require a considerable rebalancing of classroom power relations from the outset (Ito et al. 2013).

Third, actively listening to youth as they describe the problems they face online may mitigate some of the problems that emerge when adults assume that all young people approach information technologies in the same ways and for the same purposes. For this reason, the United Nations International Children's Emergency Fund (UNICEF) began to survey young people in several developing countries to understand youth Internet safety issues as they emerged from local contexts and patterns of adoption (UNICEF 2011). A number of UNICEF digital citizenry and safety research projects have been completed internationally, and they have demonstrated significant differences in the risks and potentials of information technologies faced by children and teenagers in various countries. These trends of technology use can be seen at the more local level as well, and the needs of young people are poorly served when they are provided with curricula that fail to connect broader social concerns to local problems and challenges.

Crashing Youth Internet Safety

In constituting youth Internet safety problems as a dangerous combination of the endless potentialities of information technologies and developing brains, we mask the complexities of youth/adult social interactions that produce forms of victimization and violence, and we squander an important opportunity. In describing technologies as a "form of life," Langdon Winner (1986, 6–7) sees a similar form of opportunity:

The kinds of things we are apt to see as "mere" technological entities become much more interesting and problematic if we begin to observe how broadly they are involved in conditions of social and moral life. It is true that recurring patterns of life's activity (whatever their origins) tend to become unconscious processes taken for granted. ... There is, however, one point at which we may become aware of a pattern taking shape—the very first time we encounter it.

Winner provides an example of an encounter with a student who requested an extension on his homework deadline after a computer crash—the first of many similar requests that Winner has received. The disorientation of being confronted with a new form of technology-mediated situation allowed Winner to examine the network of social and technical relations at work in the moral negotiation of extending a deadline. Winner extends the concept of the "crash" by using the term to describe the abrupt collision of everyday, unconscious social life with new, technology-mediated forms of interaction.

For Winner, the crash is a moment for reflecting primarily on the forms of life that technology makes possible and is something of an underdeveloped concept in his work. I argue that crashes are events that throw the social relations made possible by a form of technology into relief and that problematize relations that have been otherwise hidden as everyday elements of social life. Youth Internet safety panics can be read as the means for making sense of technological crashes as the smooth functioning of entrenched disciplinary institutions is interrupted by the introduction of control technologies. They represent the "moral negotiations that accompany technological change" (Winner 1986, 7) if the negotiations are notably brief and reproduce dominant power/knowledge relations. The practices and risks of online sociality lend new visibility to existing social practices, and youth Internet safety discourses renaturalize those practices through psychological and technological explanations. They create biologically and technologically determinist narratives of risk that claim that the "natural" states of childhood are affected negatively by technology and require the further regulation. Explaining online sociality in terms of youth Internet safety diverts attention away from social explanations and shields and reconstitutes the disciplinary technologies of governance. The disorienting experience of the crash becomes not a moment for critical reflection but rather a moment for panicked action and new control technologies that extend entrenched disciplinary technologies. Rather than examining the power relations that produce youth violence or career-ending inappropriate youth behaviors, we instead sensitize youth to the presence of cyberbullies and explain to them that there can be no mistakes in a newly technologized world.

In a parent focus group, one participant told a story from his own youth that contrasted the familiar actions of his generation against those of today's young people:

What used to be an embarrassment that was localized may be spread a little bit like a virus, and more people find out about it. It's instantaneous now. When I went to high school on Long Island, there was these guys who made a sex tape in someone's basement. ... Back then it was mortifying. My parents were devout Catholics: "We don't talk about that. It's a sin." But it got isolated, and they basically—the parents— and the school was able to clamp down the information. That was it. Nobody saw it. A few select people saw it. It never went beyond. Now it's online.

This is a key example of a crash. This parent described interlocking disciplinary institutions—the family, the school, the church—that mobilized to "clamp down" on the otherwise "mortifying" actions of youth, limiting the number of people who saw the sex tape and preventing the spread of information to future employers. Today, the uncontrolled reach of networked publics problematizes the disciplinary machinery of citizenship, and information escapes before it can be "clamped down," producing a permanent and public online record. The parent seemed to acknowledge that young people (and adults) engage in behavior that can be considered inappropriate or career-ending and that such behavior need not be the end of an otherwise productive life. The larger problem was not in the act itself but in the possibility that the act would become public.

Again, the focus group sessions that I conducted were on online safety, and the parent provided this story only when considering the potential problems of online safety. By examining the crash of disciplinary technology and information technology, the social positioning of adults and youth became visible. In this case, youth Internet safety discourses renegotiated the moral boundaries of youth behavior in ways that sought to prevent children and teenagers from posting inappropriate content online and, by extension, from engaging in such behavior at all. Online social applications have become the new basement, and youth Internet safety discourses do not question whether they should be policed or why we do the policing in the first place.

Through the limits placed on youth mobility and autonomy, combined with the visibility afforded by new technologies, we find ourselves confronted with the social realities of youth life. For generations, the social lives of young people have been cordoned off, forced into the invisible spaces between the school and home, and otherwise made problematic in ways that have been made invisible as good parenting practices. We both can and should use the critical moments provided by the crash of technologies to reexamine the normally invisible social construction of childhood, the ways in which we police the lives of youth, and the potential harms these forms of policing might produce. As Valerie Walkerdine (2004, 117–118) explains:

The issue is rather to understand that childhood is always produced as an object in relation to power. Thus, there can be no timeless truth, sociological or psychological, about childhood. There can rather be understandings of how childhood is produced at any one time and place and an imperative to understand what kinds of childhood we want to produce, if indeed we want childhood at all.

Winner suggests that tangible technologies and technological systems should be examined as producers of social life, and so too should the technologies of childhood and citizenship. The crash of technology therefore becomes not a moment for examining the forms of childhood that we create for youth or the ways that doing so produces various forms of citizenry but instead a moment for further penetrating into and policing the lives of youth. As the moral negotiations that surround youth and information technologies settle and as the technologies themselves increasingly become taken for granted, we slowly lose the opportunities for critical change that such crashes and critical moments afford.

References

Abernathy, J. 1990. "Computer Porno: A Keystroke Away. Tax-Funded Research Link Also Home to the Sexually Explicit." *Houston Chronicle*, June 10, 1.

Abukhadra, L. 2013. "Rachel's Challenge Won't Solve Our Problems." *South High Southerner*, March 13. http://www.shsoutherner.net/opinion/2013/03/13/rachels -challenge-wont-solve-our-problems.

Adams, P. C. 1997. "Cyberspace and Virtual Places." *Geographical Review* 87 (2): 155–171. doi:10.2307/216003.

Adams, V., M. Murphy, and A. E. Clarke. 2009. "Anticipation: Technoscience, Life, Affect, Temporality." *Subjectivity* 28 (1): 246–265. doi:10.1057/sub.2009.18.

Albrechtslund, A. 2008. "Online Social Networking as Participatory Surveillance." *First Monday* 13 (3). http://firstmonday.org/ojs/index.php/fm/article/view/2142.

Allen, C., dir. 1983. "Programmed for Murder." *Whiz Kids*. CBS, October 5.

Allen, K. P. 2014. "Tweeting, Texting, and Facebook Postings: Stirring the Pot with Social Media to Make Drama. Case Study and Participant Observation." *Qualitative Report* 19 (2): 1–24.

Alparone, F. R., and M. G. Pacilli. 2012. "On Children's Independent Mobility: The Interplay of Demographic, Environmental, and Psychosocial Factors." *Children's Geographies* 10 (1): 109–22. doi:10.1080/14733285.2011.638173.

Ambert, A.-M. 1986. "Sociology of Sociology: The Place of Children in North American Sociology." *Sociological Studies of Child Development* 1: 11–31.

Ariès, P. 1965. *Centuries of Childhood: A Social History of Family Life*. Trans. R. Baldick. New York: Vintage.

Arnett, J. J. 2000. "Emerging Adulthood: A Theory of Development from the Late Teens through the Twenties." *American Psychologist* 55 (5): 469–480. doi:10.1037/0003-066X.55.5.469.

Baez, B., and S. Talburt. 2008. "Governing for Responsibility and with Love: Parents and Children between Home and School." *Educational Theory* 58 (1): 25–43. doi:10.1111/j.1741-5446.2007.00274.x.

Bauman, A. S. 1994. "Computer at Nuclear Lab Used for Access to Porn." *Los Angeles Times*, July 12. http://articles.latimes.com/print/1994-07-12/news/mn-14800 _1_computer-crime.

Bauman, S., and A. Bellmore. 2014. "New Directions in Cyberbullying Research." *Journal of School Violence* 14 (1): 1–10. doi:10.1080/15388220.2014.968281.

Being Mommy. 2013. "Our Moms Just Had an Internet Safety Talk" (photos). Facebook, December 3. https://www.facebook.com/beingmommy/photos/a.11166 1798905203.16443.102662719805111/595445913860120/?type=1, accessed February 12, 2015.

Belsey, B. 2003. www.cyberbullying.ca,accessed March 10, 2013.

Bennett, S., K. Maton, and L. Kervin. 2008. "The 'Digital Natives' Debate: A Critical Review of the Evidence." *British Journal of Educational Technology* 39 (5): 775–786. doi:10.1111/j.1467-8535.2007.00793.x.

Bergstein, B. 2013. "Parents: Don't Panic about Your Kids' Social Media Habits." *MIT Technology Review*, December 12. http://www.technologyreview.com/qa/522421/ parents-dont-panic-about-your-kids-social-media-habits, accessed March 11, 2015.

Berson, I. R., and M. J. Berson. 2005. "Challenging Online Behaviors of Youth: Findings from a Comparative Analysis of Young People in the United States and New Zealand." *Social Science Computer Review* 23 (1): 29–38. doi:10.1177/ 0894439304271532.

Blackburn, M. 2012. "Tech #20: Computers—Making Stupid Kids Smart." *Miriam L. Blackburn Life* (blog). http://miriaml-blackburnlife.blogspot.com/2012/10/tech-20 -computers-making-stupid-kids.html, accessed February 18, 2015.

Blake, J. 2009. "How I Got Taken by a Work-at-Home Scam." CNN.com, January 7. http://articles.cnn.com/2009-01-07/living/home.scams_1_work-at-home-scammers -data-entry-job?_s=PM:LIVING, accessed March 21, 2011.

BloomBecker, J. 1984. "Computer Crime Update: The View as We Exit 1984." *Western New England Law Review* 7: 627.

Boser, S. 2007. "Power, Ethics, and the IRB Dissonance over Human Participant Review of Participatory Research." *Qualitative Inquiry* 13 (8): 1060–1074.

Boston Globe Glossary. 1983. Glossary, s.v. "hacker." *Boston Globe*, November 14, 1.

boyd, d. 2007. "Why Youth (Heart) Social Network Sites: The Role of Networked Publics in Teenage Social Life." In *Youth, Identity, and Digital Media*, ed. David Buckingham, 119–142. Cambridge, MA: MIT Press.

boyd, d. 2008. "Taken out of Context: American Teen Sociality in Networked Publics." PhD diss., University of California, Berkeley. http://www.danah.org/papers/TakenOutOfContext.pdf.

boyd, d. 2009. "Internet Safety Technical Task Force Report." *Apophenia* (blog), February 20. http://www.zephoria.org/thoughts/archives/2009/01/20/internet_safety.html

boyd, d. 2012. "White Flight in Networked Publics: How Race and Class Shaped American Teen Engagement with MySpace and Facebook." In *Race after the Internet*, ed. L. Nakamura and P. Chow-White, 203–222. New York: Routledge.

boyd, d. 2014. *It's Complicated: The Social Lives of Networked Teens*. New Haven, CT: Yale University Press.

Brand, S. 1974. *II Cybernetic Frontiers*. New York: Random House.

Brown, S. 2005. *Understanding Youth and Crime: Listening to Youth?* 2nd ed. Philadelphia: Open University Press.

Buckingham, D., and H. Strandgaard Jensen. 2012. "Beyond 'Media Panics.'" *Journal of Children and Media* 6 (4): 413–429. doi:10.1080/17482798.2012.740415.

Buzan, B., O. Wæver, and J. de Wilde. 1998. *Security: A New Framework for Analysis*. Boulder, CO: Lynne Rienner.

Callon, M. 1986. "Some Elements of a Sociology of Translation: Domestication of the Scallops and the Fishermen of St Brieuc Bay." In *Power, Action and Belief: A New Sociology of Knowledge?*, ed. J. Law, 196–223. London: Routledge; http://ionesco.sciences-po.fr/com/moodledata/3/Callon_SociologyTranslation.pdf.

Campbell, N. 2000. *Using Women: Gender, Drug Policy, and Social Justice*. New York: Routledge.

Campbell, N. 2004. "Technologies of Suspicion: Coercion and Compassion in Post-Disciplinary Surveillance Regimes." *Surveillance and Society* 2 (1): 78–92.

Cannon, R. 1996. "The Legislative History of Senator Exon's Communications Decency Act: Regulating Barbarians on the Information Superhighway." *Federal Communications Law Journal* 49 (1996): 51–94. http://www.repository.law.indiana.edu/fclj/vol49/iss1/3.

Castañeda, C. 2002. *Figurations: Child, Bodies, Worlds*. Durham, NC: Duke University Press.

Child Online Protection Act (COPA). 1998. Hearing on the Child Online Protection Act, Pub. L. No. H.R. 3783, statement of M. Oxley. http://www.copacommission.org/commission/amended.shtml.

Children's Internet Protection Act (CIPA). 2000a. Hearing on Pub. L. No. S97, statement of Senator John McCain (Republican, Arizona). http://thomas.loc.gov/cgi-bin/query/D?c106:1./temp/~c106ipqhyW.

Children's Internet Protection Act (CIPA). 2000b. Senate Report 106-141 on the Children's Internet Protection Act (No. 106-141). Senate Committee on Commerce, Science, and Transportation. http://www.gpo.gov/fdsys/pkg/CRPT-106srpt141/html/CRPT-106srpt141.htm.

Clapton, G., V. Cree, and M. Smith. 2013. "Moral Panics, Claims-Making and Child Protection in the UK." *British Journal of Social Work* 43 (4): 803–812. doi:10.1093/bjsw/bct061.

Clark, L. S. 2009. "Digital Media and the Generation Gap." *Information Communication and Society* 12 (3): 388–407. doi:10.1080/13691180902823845.

Clark, M. 2013. "Forty-nine States Now Have Anti-Bullying Laws. How's That Working Out?" Governing.com, November 4. http://www.governing.com/news/headlines/49-States-Now-Have-Anti-Bullying-Laws-Hows-that-Working-Out.html, accessed March 15, 2015.

Clinton, B. 1996. President's Statement on the U.S. Supreme Court's Communications Decency Act (CDA) Decision. June 26. http://epic.org/free_speech/cda/clinton_cda_decision.html, accessed March 1, 2011.

Club Penguin. 2010. "Trolling." YouTube.com. http://www.youtube.com/watch?v=riWbGYZ2DGk&feature=youtube_gdata_player.

Club Penguin. n.d. "Parents." http://www.clubpenguin.com/parents, accessed February 17, 2015.

Cohen, J. E. 2012. *Configuring the Networked Self: Law, Code, and the Play of Everyday Practice*. New Haven, CT: Yale University Press.

Cohen, S. 1980. *Folk Devils and Moral Panic: The Creation of the Mods and Rockers*. Oxford: Martin Robertson.

Collins, G. 1983. "Children's Magazines for a Computer Age." *New York Times*, September 10, A48.

Common Sense Media. 2014. *Digital Bytes* . https://www.commonsensemedia.org/educators/digital-bytes, accessed March 15, 2015.

Communications Decency Act. 1994a. Senate Hearing on Exon Amendment No. 2404. *Congressional Record*, July 26, S40. http://www.gpo.gov/fdsys/pkg/CREC-1994-07-26/html/CREC-1994-07-26-pt1-PgS40.htm.

Communications Decency Act. 1994b. Senate Hearing on Amendments, item 491, comments by Senator Jim Exon (D-NE), August 9. http://www.exonlibrary.com/pdf/ip103con.pdf.

Computer Pornography and Child Exploitation Prevention Act. 1985a. Hearing on Pub. L. No. J-99-59, Senate Subcommittee on Juvenile Justice, Committee on the Judiciary, statement of Senator Paul Trible (R-VA). https://www.ncjrs.gov/pdffiles1/Digitization/103808NCJRS.pdf.

Computer Pornography and Child Exploitation Prevention Act. 1985b. S.1305. https://www.congress.gov/bill/99th-congress/senate-bill/1305, accessed January 20, 2015.

Connolly, M., and J. Ennew. 1996. "Introduction: Children out of Place." *Childhood: A Global Journal of Child Research* 3 (2): 131–145. doi:10.1177/0907568296003002001.

Corcoran, E. 1995. "Cybersensitivity? Did the Media Overreact to Pornography on the Internet?" *Washington Post*, June 28, C1.

Critcher, C. 2008. "Moral Panic Analysis: Past, Present and Future." *Sociology Compass* 2 (4): 1127–1144. doi:10.1111/j.1751-9020.2008.00122.x.

"Cyberbullying: Responding to the Challenges of Teens and Technology." 2010. Bethlehem Central School District, October. http://bethlehemschools.org/antibullying/cyberbullyingpanel_video.html.

"Cyberbullying Suicides." 2012. *USA Today*. http://mediagallery.usatoday.com/Cyberbullying+suicides/G3221, accessed March 15, 2015.

"Cyber Porn." 1995. *Time*, June 3, cover. http://www.time.com/time/covers/0,16641,19950703,00.html, accessed February 17, 2011.

Cyberporn and Children: The Scope of the Problem, the State of the Technology and the Need for Congressional Action. 1995a. Hearing before the Senate Judiciary Committee, statement of Senator Russ Feingold (D-WI). http://old.cdt.org/speech/cda/950724fein.html.

Cyberporn and Children: The Scope of the Problem the State of the Technology and the Need for Congressional Action. 1995b. Hearing on S. 892, Senate Committee on the Judiciary, statement of Senator Chuck Grassley (R-IA), July 24. http://www.eric.ed.gov/ERICWebPortal/contentdelivery/servlet/ERICServlet?accno=ED400779.

Cyberporn and Children: The Scope of the Problem, the State of the Technology and the Need for Congressional Action. 1995c. Hearing on Cyberporn and Children, Senate Committee on the Judiciary, statement of Senator Strom Thurmond (R-SC), July 24. http://www.eric.ed.gov/ERICWebPortal/contentdelivery/servlet/ERICServlet?accno=ED400779.

de Certeau, M. 1984. *The Practice of Everyday Life*. Trans. S. Rendall. Berkeley: University of California Press.

Deleting Online Predators Act. 2006. Hearing on H.R. 5319 before the House Committee on Energy and Commerce, statement of Greg Abbott, Texas district attorney.

Deleuze, G. 1992a. "Postscript on the Societies of Control." *October* 59: 3–7.

Deleuze, G. 1992b. "What Is a Dispositif?" In *Michel Foucault, Philosopher: Essays Translated from the French and German*, trans. T. J. Armstrong, 159–168. New York: Harvester Wheatsheaf.

Deleuze, G., and F. Guattari. 1987. *A Thousand Plateaus: Capitalism and Schizophrenia*. Minneapolis: University of Minnesota Press.

Deleuze, G., and D. Lapoujade. 2006. *Two Regimes of Madness: Texts and Interviews 1975–1995*, ed. D. Lapoujade. Trans. A. Hodges and M. Taormina. New York: Semiotext(e).

Denning, P. J. 1983. "Editorial: Moral Clarity in the Computer Age." *Communications of the ACM* 26 (10): 709–710. doi:10.1145/358413.358415.

Department of Homeland Security. 2015. "About the Critical Infrastructure Cyber Community C3 Voluntary Program." February 12. http://www.dhs.gov/about-critical-infrastructure-cyber-community-c%C2%B3-voluntary-program, accessed March 4, 2015.

Derbyshire, D. 2007. "How Children Lost the Right to Roam in Four Generations." *Daily Mail*, June 15. http://www.dailymail.co.uk/news/article-462091/How-children-lost-right-roam-generations.html, accessed April 27, 2011.

Dewitt, P. E., H. Block, W. Cole, and S. E. Epperson. 1995. "Online Erotica: On a Screen Near You." *Time*, July 3, 38–44. http://www.time.com/time/magazine/article/0,9171,983116,00.html.

DiAngelo, S. 2010. "Cyberbullying: Responding to the Challenges of Teens and Technology." Bethlehem Central School District, October. http://bethlehemschools.org/antibullying/cyberbullyingpanel_video.html.

DiNicola, L. 2006. "The Bundling of Geospatial Information with Everyday Experience." In *Surveillance and Security: Technological Politics and Power in Everyday Life*, ed. T. Monahan, 243–264. New York: Routledge.

Dolnick, E. 1983. "Technology Codes May Stop Computer Theft." *Boston Globe*, December 12, 1.

Donzelot, J. 1979. *The Policing of Families*. Trans. R. Hurley. New York: Pantheon Books.

Duggan, M., N. B. Ellison, C. Lampe, A. Lenhart, and M. Madden. 2015. "Social Media Update 2014." Pew Research Center, Berkman Center for Internet and Society, Harvard University, Cambridge, MA, January 9. http://www.pewinternet.org/2015/01/09/social-media-update-2014.

Eglash, R., J. L. Croissant, G. Di Chiro, and R. Fouché. 2004. *Appropriating Technology: Vernacular Science and Social Power*. Minneapolis: University of Minnesota Press.

Eskow, D., and L. Green. 1984. "Catching Computer Crooks." *Popular Mechanics* 161 (6): 63.

"Facebook to Texting: Parent Your Child's Digital Life." 2013. Presentation at PS 149, Queens, NY, October 4. http://events.nydailynews.com/jackson_heights_ny/ events/show/354141223-facebook-to-texting-parent-your-childs-digital-life, accessed October 8, 2013.

Farr, R. 1975. *The Electronic Criminals*. New York: McGraw-Hill.

Feingold, R. 1995. "House-Senate Conference on Telecommunications Reform Has Implications for First Amendment Application to the Internet." *Congressional Record*, October 13, S15152–S15153. http://www.gpo.gov/fdsys/pkg/CREC-1995-10-13/pdf/ CREC-1995-10-13-pt1-PgS15152.pdf

Fisk, N. W. 2011. "Trash Talk and Trusted Adults: An Analysis of Youth Internet Safety Discourses in New York State." PhD diss., Rensselaer Polytechnic Institute, Troy, NY.

Foucault, M. 1977. *Discipline and Punish: The Birth of the Prison*. Trans. A. Sheridan. New York: Pantheon Books.

Foucault, M. 1978. *The History of Sexuality*. Trans. R. Hurley. New York: Pantheon Books.

Foucault, M. 1980. *Power/Knowledge: Selected Interviews and Other Writings, 1972–1977*, ed. C. Gordon. Trans. C. Gordon, L. Marshall, J. Mepham, and K. Soper. New York: Pantheon Books.

Foucault, M. 1988. "The Danger of Child Sexuality." In *Politics, Philosophy, Culture: Interviews and Other Writings, 1977–1984*, ed. L. Kritzman. New York: Routledge.

Freire, P. 1968. *Pedagogy of the Oppressed*. New York: Seabury Press.

Frontline: Growing Up Online. 2008. *Frontline*. PBS Video. DVD.

Gabriel, F. 2013. *Deconstructing Youth: Youth Discourses at the Limits of Sense*. London: Palgrave Macmillan.

Galloway, A. R. 2004. *Protocol: How Control Exists after Decentralization*. Cambridge, MA: MIT Press; http://www.books24x7.com/marc.asp?bookid=12929.

Gardner, H., and K. Davis. 2013. *The App Generation: How Today's Youth Navigate Identity, Intimacy, and Imagination in a Digital World*. New Haven, CT: Yale University Press.

Garland, D. 2008. "On the Concept of Moral Panic." *Crime, Media, Culture* 4 (1): 9–30.

Gibson, W. 1982. "Burning Chrome." *Omni* 4 (10): 72.

Gillespie, T. 2007. *Wired Shut: Copyright and the Shape of Digital Culture*. Cambridge, MA: MIT Press. http://search.ebscohost.com/login.aspx?direct=true&scope=site&db=nlebk&db=nlabk&AN=190972.

Glickman, D. 1984. *Computer and Communications Security and Privacy*. Washington, DC: Science and Technology, Subcommittee on Transportation, Aviation and Materials.

Guins, R. 2009. *Edited Clean Version: Technology and the Culture of Control*. Minneapolis: University of Minnesota Press.

Gunkel, D. J. 2001. *Hacking Cyberspace*. Boulder, Colo.: Westview Press.

Hall, S., C. Critcher, T. Jefferson, J. Clarke, and B. Roberts. 1978. *Policing the Crisis: Mugging, the State, and Law and Order*. London: Macmillan.

Hansen, C. 2004a. "Dangerous Web." *Dateline NBC*, November 11. NBC. YouTube.com. https://www.youtube.com/watch?v=9AXDvE_d6ow&feature=youtube_gdata_player.

Hansen, C. 2004b. "Dangers Children Face Online." *Dateline NBC*, November 11. NBC. http://www.msnbc.msn.com/id/6083442, accessed April 27, 2009.

Hansen, C. 2007. "Online Enemies Already in Your Home." *Dateline NBC*, March 14. http://www.msnbc.msn.com/id/17584928, accessed February 19, 2009.

Haraway, D. 1994. *Modest Witness, Second Millennium: FemaleMan Meets OncoMouse*. New York: Routledge.

Harmetz, A. 1983. "Hollywood Forecast: Best Summer at Box Office." *New York Times*, May 16, C15.

Hayasaki, E., and J.-R. Chong. 2003. "Parents Rally to Stop 'Cyber Bullying.'" *Los Angeles Times*, April 17, B1.

Hebdige, D. 1993. *Subculture: The Meaning of Style*. London: Routledge.

Heins, M. 2008. *Not in Front of the Children: Indecency, Censorship, and the Innocence of Youth*. Piscataway, NJ: Rutgers University Press.

Henderson, A. C., S. M. Harmon, and J. Houser. 2010. "A New State of Surveillance? An Application of Michel Foucault to Modern Motherhood." *Surveillance and Society* 7 (3–4): 231–247.

Hendrick, H. 1997. "Constructions and Reconstructions of British Childhood: An Interpretative Survey, 1800 to the Present." In *Constructing and Reconstructing Childhood: Contemporary Issues in the Sociological Study of Childhood*, 2nd ed., ed. A. James and A. Prout, 33–60. London: Routledge.

Herring, S. 2008. "Questioning the Generational Divide: Technological Exoticism and Adult Constructions of Online Youth Identity." In *Youth, Identity and Digital Media*, ed. D. Buckingham, 71–92. Cambridge, MA: MIT Press.

Hess, D. 1995. *Science and Technology in a Multicultural World*. New York: Columbia University Press.

Hillman, M. 2006. "Children's Rights and Adults' Wrongs." *Children's Geographies* 4 (1): 61–67. doi:10.1080/14733280600577418.

Hinduja, S., and J. W. Patchin. 2015. "State Cyberbullying Laws: A Brief Review of State Cyberbullying Laws and Policies." Cyberbullying Research Center, January 1. http://cyberbullying.us/state-cyberbullying-laws-a-brief-review-of-state-cyberbullying-laws-and-policies, accessed March 3, 2015.

Hofer, B., C. Souder, E. Kennedy, N. Fullman, and K. Hurd. 2009. "The Electronic Tether: Communication and Parental Monitoring during the College Years." In *Who's Watching? Daily Practices of Surveillance among Contemporary Families*, ed. M. K. Nelson and A. I. Garey, 277–294. Nashville, TN: Vanderbilt University Press.

Hollinger, R., and L. Lanza-Kaduce. 1988. "The Process of Criminalization: The Case of Computer Crime Laws." *Criminology* 26 (1): 101–126. doi:10.1111/j.1745-9125.1988.tb00834.x.

Holloway, S., and G. Valentine. 2001. *Cyberkids: Youth Identities and Communities in an On-line World*. Abingdon, UK: Routledge.

Hunter, M. 1983. "The Calendar." *New York Times*, September 26, B10.

International Pedophile and Child Emancipation (IPCE). 2010. "Welcome." http://www.ipce.info, accessed March 15, 2011.

Internet Keep Safe Coalition (IKSC). 2009a. "Privacy and Reputation Online: Parents." YouTube.com. https://www.youtube.com/watch?v=fvA8zza6njA&feature=youtube_gdata_player.

Internet Keep Safe Coalition (IKSC). 2009b. "Privacy and Reputation Online: Parents." iKeepSafe. http://www.ikeepsafe.org/videos/privacy-and-reputation-online-parents, accessed January 2, 2015.

Internet Online Summit: Focus on Children. 1997. Remarks of Vice President Al Gore, Washington, DC, December 2. http://www.kidsonline.org/archives/gore.shtml.

Internet Safety Technical Task Force. 2008. *Enhancing Child Safety and Online Technologies: Final Report of the Internet Safety Technical Task Force to the Multi-State Working Group of State Attorneys General of the United States*. Cambridge, MA: Berkman Center for Internet and Society, Harvard University, December 31. http://cyber.law.harvard.edu/sites/cyber.law.harvard.edu/files/ISTTF_Final_Report.pdf, accessed February 18, 2009.

"Internet 'Virus' Was Spawned by Our Rude Culture." 2010. *Wall Street Journal*, January 5, A16.

"It Gets Better." 2010. Dan and Terry. YouTube.com. http://www.youtube.com/watch?v=7IcVyvg2Qlo&feature=youtube_gdata_player.

Ito, M., S. Baumer, M. Bittanti, d. boyd, R. Cody, B. Herr-Stephenson, … L. Tripp. 2009. *Hanging Out, Messing Around, and Geeking Out: Kids Living and Learning with New Media*. Cambridge, MA: MIT Press.

Ito, M., K. Gutiérrez, S. Livingstone, B. Penuel, J. Rhodes, K. Salen, J. Schor, J. Sefton-Green, and S. C. Watkins. 2013. "Connected Learning: An Agenda for Research and Design." The Digital Media and Learning Research Hub Reports on Connected Learning. Irvine, CA: Digital Media and Learning Research Hub. http://dmlhub.net/wp-content/uploads/files/Connected_Learning_report.pdf.

Jacobs, J. 1961. *The Death and Life of Great American Cities*. New York: Random House.

James, A., C. Jenks, and A. Prout. 1998. *Theorizing Childhood*. New York: Teachers College Press.

James, A., and A. Prout, eds. 1997. *Constructing and Reconstructing Childhood: Contemporary Issues in the Sociological Study of Childhood*. 2nd ed. London: Routledge.

Jenkins, P. 1992. *Intimate Enemies: Moral Panics in Contemporary Great Britain*. New York: Aldine de Gruyter.

Johns, A. 2009. *Piracy: The Intellectual Property Wars from Gutenberg to Gates*. Chicago: University of Chicago Press.

Joint Statement on Key Principles of Social Networking Sites Safety. 2008. Statement signed by the Facebook chief privacy officer and the state attorneys general, May 8. http://www.state.tn.us/attorneygeneral/cases/facebook/facebookstatement.pdf.

Just the Facts about Online Youth Victimization. 2007. Congressional Internet Advisory Committee Forum. http://www.netcaucus.org/events/2007/youth/20070503transcript.pdf.

Karsten, L. 2005. "It All Used to Be Better? Different Generations on Continuity and Change in Urban Children's Daily Use of Space." *Children's Geographies* 3 (3): 275. doi:10.1080/14733280500352912.

Karsten, L., and W. van Vliet. 2006. "Increasing Children's Freedom of Movement: Introduction." *Children, Youth and Environments* 16 (1): 69–73.

Kellner, D., and J. Share. 2005. "Toward Critical Media Literacy: Core Concepts, Debates, Organizations, and Policy." *Discourse* 26 (3): 369–386. doi:10.1080/01596300500200169.

Kellner, D., and J. Share. 2007. "Critical Media Literacy Is Not an Option." *Learning Inquiry* 1 (1): 59–69. doi:10.1007/s11519-007-0004-2.

Kerrey, B. 1995. "Telecommunications Bill." *Congressional Record*, June 9, S8092–S8094. http://www.gpo.gov/fdsys/pkg/CREC-1995-06-09/pdf/CREC-1995-06-09-pt1-PgS8087-4.pdf.

Kik. 2015. "Partners: A New Way to Engage." Kik.com. http://www.kik.com/partners, accessed February 14, 2015.

Knowles, C. 1996. *Family Boundaries: The Invention of Normality and Dangerousness*. Toronto: University of Toronto Press.

Kornblum, J. 2007. "The Net: A Circuit of Safety Concerns." *USA Today*, November 8, 9D.

Kozakiewicz, A. 2007. Sex Crimes and the Internet: Hearing before the Committee on the Judiciary, 110th Congress, Washington, DC.

Krance, M., J. Murphy, and P. Elmer-Dewitt. 1983. "The 414 Gang Strikes Again." *Time*, August 29. http://www.time.com/time/magazine/article/0,9171,949797,00.html.

Kupchik, A., and T. Monahan. 2006. "The New American School: Preparation for Post-industrial Discipline." *British Journal of Sociology of Education* 27 (5): 617–622. doi:10.1080/01425690600958816.

Kurz, D. 2009. "'I Trust Them but I Don't Trust Them': Issues and Dilemmas in Monitoring Teenagers." In *Who's Watching? Daily Practices of Surveillance among Contemporary Families*, ed. M. K. Nelson and A. I. Garey, 260–276. Nashville, TN: Vanderbilt University Press.

Lair, D. J., K. Sullivan, and G. Cheney. 2005. "Marketization and the Recasting of the Professional Self: The Rhetoric and Ethics of Personal Branding." *Management Communication Quarterly: McQ* 18 (3): 307–343.

Lareau, A. 2003. *Unequal Childhoods: Class, Race, and Family Life*. Berkeley: University of California Press.

Lawson, S. 2012. "Putting the 'War' in Cyberwar: Metaphor, Analogy, and Cybersecurity Discourse in the United States." *First Monday* 17 (7). http://firstmonday.org/ojs/index.php/fm/article/view/3848.

Leahy, P. 1995. "Child Protection, User Empowerment, and Free Expression in Interactive Media Study Act." *Congressional Record*, April 7, S5548.

Lessig, L. 2008. *Remix: Making Art and Commerce Thrive in the Hybrid Economy*. New York: Penguin Press.

Levy, S. 2001. *Hackers: Heroes of the Computer Revolution*. New York: Penguin. (Originally published in 1984)

Levy, S. 2014. "'Hackers' and 'Information Wants to Be Free.'" *Backchannel*, November 21. https://medium.com/backchannel/the-definitive-story-of-information-wants-to-be-free-a8d95427641c, accessed January 26, 2015.

Ling, R. S. 2012. *Taken for Grantedness: The Embedding of Mobile Communication into Society*. Cambridge, MA: MIT Press. http://search.ebscohost.com/login.aspx?direct=true&scope=site&db=nlebk&db=nlabk&AN=502781.

Livingstone, S. 2002. *Young People and New Media Childhood and the Changing Media Environment*. Thousand Oaks, CA: Sage. http://public.eblib.com/EBLWeb/patron/?target=patron&extendedid=E_816287_0.

Livingstone, S. 2009. *Children and the Internet*. Cambridge, UK: Polity.

Livingstone, S., and M. Bober. 2006. "Regulating the Internet at Home: Contrasting the Perspectives of Children and Parents." In *Digital Generations: Children, Young People, and New Media*, ed. D. Buckingham and R. Willett, 93–114. Mahwah, NJ: Lawrence Erlbaum.

Livingstone, S., L. Haddon, A. Görzig, and K. Ólafsson. 2011. *Risks and Safety on the Internet: The Perspectives of European Children. Full Findings*. London: London School of Economics and EU Kids Online.

Livingstone, S., and E. Helsper. 2007. "Gradations in Digital Inclusion: Children, Young People and the Digital Divide." *New Media and Society* 9 (4): 671–696. doi:10.1177/1461444807080335.

Loveridge, J., and S. Cornforth. 2014. "The Ages of Consent: Re-working Consensual Frameworks in Postmodern Times." *International Journal of Qualitative Studies in Education* 27 (4): 454–471.

Lyon, D. 1993. "An Electronic Panopticon? A Sociological Critique of Surveillance Theory." *Sociological Review* 41 (4): 653–678. doi:10.1111/j.1467-954X.1993.tb00896.x.

Lyon, D. 2007. *Surveillance Studies: An Overview*. Malden, MA: Polity.

Mace, S. 1985. "Federal Bill Seeks to Ban Porno Boards." *InfoWorld* 7 (40) (October 7): 1.

Madden, M. 2013. "Teens Haven't Abandoned Facebook (Yet)." Pew Research Center, Berkman Center for Internet and Society, Harvard University, Cambridge, MA, August 15. http://www.pewinternet.org/2013/08/15/teens-havent-abandoned-facebook-yet.

Madden, M., A. Lenhart, S. Cortesi, U. Gasser, M. Duggan, A. Smith, and M. Beaton. 2013. "Teens, Social Media, and Privacy." Pew Research Center, Berkman Center for

Internet and Society, Harvard University, Cambridge, MA, May 21. http://www
.pewinternet.org/2013/05/21/teens-social-media-and-privacy.

Maitland, C., G. Stratton, S. Foster, R. Braham, and M. Rosenberg. 2013. "A Place for
Play? The Influence of the Home Physical Environment on Children's Physical
Activity and Sedentary Behaviour." *International Journal of Behavioral Nutrition and
Physical Activity* 10 (1): 99. doi:10.1186/1479-5868-10-99.

Making the Internet Safe for Kids: The Role of ISP's and Social Networking Sites.
2006a. House Committee on Energy and Commerce Hearing on Pub. L. No. 109-
123, statement of Representative Diana DeGette (D-CO). http://www.gpo.gov/fdsys/
pkg/CHRG-109hhrg30530/html/CHRG-109hhrg30530.htm.

Making the Internet Safe for Kids: The Role of ISP's and Social Networking Sites.
2006b. Hearing on Pub. L. No. 109-123, House Committee on Energy and Commerce, statement of Representative Bart Stupak (D-WI). http://www.gpo.gov/fdsys/
pkg/CHRG-109hhrg30530/html/CHRG-109hhrg30530.htm.

Making the Internet Safe for Kids: The Role of ISP's and Social Networking Sites.
2006c. Hearing on Pub. L. No 109-123, House Committee on Energy and Commerce, statement of Representative Ed Whitfield (R-KY). http://www.gpo.gov/fdsys/
pkg/CHRG-109hhrg30530/html/CHRG-109hhrg30530.htm.

MamaBear. 2015. MamaBear Family Safety. geoWaggle, Tampa, FL. https://play
.google.com/store/apps/details?id=com.geowaggle.mamabear&hl=en.

Marwick, A. E. 2008. "To Catch a Predator? The MySpace Moral Panic." *First
Monday* 13 (6). http://www.uic.edu/htbin/cgiwrap/bin/ojs/index.php/fm/article/
view/2152/1966.

Marwick, A. E. 2012. "The Public Domain: Surveillance in Everyday Life." *Surveillance and Society* 9 (4): 378–393.

Marwick, A. E., and d. boyd. 2011. "The Drama! Teen Conflict, Gossip, and Bullying
in Networked Publics." SSRN Scholarly Paper No. ID 1926349. Social Science
Research Network, Rochester, NY. http://papers.ssrn.com/abstract=1926349.

Marwick, A. E., and d. boyd. 2014. "'It's Just Drama': Teen Perspectives on Conflict
and Aggression in a Networked Era." *Journal of Youth Studies* 17 (9): 1187–1204. doi:1
0.1080/13676261.2014.901493.

McCarthy, C. 2007. "New Jersey Attorney General Subpoenas Facebook over Sex
Offender Data." *c/net*, October 2. http://www.cnet.com/news/new-jersey-attorney
-general-subpoenas-facebook-over-sex-offender-data, accessed March 1, 2015.

McDonald, N. C., A. L. Brown, L. M. Marchetti, and M. S. Pedroso. 2011. "U.S.
School Travel, 2009: An Assessment of Trends." *American Journal of Preventive Medicine* 41 (2): 146–51. doi:10.1016/j.amepre.2011.04.006.

McKean, K. 1983. "Whiz Kids in the Fast Lane." *Discover* 4 (5): 20–22, 27.

Miller, L. 1995. "Products Shield Kids from Adult Material On-line." *USA Today*, June 27, D1.

Miller, M. 1980. "Computer Whiz Kids at Work: They're Pros in a Whole New World." *Boston Globe*, October 12, 1.

"Milwaukee Discovers 'WarGamesmanship.'" 1983. *Newsweek*, August 22.

MinorMonitor. 2012. "About MinorMonitor: Parental Control Software, Internet Control, Online Predators." MinorMonitor. http://www.minormonitor.com/about, accessed February 1, 2015.

Mitchell, K. J., D. Finkelhor, and J. Wolak. 2003. "The Exposure of Youth to Unwanted Sexual Material on the Internet: A National Survey of Risk, Impact, and Prevention." *Youth and Society* 34 (3): 330–358. doi:10.1177/0044118X02250123.

Mitchell, K. J., L. Jones, D. Finkelhor, and J. Wolak. 2014. "Trends in Unwanted Sexual Solicitations: Findings from the Youth Internet Safety Studies." Crimes against Children Research Center, University of New Hampshire. http://www.unh
.edu/ccrc/pdf/Sexual%20Solicitation%201%20of%204%20YISS%20Bulletins%20
Feb%202014.pdf.

Monahan, T. 2006. "The Surveillance Curriculum: Risk Management and Social Control in the Neoliberal School." In *Surveillance and Security: Technological Politics and Power in Everyday Life*, ed. T. Monahan, 109–124. New York: Routledge.

Montgomery, K. 2007. *Generation Digital: Politics, Commerce, and Childhood in the Age of the Internet*. Cambridge, MA: MIT Press.

Morrow, V., and M. Richards. 1996. "The Ethics of Social Research with Children: An Overview1." *Children and Society* 10 (2): 90–105. doi:10.1111/j.1099-0860.1996.
tb00461.x.

Nathan, L., and F. Gallagher. 2015. "Why We're Moving from Online Safety to Digital Citizenship … and You Should Too." Webinar, January. http://engage.vevent.
com/production?eid=2519&seid=62.

National Center for Missing and Exploited Children (NCMEC). 2007. "Think Before You Post (Sarah)." YouTube.com. https://www.youtube.com/watch?v=4w4
_Hrwh2XI&feature=youtube_gdata_player.

National Center for Missing and Exploited Children (NCMEC). 2008. "Think before You Post (photo)." YouTube.com. https://www.youtube.com/watch?v=CE2Ru
-jqyrY&feature=youtube_gdata_player.

National Center for Missing and Exploited Children (NCMEC). 2011. "Out of Your Hands." YouTube.com. https://www.youtube.com/watch?v=DDiuR819EVU&feature
=youtube_gdata_player.

National Information Infrastructure. 1993. "Agenda for Action." http://clinton6 .nara.gov/1993/09/1993-09-15-the-national-information-infrastructure-agenda-for -action.html, accessed February 21, 2015.

National Research Council. 2002. *Youth, Pornography and the Internet*, ed. D. Thornburgh and H. Lin. Washington, DC: National Academies Press.

Nelson, M. K. 2010. *Parenting out of Control: Anxious Parents in Uncertain Times*. New York: New York University Press. http://site.ebrary.com/id/10386276.

Ness, C. D. 2010. *Why Girls Fight: Female Youth Violence in the Inner City*. New York: New York University Press. http://site.ebrary.com/id/10409385.

Net Nanny. 2002a. Home Page. NetNanny.com, October 28. https://web.archive. org/web/20021028124910/http://www.netnanny.com/index.html, accessed February 1, 2015.

Net Nanny. 2002b. Site Map. NetNanny.com, October 14. https://web.archive.org/ web/20021014212232/http://www.netnanny.com/index.html, accessed February 1, 2015.

Net Nanny. 2003. Home Page. NetNanny.com, April 1. https://web.archive.org/ web/20030401091331/http://www.netnanny.com/index.html, accessed February 1, 2015.

Net Nanny. 2014a. "Cyberbullies: Are You Creating Them?" NetNanny.com. http:// www.netnanny.com/assets/brochures/NetNanny-Infographic-Cyberbullies.jpg, accessed February 1, 2015.

Net Nanny. 2014b. Home Page. NetNanny.com. https://www.netnanny.com, accessed February 1, 2015.

NetSmartz. 2006a. "Profile Penalty." NSTeens.org. http://www.nsteens.org/Videos/ ProfilePenalty, accessed March 14, 2015.

NetSmartz. 2006b. "Survivor Diaries." NSTeens.org. http://www.nsteens.org/Videos/ SurvivorDiaries, accessed March 14, 2015.

NetSmartz. 2006c. "You Can't Take It Back." NSTeens.org. http://www.nsteens.org/ Videos/YouCantTakeItBack, accessed March 14, 2015.

NetSmartz. 2007. "Teens Talk Back: Cyberbullying." NSTeens.org. http://www .nsteens.org/Videos/Cyberbullying, accessed September 11, 2010.

NetSmartz. 2010a. "Internet Safety Basics." NetSmartz.org. http://www.netsmartz .org/StreamingPresentations/InternetSafetyBasics, accessed October 2, 2013.

NetSmartz. 2010b. "Know the Rules: Tell a Trusted Adult (Intermediate)." NetSmartz.org. http://cdn.netsmartz.org/activitycards/RWS_IM_KTR_TellTrustedAdult .pdf, accessed May 5, 2016.

NetSmartz. 2010c. "NetSmartz Workshop Resource Manual." NetSmartz.org. http://www.michaelcary.com/uploads/6/8/9/2/6892764/resourcemanual.pdf, accessed May 5, 2016.

NetSmartz. 2010d. "Tell a Trusted Adult." NetSmart.org. http://www.netsmartz.org/NetSmartzKids/TellAnAdult, accessed October 6, 2013.

NetSmartz. 2012a. "Tips for Teens." NetSmartz.org. http://cdn.netsmartz.org/tipsheets/tips_for_teens.pdf, accessed February 21, 2015.

NetSmartz. 2012b. "Two Kinds of Stupid." NSTeens.org. http://www.nsteens.org/Videos/TwoKindsOfStupid, accessed March 14, 2015.

NetSmartz. 2013a. "Internet Safety Presenter's Guide." NetSmartz.org. http://cdn.netsmartz.org/presentersguides/Presentation_Guide_Parents_EN.pdf, accessed May 5, 2016.

NetSmartz. 2013b. "Parents' Presentation." NetSmartz.org. http://www.netsmartz.org/Presentations/Parents,accessed January 2, 2015.

NetSmartz. 2013c. "Why Bystanders Matter." NetSmartz.org (blog), November 18. http://blog.netsmartz.org/post/67372269813/why-bystanders-matter, accessed March 16, 2015.

NetSmartz. 2014. "Stand by or Stand Up?" NSTeens.org. http://www.nsteens.org/Comics/StandByOrStandUp, accessed March 16, 2015.

NetSmartz. 2015. "Teaching Digital Citizenship." NetSmartz.org, January. http://www.netsmartz.org/Training., accessed March 16, 2015.

NetSmartz. (n.d.-a). "Offline Consequences." NSTeens.org. http://www.nsteens.org/Videos/OfflineConsequences, accessed September 11, 2010.

NetSmartz. (n.d.-b). "Parents and Guardians." NetSmartz.org. http://www.netsmartz.org/Parents, accessed January 2, 2015.

New York State Office of the Attorney General (NYS OAG). n.d. "Your Child's D.I.G.I.T.A.L. Life: Safety Tips for Parents." http://www.oag.state.ny.us/sites/default/files/pdfs/bureaus/internet_bureau/Handout_FINAL_Proof.pdf.

Nissenbaum, H. 2005. "Where Computer Security Meets National Security." *Ethics and Information Technology* 7 (2): 61–73. doi:10.1007/s10676-005-4582-3.

Norman, D. A. 2009. "The Way I See It: When Security Gets in the Way." *Interaction* 16 (6): 60–63. doi:10.1145/1620693.1620708.

Nunes, M. 1999. "Virtual Topographies: Smooth and Striated Cyberspace." In *Cyberspace Textuality: Computer Technology and Literary Theory*, ed. M.-L. Ryan, 61–77. Bloomington: Indiana University Press. http://www.cyberhead2010.net/nunes.html.

Obama, B. 2010. "It Gets Better." Speech. YouTube.com. https://www.youtube.com/watch?v=geyAFbSDPVk&feature=youtube_gdata_player.

Olweus, D. 2012. "Cyberbullying: An Overrated Phenomenon?" *European Journal of Developmental Psychology* 9 (5): 520–538. doi:10.1080/17405629.2012.682358.

Online Safety and Technology Working Group. 2010. "Youth Safety on a Living Internet." National Telecommunications and Information Administration, Washington, DC. http://www.ntia.doc.gov/advisory/onlinesafety/index.html.

Oswell, D. 1999. "The Dark Side of Cyberspace." *Convergence* 5 (4): 42–62. doi:10.1177/135485659900500404.

Palmås, K. 2010. "Predicting What You'll Do Tomorrow: Panspectric Surveillance and the Contemporary Corporation." *Surveillance and Society* 8 (3): 338–354.

Parker, D. B. 1976. *Crime by Computer*. New York: Scribner's.

Pasquale, F. 2015. *The Black Box Society: The Secret Algorithms That Control Money and Information*. Cambridge: Harvard University Press.

Paulson, A. 2003. "Internet Bullying." *Christian Science Monitor*, December 30. http://www.csmonitor.com/2003/1230/p11s01-legn.html.

Payne, R. 2008. "Virtual Panic: Children Online and the Transmission of Hharm." In *Moral Panics over Contemporary Children and Youth*, ed. C. Krinsky, 31–46. Farnham, UK: Ashgate.

Perez, S. 2014. "Mamabear Raises $1.4 Million for a Parenting App That Monitors Children's Social Media Use and More." *Tech Crunch*, July 21. http://social.techcrunch.com/2014/07/21/mamabear-raises-1-4-million-for-a-parenting-app-that-monitors-childrens-social-media-use-and-more.

Perverted Justice. 2014. Home Page. Perverted-Justice.com, August 5. http://www.perverted-justice.com, accessed March 1, 2015.

Piaget, J. 1971. "The Theory of Stages in Cognitive Development." *Measurement and Piaget: Proceedings of the CTB/McGraw-Hill Conference on Ordinal Scales of Cognitive Development*, ed. D. B. Green, M. P. Ford, and G. B. Flamer, 1–11. New York: McGraw-Hill.

Pollack, A. 1983. "Electronic Trespassers." *New York Times*, November 10, D2.

Poster, M. 2001. *What's the Matter with the Internet?* Minneapolis: University of Minnesota Press.

Pountain, D., and D. Robins. 2000. *Cool Rules: Anatomy of an Attitude*. London: Reaktion.

Prensky, M. 2001a. "Digital Natives, Digital Immigrants Part 1." *On the Horizon* 9 (5): 1–6.

Prensky, M. 2001b. "Digital Natives, Digital Immigrants Part 2." *On the Horizon* 9 (5): 1–6.

Protection of Children from Computer Pornography Act. 1995. Hearing on the Protection of Children from Computer Pornography Act of 1995, S. 892, comments of Senator Chuck Grassley (R-IA). *Congressional Record*, June 26, S9017–S9023. http://www.gpo.gov/fdsys/pkg/CREC-1995-06-26/pdf/CREC-1995-06-26-pt1-PgS9017-2.pdf.

Prout, A. 2003. "Participation, Policy and the Changing Conditions of Childhood." In *Hearing the Voices of Children: Social Policy for a New Century*, ed. C. Hallett and A. Prout. London: Routledge.

Rader, W. 2015. *Online Slang Dictionary*. http://onlineslangdictionary.com, accessed February 23, 2015.

Rainie, L. 2014. "Thirteen Things to Know about Teens and Technology." Pew Research Center, Berkman Center for Internet and Society, Harvard University, Cambridge, MA, July 23. http://www.pewinternet.org/2014/07/23/13-things-to-know-about-teens-and-technology.

Reno v. American Civil Liberties Union. 1997. 521 U.S. 844.

ReputationDefender. 2015. "If It's Online, It Matters." Reputation.com. http://manage.reputation.com/reputation-defender-br/?code=rep-brand&mm_campaign=511e038c9be0b367211fab78b4f9325d&utm_source=google&utm_medium=cpc&keyword=reputation%20defender&gclid=Cj0KEQjwuI-oBRCEi87g0K3O8OoBEiQAb25WAe35vfsomSb5FsB0-UzqpIW_pzHDlHLil50lsA9eMSEaAlTl8P8HAQ, accessed March 14, 2015.

Richtel, M. 2006. "MySpace.com Moves to Keep Sex Offenders off of Its Site." *New York Times*, December 6, 3.

Rideout, V. J., U. G. Foehr, and D. F. Roberts. 2010. *Generation M2: Media in the Lives of Eight- to Eighteen-Year-Olds*. Menlo Park, CA: Kaiser Family Foundation. http://kff.org/other/event/generation-m2-media-in-the-lives-of.

Rose, N. 1985. *The Psychological Complex: Psychology, Politics and Society in England, 1869–1939*. London: Routledge Kegan & Paul.

Rose, N. 1990. *Governing the Soul: The Shaping of the Private Self*. London: Routledge.

Rose, N. 2000. "Government and Control." *British Journal of Criminology* 40 (2): 321–339. doi:10.1093/bjc/40.2.321.

Rose, N. 2008. "Psychology as a Social Science." *Subjectivity* 25 (1): 446–462.

Santos, M. P., A. N. Pizarro, J. Mota, and E. A. Marques. 2013. "Parental Physical Activity, Safety Perceptions and Children's Independent Mobility." *BMC Public Health* 13 (1): 584. doi:10.1186/1471-2458-13-584.

Saul, D. 2014. "Three Million Teens Leave Facebook in Three Years: The 2014 Facebook Demographic Report." I Strategy Labs (ISL), January 15. http://istrategylabs .com/2014/01/3-million-teens-leave-facebook-in-3-years-the-2014-facebook -demographic-report.

Scalet, S. 2007. "Hemanshu Nigam: Mr. Safety for MySpace." *CSO*, March 1, 24–32.

Scheff, S. 2013. "Smile, Snap, Click and Post (or Not): Graduation and Prom Party Digital Drama Footprints." *Huffington Post*, April 12. http://www.huffingtonpost .com/sue-scheff/smile-snap-click-and-post_b_3067990.html, accessed March 14, 2015.

Schmidt, P. 1983. "The Education Consumer: The Computer—A Primer for Parents." *New York Times*, April 24, A3.

Schneider, C. 2015. *The Censor's Hand: The Misregulation of Human-Subject Research.* Cambridge, MA: MIT Press.

Schoeppe, S., M. J. Duncan, H. M. Badland, M. Oliver, and M. Browne. 2014. "Associations between Children's Independent Mobility and Physical Activity." *BMC Public Health* 14 (1): 91. doi:10.1186/1471-2458-14-91.

Schrag, Z. M. 2010. *Ethical Imperialism: Institutional Review Boards and the Social Sciences, 1965–2009.* Baltimore, MD: Johns Hopkins University Press.

Schulte, S. R. 2008. "'The *WarGames* Scenario': Regulating Teenagers and Teenaged Technology (1980–1984)." *Television and New Media* 9 (6): 487–513. doi:10.1177/1527476408323345.

Shea, T. 1983. "Computer 'Whiz Kids' Will Star in Fall TV Series." *InfoWorld* 5 (26) (June 27): 1–6.

Simmons, R. 2003. "Cliques, Clicks, Bullies and Blogs." *Washington Post*, September 28, B01.

Simon, R. 1995. "New York City's Restrictive Zoning of Adult Businesses: A Constitutional Analysis." *Fordham Urban Law Journal* 23: 187.

Singer, B. n.d. "Ten Best Apps for Paranoid Parents: Find My Kids—Footprints." *Parents* . http://www.parents.com/parenting/technology/best-apps-for-paranoid-parents, accessed February 25, 2015.

Small, G., and G. Vorgan. 2008. *iBrain: Surviving the Technological Alteration of the Modern Mind.* New York: Collins Living.

Smith, G. J. D. 2012. "Surveillance Work(ers)." In *Routledge Handbook of Surveillance Studies*, ed. K. Ball, K. D. Haggerty, and D. Lyon, 107–115. Abingdon, UK: Routledge.

Spilsbury, J. C. 2005. "'We Don't Really Get to Go out in the Front Yard': Children's Home Range and Neighborhood Violence." *Children's Geographies* 3 (1): 79–99. doi:10.1080/14733280500037281.

Steel, E. 2009. "The Case for Age Verification." *Wall Street Journal*, January 13. http://blogs.wsj.com/digits/2009/01/13/the-case-for-age-verification, accessed April 15, 2009.

Steeves, V. 2009. "Online Surveillance in Canadian Schools." In *Schools under Surveillance: Cultures of Control in Public Education*, ed. T. Monahan and R. D. Torres, 87–103. New Brunswick, NJ: Rutgers University Press.

Stein, A. 1982. "Micros vs. the Moral Majority." *InfoWorld* 4 (25) (September 27): 41–41.

Stelter, B. 2007. "*To Catch a Predator* Is Falling Prey to Advertisers' Sensibilities." *New York Times*, August 27. http://www.nytimes.com/2007/08/27/business/media/27predator.html.

Sterling, B. 1992. *The Hacker Crackdown: Law and Disorder on the Electronic Frontier*. New York: Bantam Books.

Strasburger, V. C., M. J. Hogan, D. A. Mulligan, N. Ameenuddin, D. A. Christakis, C. Cross, et al. 2013. "Children, Adolescents, and the Media." *Pediatrics* 132 (5): 958–961. doi:10.1542/peds.2013-2656.

"Study: Kids Too Tethered to Technology." 2010. *ABC News*, January 21. http://abcnews.go.com/WN/kids-electronics-study-shows-kids-spend-hours-day/story?id=9616699, accessed March 7, 2015.

Swauger, M. 2009. "No Kids Allowed!!! How IRB Ethics Undermine Qualitative Researchers from Achieving Socially Responsible Ethical Standards." *Race, Gender, and Class* 16 (1–2): 63–81.

"Teens Continue to Flee Facebook, Study Shows." 2015. *c/net*, January 7. http://www.magid.com/node/269, accessed February 14, 2015.

"There's an X-Rated Side to Home Computers, Parents Warned." 1987. *Los Angeles Times*, December 25, 47.

Thomas, D. 1998. "Criminality on the Electronic Frontier: Corporality and the Judicial Construction of the Hacker." *Information Communication and Society* 1 (4): 382–400. doi:10.1080/13691189809358979.

Thomas, D. 2002. *Hacker Culture*. Minneapolis: University of Minnesota Press.

Thomas, J. 2005. "The Moral Ambiguity of Social Control in Cyberspace: A Retro-Assessment of the 'Golden Age' of Hacking." *New Media and Society* 7 (5): 599–624. doi:10.1177/1461444805056008.

Thomas, K. 2000. "Kids Run a 20% Risk of 'Cybersex' Advances." *USA Today*, June 8, 1A.

Thomas, M. 2011. *Deconstructing Digital Natives: Young People, Technology, and the New Literacies*. London: Routledge.

United Nations International Children's Emergency Fund (UNICEF). 2011. *Child Safety Online: Global Challenges and Strategies.* UNICEF Publication No. 650. Florence, Italy: UNICEF Innocenti Research Center.

United States Congress, Office of Technology Assessment. 1986. *Federal Government Information Technology: Management, Security, and Congressional Oversight.* No. OTA-CIT-297. Washington, DC: U.S. Government Printing Office.

United States Department of Health and Human Services. 2013. "Facts about Bullying." StopBullying.gov, September 13. http://www.stopbullying.gov/news/media/facts, accessed March 15, 2015.

Valentine, G., and S. L. Holloway. 2002. "Cyberkids? Exploring Children's Identities and Social Networks in On-line and Off-line Worlds." *Annals of the Association of American Geographers* 92 (2): 302. doi:10.1111/1467-8306.00292.

Walkerdine, V. 1984. "Developmental Psychology and the Child-Centred Pedagogy: The Insertion of Piaget into Early Education." In *Changing the Subject: Psychology, Social Regulation and Subjectivity,* ed. J. Henriques, 153–202. London: Methuen.

Walkerdine, V. 2004. "Developmental Psychology and the Study of Childhood." In *An Introduction to Childhood Studies,* ed. M. J. Kehily, 96-107. Maidenhead, UK: Open University Press; http://search.ebscohost.com/login.aspx?direct=true&scope=site&db=nlebk&db=nlabk&AN=265852.

Wan, J. 2010. "Cyberbullying: Responding to the Challenges of Teens and Technology." Bethlehem Central School District, October. http://bethlehemschools.org/antibullying/cyberbullyingpanel_video.html.

WarGames. 1983. Directed by J. Badham. Beverly Hills, CA: United Artists.

Wesson, R. 1983. "Computer Hackers Deserving of Medals." *New York Times,* November 14, A18.

Wetzstein, C. 2001. "Survey: Fifth of Youth Solicited on Sex Online." *Washington Times,* June 20, A6.

"What Is the It Gets Better Project? 2010. It Gets Better, October 6. http://www.itgetsbetter.org/pages/about-it-gets-better-project, accessed March 12, 2013.

White, N., and J. Lauritsen. 2012. "Violent Crime against Youth, 1994–2010." NCJ 240106. Patterns & Trends. U.S. Bureau of Justice Statistics. http://www.bjs.gov/content/pub/pdf/vcay9410.pdf.

Whiteley, M. 2010. "Cyberbullying: Responding to the Challenges of Teens and Technology." Bethlehem Central School District, October. http://bethlehemschools.org/antibullying/cyberbullyingpanel_video.html.

Wieden & Kennedy. 1994. Microsoft TV ad. YouTube.com. https://www.youtube.com/watch?v=OG4mqqB1E3I&feature=youtube_gdata_player.

Wiener, N. 1948. *Cybernetics: Control and Communication in the Animal and the Machine*. New York: Wiley.

Willard, N. 2008. "Introducing Digi-Parent: And Comments on the Effectiveness of Technology Approaches to Address Human Behavior Concerns." Paper presented at the Internet Safety Technical Task Force, Berkman Center for Internet and Society, Harvard University, Cambridge, MA, September 23.

Winchester, S. 1995. "An Electronic Sink of Depravity." *Spectator*, February 4.

Winner, L. 1986. *The Whale and the Reactor: A Search for Limits in an Age of High Technology*. Chicago: University of Chicago Press.

Witt, H. 1985. "Hacker Hysteria Teenage Computer Pirates Are More Nuisance Than National Security Risks." *Chicago Tribune*, October 25, 1.

Wolak, J., K. Mitchell, and D. Finkelhor. 2006. "Online Victimization of Youth: Five Years Later." National Center for Missing and Exploited Children Bulletin.

Wolak, J., K. Mitchell, and D. Finkelhor. 2007. "Unwanted and Wanted Exposure to Online Pornography in a National Sample of Youth Internet Users." *Pediatrics* 119 (2): 247–257. doi:10.1542/peds.2006-1891.

Wolf, H. 1982. "Students of the '80s: Survival and Escape." *Christian Science Monitor*, September 24. http://search.proquest.com.ezproxy.rit.edu/news/docview/1038368592/5822BB80BE24FBEPQ/11?accountid=108.

Woogi World. 2011. "Woogi World: Parents." WoogiWorld.com. http://www.woogiworld.com/parents, accessed February 4, 2011.

Woolley, H. E., and E. Griffin. 2015. "Decreasing Experiences of Home Range, Outdoor Spaces, Activities and Companions: Changes across Three Generations in Sheffield in North England." *Children's Geographies* 13 (6): 677–691. doi:10.1080/14733285.2014.952186.

"The World of Data Confronts the Joy of Hacking." 1983. *New York Times*, August 28, E20.

Wrennall, L. 2010. "Surveillance and Child Protection: De-mystifying the Trojan Horse." *Surveillance and Society* 7 (3–4): 304–324.

Wyness, M. G. 2000. *Contesting Childhood*. London: Falmer Press.

Young, J. 1971. *The Drugtakers: The Social Meaning of Drug Use*. London: MacGibbon and Kee.

"Your Child's D.I.G.I.T.A.L Life." 2010. Hudson Falls Intermediate School, March. Hudson Falls, NY.

Zittrain, J. 2008. *The Future of the Internet and How to Stop It*. New Haven, CT: Yale University Press.

Index

Evelyn S. Field Library
Raritan Valley Community College
118 Lamington Road
North Branch, NJ 08876-1265